Last	First	4/13/19	5/11/19	6/1/19	Partic
Anan	Baramee	*Pepp*			
Aquino	Bruce				
Bazyar	Melody	*me /*			
Campbell	McKenzie	✓			
Diaz	Jose	✓			
Goldstone	Jennie	✓			
Hunter	Alexandria	✓			
Kocour	Michelle	✓			
Martinez	Julia	✓			
Rsesendez-Orozco	Jessica	✓			
Rockwell .	Dean	✓			
Singleton-Daniel	Felicia	✓			
Sorrem	Angela	✓			
Schartz	Anne	✓			
Tan	Cristobelle	*Bell*			

pation	IRR 1	IRR 2	Book	AG	

The Politics of Survival in Academia

Immigration and the Transnational Experience
Series Editors: Enrique (Henry) T. Trueba,
Pedro Reyes, and Yali Zou

The Power of Community: Mobilizing for Family and Schooling
by Concha Delgado-Gaitan

Ethnography and Schools: Qualitative Approaches to the Study of Education
edited by Yali Zou and Enrique (Henry) T. Trueba

The Politics of Survival
in Academia

Narratives of
Inequity, Resilience, and Success

EDITED BY LILA JACOBS, JOSÉ CINTRÓN,
AND CECIL E. CANTON

ROWMAN & LITTLEFIELD PUBLISHERS, INC.
Lanham • Boulder • New York • Toronto • Plymouth, UK

ROWMAN & LITTLEFIELD PUBLISHERS, INC.

Published in the United States of America
by Rowman & Littlefield Publishers, Inc.
A wholly owned subsidiary of The Rowman & Littlefield Publishing Group, Inc.
4501 Forbes Boulevard, Suite 200, Lanham, Maryland 20706
www.rowmanlittlefield.com

Estover Road
Plymouth PL6 7PY
United Kingdom

British Library Cataloguing in Publication Information Available

Library of Congress Cataloging-in-Publication Data

The politics of survival in academia : narratives of inequity, resilience, and success / edited by Lila Jacobs, José Cintrón, and Cecil E. Canton.
    p. c.m. — (Immigration and the transnational experience)
    Includes bibliographical references and index.
    ISBN 0-7425-2368-3 (alk. paper) — ISBN 0-7425-2369-1 (pbk. : alk. paper)
    1. Minority college teachers—United States—Case studies. 2. Discrimination in higher education—United States—Case studies. 3. Minorities—Education (Higher)—United States—Case studies. I. Jacobs, Lila. II. Cintrón, José, 1953– III. Canton, Cecil E. 1946– IV. Series.

LC212.42 .P65 2002
378.1'2'087—dc21   2002069690

Printed in the United States of America

♾™ The paper used in this publication meets the minimum requirements of American National Standard for Information Sciences—Permanence of Paper for Printed Library Materials, ANSI/NISO Z39.48-1992.

The editors of the volume would like to dedicate this effort to Dr. Enrique (Henry) Torres Trueba. "Dr. T," your inspiring and brilliant scholarship, your relentless affirmation of students and faculty of color, your generous and strong mentorship, and your tireless dedication to the struggle for equity and justice have made many people proud to have kept your company. On behalf of those whom you have befriended and aided over your long and illustrious academic career, we say thank you *y gracias por su amistad y apoyo. Con todo nuestro agradecimiento, respeto y cariño—hasta siempre.*

Contents

Foreword

This volume is a telling of the stories of ten ethnically diverse scholars with firsthand experience in American academia. All of them are well-known, respected academics. They got to where they are the hard way, surviving prejudice, both subtle and blatant, but keeping a good heart and an optimistic outlook.

How does it happen that in the very places one would least expect it—places where minds are held to be open, where liberal views prevail, where the tradition of intellectual judgment and rationality are maintained as the *sine qua non*?

There must be forces operating that transcend the presumed attributes of the field, that are communicated to academics of ethnic status, to the great damage of the victims and to the established academics alike.

There are many kinds of forces that might operate in this manner. I would select one as outstanding . . . the culture of academia. The culture of academia is not exactly as it is held to be, or its bearers want it to be. It is permeated by competition with varying degrees of ruthlessness giving it a special sharpened edge. It is ungenerous in mien and attitude, never giving more than the judges can afford without losing their edge. It is, as constructed in North America, essentially based on Anglo-Saxon rationality. It is production-oriented rather relational. And part of the production is efficiency.

It is not that these attributes are unknown to academics of ethnic status. But they are combined in a different matrix than in Anglo-Saxon, North European, cultures, and therefore expose ethnic academics, especially young ones, to prejudice and negative judgments that are damaging and unwarranted.

This condition is correctable and there are some signs it is being corrected, but slowly. An intensified self-consciousness is called for that can only be achieved by diligent self-monitoring and self-exposure—mere discussion will not do it.

Eventually one can hope that culture-free judgments can be made that will give the excellent people of ethnicity the same chances of security and success that are enjoyed by others. This book is a step in that direction.

George D. Spindler
Stanford University

Preface

The Politics of Survival in Academia: Narratives of Inequity, Resiliency, and Success

Edited by Lila Jacobs, José Cintrón, and Cecil E. Canton, as a volume in the *Immigrant and Transnational Families Series* (eds. H. Trueba, P. Reyes, and Yali Zou).

One of the indirect outcomes of immigration and transnational phenomena has been the rapid change in the human landscape of the academy. The increasing presence of new members from different cultural, linguistic, and economic backgrounds has been an odyssey punctuated by unexpected turns of heroic resilience among the newly accepted members. This book, however, does not bring only the happy stories of accomplishment and the successes of democracy in education, but it confronts the reader face-to-face with narratives of inequity, survival, and pain in the search for self-identity, respect, and intellectual growth. The dream that education is key to the ideals of democratic societies, that the horizons of learning and recognition are open to all, and color or accent are irrelevant to academic performance if there is quality of thought and demonstrably satisfactory performance, are a reality that is alive and well and accessible to all. This dream has a price, however. Academic success requires resilience, dedication, and skill. Furthermore, success depends on the ability of individuals to use their newly developed cultural capital, their multiple identities, and their determination to stay in the race in order to resolve conflicts and adapt to new settings. This is not to say that academic success must always be more difficult to newcomers, the ethnic members, those originally marked to fail because they come from low-income, immigrant, or transnational families who speak English as a second language. In fact, the ability to use multiple identities and languages, the skill to resolve conflicts with an abundant reservoir of patience and resilience should make it easier for the marginalized and culturally diverse people to stay on target. We often ask ethnic minorities why they persevere in their effort to succeed in school, and we frequently hear that the motivation behind their academic success is to avoid the hardships of migrant labor. Those hot summers picking cotton in South Texas are unforgettable to children of migrant families who became professional academicians, and they certainly became an incentive to study hard, achieve, and remain in school.

The collection of narratives placed in this volume is a cross section of ethnic and linguistic groups with a variety of experiences. The feelings of the authors, their worldview, and their strategies to survive in life have much to teach us. The recent use of narratives in critical ethnography brings us back to our roots and the historical significant of discourse intended to disclose and explain oppression. In fact, one could claim that the use of narrative by ethnic ethnographers has brought new light into modern life experiences faced by Americans who are members of immigrant and transnational families. These new perspectives presented by ethnic ethnographers offer epistemological nuances and calibration of meanings and interpretations that enrich our understanding of America; these perspectives either did not exist before or were previously considered unreliable, irrelevant, or unscientific. This volume should encourage all persons from marginal groups to express their views and spell out for all the public the secrets of resistance, the motivation to excel even against the expectations of others, and ultimately, their faith in the American dream. As the critical mass of new immigrants and members of transnational families enters formally the scene of American life, it does it with a clear notion that languages and cultures, previous experiences and struggles can all become an important asset in modern America. For the more recent members of our democracy, the academy has, in different terms, with different tools, and at unexpected times, opened up a new life, new vistas and great hopes for a brilliant future in the lives of persons who were viewed as classical cases of failure: mothers on welfare, poor black, Native American, Latino, and Asian students, young scholars unprepared to compete with mainstream persons and succeed. However, these individuals who keep trying and pursue again and again new avenues and strategies to overcome disabilities and overturn rejections; individuals unable to understand and communicate in the English language with mainstream persons of the academy, but determined to keep learning regardless of the outcomes. What these new academicians have in common is not only that they were supposed to fail and managed to survive and even succeed; but that they all firmly believed in their self-worth, all remained deeply attached to their cultural values, and all sincerely bought into the American dream.

This book is a contribution to critical ethnography, to epistemological flexibility rich in interpretive approaches, and a quintessential example of emancipatory narratives, that is, narratives which have the intent of helping people adopt a strong commitment to "praxis." That is, a commitment to bring to our daily lives, to our real "praxis" the beliefs and theoretical insights gained from emancipatory accounts and other related experiences. This book is also a contribution to critical pedagogy as discussed by Freire in his many contributions published by Rowman & Littlefield and elsewhere. Behind the narratives, the message is clear: the roots of empowerment are precisely in establishing this connection between theory and praxis. Academic success (via survival and resilience) provides marginalized individuals with the tools they need to adopt a new identity as members of the academy, with the literacy skills and appropriate discourse to interact successfully with populations placed in our society in polar positions: ethnic communities and mainstream folks. Educated, successful, ethnic academicians experience the advantages of their new cultural capital (their bilingualism, their biculturalism, their determination to withstand conflict, and their commitment to succeed). This capital enables them to be uniquely qualified to succeed in multicultural settings previously inaccessible to mainstream academicians. In a way this book opens small windows into the souls of the new academicians and permits everybody to witness the creation of a new academy that brings hope to those still trying to belong in school.

Racism, sexism, classism, and homophobia were enormous obstacles to academic success in the lives of previous generations. Now they have become opportunities to develop unique qualities of resilience and to acquire a new cultural capital. Illness and university neglect had been viewed as the end of academic careers, as terminal problems; now they can be seen as challenges and opportunities for higher success and deeper understanding of the nature of genuine intellectual work in democratic societies.

After the events of September 11, 2001, life in America is said to have changed drastically. But the events themselves showed the new America—the interdependency across ethnic groups and social classes, the heroic texture of simple persons, the collective commitment to resilience and democracy, and our dedication to the long-term success of our lifestyle and our cultural traditions.

Acknowledgments

Deepest appreciation to my mentors who first opened the door to academia for me: Dr. Enrique T. Trueba, Dr. Laurence Iannaccone, and Dr. George Brown. To Baba and Helene for loving guidance, and to Kahlil, Eli, Alicia, and Jivan for motivation and inspiration . . . *siempre*.

—Dr. Lila Jacobs

I would first like to acknowledge the contributors of this volume. Their courage and strength serve as an inspiration to future academics of color. I would also like to acknowledge the ongoing work toward social justice and equity of my colleagues in the bilingual/multicultural education department in the CSUS College of Education—their stories served as an impetus as well. Gracias Judy Morales-Sue from the Migrant/OLE Project for your excellent help with the formatting of the volume. Thanks also to Kärstin Painter from the Rowman & Littlefield editorial staff for your steadfast and professional assistance. Lastly, gracias Adele and Zachary for making me new.

—Dr. José Cintrón

We acknowledge the debt owed to our ancestors and all of those who came before us, who provided us with the benefit of their courage and their wisdom. I would especially like to acknowledge and thank my late mother, Mrs. Geneva M. Donadelle Canton and my late grandmother, Mrs. Dorothy (Nana) Lewis Donadelle. You may be gone, but you are never forgotten.

—Dr. Cecil E. Canton

Introduction

José Cintrón, Lila Jacobs, and Cecil E. Canton .

Over the last two decades new faculty from historically underrepresented groups such as African Americans, Latinos, Asian Americans, and Native Americans have entered the American academy and struggled to survive through the processes of evaluation, tenure, scholarly productivity, and other powerful tests of resilience. This volume, *Surviving the Politics of Academia: Narratives of Inequity, Resilience, and Success* presents the narratives of two African Americans (one from Native American parentage), two Latinas, one Jew, and three Asian Americans. Six of the authors are immigrants or first-generation born in the United States from immigrant parents and most come from humble socioeconomic backgrounds. Six of the authors are native speakers of languages other than English and therefore speakers and writers of English as a second or third language. In spite of the vast differences among the authors, there is a consistent theme evident in their accounts: resilience, in other words the ability to pursue, over a period of time, academic goals regardless of the personal sacrifices, efforts required, and obstacles confronted. Also consistent across the various accounts is a profound and personal commitment to students and colleagues of color, a complete dedication to their profession, and a clear ability to define themselves as both Americans and also active and loyal members of their ethnic groups. Most of the authors are bilingual/bicultural individuals who have retained a high level of proficiency in their home languages and strong and meaningful cultural linkages with their country and community of origin.

Chapter 1 tells the story of Dr. Lila Jacobs and her incredible journey from welfare mother to university administrator, teacher, and researcher. Born to a lower-middle-class Jewish family from Chicago, Lila worked with the Student Non-Violent Coordinating Committee as a teenager, and was called "Nigger lover" because of her strong interracial friendships. She moved to New York to study drama but returned to Chicago to participate in the protests at the National Democratic Convention of 1968. Losing faith in the American political system, she spent several years involved with theatrical work in Europe, South America, and Asia. After returning to the states, she became a single parent of two mixed-heritage boys (Jewish and Puerto Rican) and an adopted Puerto Rican, received public assistance, and was forced from one housing situation to the next as she tried to survive and take care of her children. Lila became a community activist and after attending community college, was convinced to start her graduate career. The years of poverty as a single mother gave her a powerful and creative spirit that served her well in pursuing her doctorate. Her incredible ability to care for and help others increased her motivation to achieve her goals regardless of any obstacles. She has now become a successful professor and department chair, who has dedicated her life to mentoring students and colleagues.

> My narrative does not produce new theories or themes, but it does give access to one woman beyond the façade of a department chair, a professor, or even a welfare mother. It makes my stomach tighten to do an analysis, for I know the feelings associated with the events. The adrenaline still pumps in my veins, the dryness comes to my mouth, and the tears to my eyes. Not just for me, but for the others who have experienced, are experiencing, or are yet to experience, the isolation, fear, degradation, and despair that is intertwined with the telling of this story. (Jacobs, this volume)

Chapter 2 is the subtle, elegant, and at times, painful account of Dr. Cecil Canton. He faced a lifetime of racism and discrimination but has managed to retain his optimism and integrity, as well as his extraordinary scholarship. This is an inspiring story for many faculty of color who face similar challenges and try to survive without bitterness or marginalization. Dr. Canton presents an eloquent and honest view from within, as a person insulted, distrusted, neglected, and underestimated. The endurance of his spirit and the insightful and sharp analytical skills evident in his writings match the profound respect he has garnered from students and colleagues alike. Resilience, courage, and wisdom are not in conflict with intelligent resistance in the face of academic racism. Without these qualities, intellectual growth, self-respect, and academic achievement are impossible. For Cecil dealing with racism has been the most challenging and draining task in academia. He states:

> Unless you have come face-to-face with blatant individual prejudice, it is often difficult to recognize it when it presents itself in hidden, sometimes unintentional ways. . . . Given the law enforcement backgrounds of many of my colleagues on the faculty, I was amazed that I wasn't exposed to it more often. Whatever the reason, what I found was much more organizational discrimination and institutional racism than the individual variety. (Canton, this volume)

Dr. Geni Cowan presents in Chapter 3 the personal struggles she has faced as a lesbian and a Native and black American woman in academia. The internal disagreements among faculty of color, and their conflicting expectations from female colleagues of color, resulted at times in deep disappointment and isolation for Dr. Cowan. Unwilling to pass for someone else or to hide her ancestry, she searches for a personal identity with courage and optimism. As Geni states:

> Since I didn't know of my Indian heritage in childhood, I only learned how awful it was to be me. Where I've come to now is the knowledge that being both black and Indian is rich and full; life affirming. To deny either is to engage, maybe even affirm, the comfort preferences of the dominant cultures; to support the unspoken contention that black is bad. (Cowan, this volume)

Dr. Concha Delgado-Gaitan details in Chapter 4 her encounters with academia as a scholar facing enormous health challenges due to an advanced lupus condition. Her biographical history as a child of Mexican immigrant parents and her many years of applied anthropological literacy fieldwork in poor communities provides firsthand knowledge and understanding of the resilience one needs in the face of adversity. It was family and friends she leaned on while tapping her inner cultural knowledge and strength when a health crisis called for extraordinary measures. In spite of her previous successes in academia, and her worsening medical condition, she expected that a senior professor at the University of California would receive better treatment given that the Americans with Disabilities Act requires special provisions for the disabled. She says:

> Fundamentally, I learned that while I relied on the support of my family, friends, and cultural values to strengthen me, the University of California did not consider my needs. Instead it dealt with my situation only according to their interpretation of the Americans with Disability Act—the bureaucratic law. (Delgado-Gaitan, this volume)

She describes in detail her extraordinary struggle for retaining a measure of personal dignity in light of a debilitating disease. Daily problems with insensitive university bureaucrats continued. Her growing inability to walk long distances on campus to teach classes made her appear even more impaired and walking with a cane became impossible. She recalls her course scheduling problems:

> When I first became ill, I was always assigned to teach in classrooms that were located long distances from my office and designated class hours impossible to meet because I felt too debilitated to get up very early in the morning or stay late enough in the day on campus to teach. Most quarters I fought with the administration about appropriate scheduling of my classes up to the last minute before class began. This impeded students from taking my course since time and place were often undetermined until the first week of class. (Delgado-Gaitan, this volume)

Her personal accounts of the trials that ensued when she faced physical disabilities illustrate the vulnerability of the individual against a bureaucracy and the power of cultural values and strengths that Dr. Delgado-Gaitan evoked. Currently her new career as an independent writer enables her to continue healing and sharing stories in genres other than academic.

In Chapter 5 Dr. Myriam N. Torres shares her personal attempts to uncover and discover the "secrets" of academia under adverse circumstances:

> My story is that of strange becoming familiar (or at least less strange) within the United States academia, starting in 1990. It has been a continual struggle to overcome the multiple obstacles hidden in the higher education system a person like myself, a mature Latina woman with a Spanish accent, must face as part of one's academic life. (Torres this volume)

The internalization of what it means to be a *Latina*, and increased ability to convert negative and "doubt-casting messages into self-propellers to prove the message wrong" are the basis for resilience and success. Dr. Torres describes her doctoral program, her acquisition of English discourse to present scholarly arguments, and her ongoing internal struggle to control anger and anxiety. The growing confidence in her own skills and talents eventually led her to create appropriate survival strategies:

> To awaken to one's own reality is painful and overwhelming. I became overwhelmed with cautious post-awakenings: it is better to be silent rather than to speak up, it is better to avoid using terms that identify one as a radical, it is better to appear cold rather than passionate . . . it is best to reveal to others the least possible about my work; the more secretive the better. This led me to embrace silence as the easiest way to cope with the situation—and silence is not exactly my *forte*. (Torres, this volume)

Dr. Torres' concluding remarks are clear and poignant:

> I really do not want to sugarcoat my story to appeal to those who refuse to see how reality is different for different people, not because of their abilities and potentialities, but because of their identity. To enter and move up in academia, some people need only to enter and move up in academia, some people need only push a button and the elevator door opens, while others need to take the stairs step-by-step, jumping over and through numerous hurdles and hoops on the way. (Torres, this volume)

Chapter 6 follows a different format in that Dr. Chalsa M. Loo and Maria Chun present case studies of eight different "Asian American Warriors":

> Exposing the myth that the Asian American experience in academia is exemplary and devoid of any racial/ethnic bias . . . this chapter highlights the cases of eight Asian American professors in institutions of higher education in the United States who were faced with the academic trauma of denied tenure and/or promotion and addresses one of several strategies that must be used to

make improvements in the retention of and equal treatment of faculty of color—to battle when denied. These eight faculty warriors chose "fight" rather than "flight." Their academic worth attacked, many felt their jobs, careers, or professional integrity were in jeopardy. (Loo & Chun, this volume)

This chapter "serves as a blueprint—a preparatory manual—of the Art of Academic Warfare for the faculty of color who chooses self-defense" (Loo & Chun, this volume). In one of the cases, for example, seven years after a second re-review and a positive vote, Warrior 2 comments:

> Finally, the promotion due me was recommended, seven years later, but even this victory was bittersweet. The summary contained inaccurate statements, prejudicial omissions, discriminatory criteria, and a biased tone, terminology, and biased weighting of evidence. (Loo & Chun, this volume)

The denial of tenure had different impact for different Asian Americans. In the case of Warrior 7, the following happened:

> This warrior suffered with avoidance symptoms, common to trauma victims—"an inability to recall the incident, an unwillingness to talk about it, and paranoia." He described how this denial precipitated a "loss of self-esteem, self-deprecation, a paralysis in [one's capacity] to [handle] professional responsibilities, anger and permanent bitterness toward individuals regarding the incident, desires for revenge, [feelings of] racial persecution, and the development of a stoic and impenetrable [persona]." "I became a person who would not engage with others," a symptom of detachment and estrangement of others found in most trauma victims. "I developed a kind of scar tissue, the development of cynicism." The denial represented "a total invalidation of my life, of what I pursued, my activities. They made me feel like an inferior person. They weren't judging my competence, only what they thought was relevant. . . . These were totally ignorant people judging me."

This chapter is an extraordinary account of facts we never suspected could exist in academia, and it has an intensity that contrasts with the stereotype of Asian American academicians who are presumed to accept inequities without a challenge.

Chapter 7 is written by Dr. Yali Zou who, as a teenager, had extraordinary experiences in mainland China:

> Perhaps no other experience in China had a greater impact on me than having worked in a rural village for two years during the Cultural Revolution. Being in that village changed my life completely. Although I suffered seriously physically and mentally, it nurtured my deep love for poor peasant children and established a great relationship with my students' parents, which, in turn, laid the foundation for my future career. Leaving my comfortable family life in the city for the first time when I was seventeen years old, I was sent like millions of

other educated young people to live in one of the poorest villages, where there was not enough food to eat, no running water, electricity, or gas; communication with the rest of the world was nonexistent. Everyday I worked physically in an endless field, often for up to fourteen hours under the burning sun or in the freezing winter. In addition, I had to go into the mountains to find tree branches for the evening fire and wild vegetables to supplement the community's meals . . . one day I was transplanting rice shoots in a rice field with cold water, and had worked for four hours without a break. Suddenly I felt pain in my legs. When I looked at my legs, there were several leeches. I was terrified and fell into the water. I cried and sank into the muddy field. (Zou, this volume)

Yali is eventually sent to the Shanghai Foreign Language Institute, learns Albanian, works as an interpreter for the government, and works in the Chang Chun Film Studio. Zou finally enters the Chang Chun Science and Technology Institute where she becomes a professor and is selected among thousands to go to the United States as a visiting scholar. In California, she obtains her M.A. and Ph.D. and begins the tortuous path of learning English while teaching Mandarin at the University of California. She describes in this chapter the many changes and transitions that finally led to the current position she has as director of an Asian American Studies Center in a Texas university. This chapter has important implications for the formation of self-identity among academicians from other countries. Portions of this chapter appear in other publications.

In Chapter 8, Dr. Peter Kiang, who has been instrumental in the development of Asian American studies on the East Coast, describes the intimate relationship between self-identity and institutional impact on recent Asian immigrants. He also highlights the ways in which curriculum can help Asian immigrants to overcome their academic difficulties and to rebuild and maintain vital connections with their homes, families, and communities. Dr. Kiang notes how stereotypes used to denote Asian Americans distort their lives and cultural values. He writes:

the melting pot paradigm has never adequately represented the realities of African Americans or native peoples who, after many generations, have not achieved structural assimilation in the United States because of unequal power relations, the persistence of racial inequality, and indigenous commitments to self-determination. Similarly, even though today's immigrants share some of the same challenges of adapting to a new language and culture that confronted earlier generations of European immigrants, the melting pot paradigm does not accurately describe the ways that dynamics of racism shape the adjustment process of the post-1965 immigrant waves—most of whom are nonwhite, having come from Asia, Latin America, the Caribbean, and Africa. (Kiang, this volume)

Peter contends that transnational themes ("home," "identity," and "family ties") represent an important way to use "the curriculum in order to explore the connections of culture, history, economics, and politics across time and distance for specific nationalities" (Kiang, this volume). Using actual texts composed by students, Dr. Kiang sensitizes the reader to the cultural perspectives of various Asian immigrant groups.

In brief, this volume represents an unadulterated firsthand account of the lives that many faculty of color experience in American academia. These are individuals who have managed to survive and succeed in their academic tasks by staying on course, confronting failure, racism, and neglect, and doing it with courage and resourcefulness. They persist and try again and again, always retaining their self-identity and self-respect in the face of prejudice, biases, and disrespect from colleagues, peers, and administrators. It is important that these narratives be known to other academics of color as well as nonminority faculty. It is critically important that academicians take notice and learn from them. Prejudice, racism, and inequity not only dehumanize the victims but also the oppressors. In the long run these structural injustices jeopardize substantially the intellectual value of academic endeavors and particularly the theoretical and methodological contributions made by faculty and scholars of color to the various disciplines found in the academy. Ultimately, and perhaps most importantly, systemic racist practices undermine the richness of an open, humane, and fair academy. And as the new millenium speeds forward, American universities across the country cannot afford to deny the messages or delay constructive action.

Chapter One

Redefining the Self: From AFDC to Ph.D.

Lila Jacobs, Ph.D.

Introduction

For years, my colleagues and I discussed writing a book that would tell our real stories; personal narratives that were full of drama, past struggles, and heroic journeys. These narratives were a bond that kept us pledged to each other, a bond as deep as a blood oath. We were an unusual group of professors; none of us had the background that was typical to our profession, and our lives had veered far from the path of academia. Our identities were forged by marginalization, solidarity with the oppressed, and dreams that pulled us forward.

While brainstorming ideas for an edited volume, the dare was thrown out—to reveal the elements of our lives that a good ethnographer would discover in an interview. The taboo was obvious; as educational anthropologists, we uncovered the lives of other people, writing case stories that were poignant, inspirational, or depressing, but we did not share the intimate details of our own histories in professional settings. It made us highly nervous to even consider putting on paper the details of our journeys inside academia; nevertheless, we decided to take the risk. We believed that there were important elements from our personal lives that would shed light on the process of nontraditional folks "making it" in academia.

I wrote the pages that became the foundation of my chapter just after midnight on New Year's Eve 1997. I wrote without stopping once I had given myself permission to let go of judgment, embarrassment, and speculation of how others would perceive my life. I wanted to tell my story, to see what would happen if I exposed hidden parts of myself. As the Persian poet Rumi (1250) wrote long ago:

If this me is not I, then
who am I?

If I am not the one who speaks, then
who does?
If this me is only a robe then
who is
The one I am covering?

I felt compelled to tell my story for a number of deeply felt reasons: the complexity of the struggle for those of us who have fought against the injustice of the system, yet chose to work within it; for other single mothers who felt inspired by my success; and to testify to the importance of giving help and support to those who need it by showing how that made a critical difference for me. There is a great need for the insight gained from hard times to be used to improve conditions for others that have not yet found a way to have their voices heard. On a more personal level, it became clear to me that I was surviving, but at a marginal level, that I had to find a way to change my situation. Maybe it was when I could not find someone who would rent to me, or maybe when I could not find a doctor to treat my child, or when the electricity was turned off for late payment, but there was no way I could deny the potential for danger. Entering the educational arena initially gave me some degree of security and legitimacy, limited power, financial stability, and medical benefits. Once basic needs were met, I was able to take advantage of the intellectually rich environment and the opportunity to develop the art of teaching at a higher level.

I have kept parts of this chapter in a personal tone, unable to find academic language that did not distance me from the reader. This chapter was painful to write—excruciating at times—as the feelings flooded back over me. For years, I was incapable of editing my work because I could not bear to read my own story. Even now, the feelings interwoven with the facts make me ill; my adrenalin rushes prepared for battle, my breath is short and painful, as if not breathing fully will protect me from taking in the toxic memories. The pain is not just for me, but also for others who have experienced the isolation, fear, degradation, and despair of being a single parent on welfare in this country.

My Story Part 1: AFDC to Ph.D.

Most people think I am being humble when I say that I would never have my Ph.D. without the help of my mentor, Dr. Enrique Trueba, but in fact, it is the unembellished truth. He felt I had the skills and motivation to complete a doctoral program, and he saw my life experiences as an additional resource. He well deserved the *vela* (candle) I gave him at the end of my graduate work that was inscribed, "To the Patron Saint of Ph.D.s."

How I changed the initials after my name—from the stigma of Aid to Families with Dependent Children to having a doctorate in education—is a chronicle of events, some might say a gain in social capital, others might say the hand of destiny, and I must say it is a part of the mysteries, the part of our lives that is inexplicable.

I was raised in a lower-middle-class family in Chicago, Jewish in culture, and progressive for the times. Although my parents were both first generation Americans, to me they seemed a part of the majority culture. I grew to recognize the boundaries created by discrimination and anti-Semitism towards Jews. My family believed in equality and was strongly in support of the Civil Rights movement. I read Sartre and Camus when I was sixteen, worked for the Student Non-Violent Coordinating Committee, and was called "nigger lover" by my high school classmates. I never understood how people that suffered from stereotyping, discrimination, and racism could so easily participate in subjecting another group of people to this pain.

I attended the University of Wisconsin in Madison in 1965, where student activities included politics, music, and getting high. I dropped out of college to examine my goals and to explore the counterculture and left for California, arriving in Haight-Ashbury at the height of the Summer of Love in 1966. It was the '60s, and we thought that we had found the solution to the world's problems. The alternative movement had potential, we believed in peace, and we understood that economics played a major part in creating and sustaining war. Doing things for free was our response to the unjust distribution of wealth, and love was our answer to historical, psychological, and political problems. This was a radically different way to live, but by the end of the summer it was obvious to me that the change in consciousness we desired had happened only for a few.

I moved to the other end of the earth, as I saw it, and rented an apartment on the Lower East Side of New York City. The city was having its own version of love-ins in Central Park, and I continued my work toward a major in theater at New York University. My idealism was shattered when a local hippie named Groovy was murdered outside the jazz club on Avenue A. By then, our dreams had been co-opted by television advertising campaigns, the FBI had been successful in setting up a barter system of reduced sentencing for turning in others, drugs had become big business rather than tokens of exchange, and violence had found a way into our peace movement.

I returned to the Madison campus to finish my degree with a sense of having outgrown my naiveté but still valuing the same fundamental principles. Soon, I was confronted with the growing U.S. military presence in Vietnam and I became deeply committed to the antiwar movement. The entire campus was often a battleground between the police and protesting students. Protesters became adept at throwing tear-gas canisters back at the police. By the Chicago Democratic Convention in 1968, which I attended, the police had perfected their attacks. I was shocked and horrified by the clubbing and gassing of innocent people by the police.

By this time, my friends were carrying guns; they had become political hippies dedicated to changing society by any means. Cointel-pro was in full effect, activists were being murdered in their sleep, it seemed like the revolution had begun. I experienced profound conflict as I remained committed to nonviolence learned from my time in SNCC and could not bring myself to participate in armed struggle. In 1969, I decided to leave the United States to live in the Netherlands, a country that had a reputation for moderation and freedom (not including their colonial history). I worked as an artist in avant-garde theaters and music productions for the next four years. I had no regrets about not owning a weapon, but it was not so easy to be nonviolent in my thoughts. I returned to New York City to do special effects for a Broadway play, still with unresolved conflicts about art, money, and politics. Living in the Chelsea Hotel, working at the Ambassador Theater, yet my soul was not satisfied. If this was "making it," then I needed something more.

In a sequence of magical reality, I crossed paths with a Puerto Rican musician I had met in Amsterdam and traveled to Mexico with him and a troupe of performers. For the next three years we traveled through India, Nepal, Thailand, Bali, Australia, and South America performing in theaters and schools. I saw firsthand and heard the stories of the beggars in Calcutta, the Tibetans in exile, the heroin-addicted prostitutes in Bangkok left over from the rest-and-recreation jaunts of American soldiers fighting in Vietnam, the Aborigines trapped in Australian cities, and the Quechua Indians in the Andes Mountains of Peru.

Life did not make sense to me; incredible beauty and kindness always juxtaposed with poverty, immoral laws, oppression, and limited opportunities. Ultimately, being exposed to indigenous and Eastern ways of thought opened up new possibilities for me. Finding a philosophy that was based on a circle, or spiral, allowed me to explore the purpose of life at a different level. I recognized that the negativity that repulsed me was also inside myself. While this realization did not change all my attitudes and biases, on a very deep level, it allowed compassion to become a part of my understanding.

Something changed in me, and I was ready to participate in the fullness of life. I continued my travels and visited temples throughout India, Stupas in Nepal, Borabadour in Indonesia, and Machu Pichu in Peru. I felt we had reclaimed the magic of life when I found out I was pregnant. We returned to New York and traveled across the United States in a van, arriving in Santa Barbara when I was eight months pregnant. In 1976, I gave birth at home to our firstborn son. We continued traveling across the country with theater and music productions until we moved to Maui, Hawaii, where our second son was born in 1978.

Unfortunately, the magic did not last in the new environment. Different demands impacted our relationship, and we responded in very different ways. I returned to California with my two infant sons, soon to informally adopt their cousin from their father's side of the family. In just months, I became a single parent of three children with no job and no place to live.

I settled in Santa Barbara, went on welfare, and did not report that I also had my sons' five-year-old cousin living with me. I was afraid social workers would take her away. We lived on $500 per month, renting a house and then subletting rooms to make enough money to pay the bills. Moving from place to place, my children attended eight schools by eighth grade. My children were brown skinned, growing up in an elitist city that expected people to be blonde and rich, or gardeners and service providers. I became a community activist organizing for indigenous rights, against nuclear power plants, and for single parents.

My circumstances made each day a struggle, but I did not see it as an individual situation. I was acutely aware of the larger picture of inequity between the rich and the poor, the landowners and indigenous peoples, and the business of war and the need for peace. I volunteered at the intertribal Urban Indian Center and decided to take a course at the City College to become better skilled at handling crisis situations. I did not know the college system, and my first attempts at enrolling were exhausting. I had to fight to get into the Educational Opportunity Program, I had to fight to get into the childcare center, I had to fight to get into the counseling course I needed.

The instructor for the course was Art Sanchez, a Chicano graduate student from the nearby university. He saw potential in me, and when he found out I had earned a B.A. degree twelve years earlier, he strongly encouraged me to go to graduate school. I was reluctant, my undergraduate experience was over a decade prior, but he persisted. The university sent me to a special re-entry counselor, who was supposed to assist me with admissions. When she found out I had three children, no child support, and was on welfare, she told me I would never make it at the university and that it was useless to fill out the forms. This was devastating to me; I lost my confidence and did not proceed with my paperwork. By chance, the ombudsman of the university heard my story and was outraged. He tracked me down, encouraged me to reapply, used my case to get the counselor fired, and helped me gain admission. At this time, there was a unique progressive humanistic department, Confluent Education, whose professors valued my resilience. They took a chance and admitted me to their department, and I found a niche at the university.

Unfortunately, at the same time I was forced to leave my residence and could not come up with the prohibitive fee of first month, last month, and deposit required for a new rental. My children and I stayed in my car and on the floors of friends' apartments. The only people who helped me were other poor people. Folks that were doing well thought my hard times were contagious. Circumstances forced us to live at the women's shelter. I told no one; I was mortified, afraid that I would have to quit school and felt completely disappointed in myself. By this time I had foster custody of my niece and risked losing her if I did not have secure housing. I went to the vice president of the university, the only woman in the administrative cabinet, and refused to leave her office until she would see me. She was moved by the urgency of the situation and allowed me to move into student housing. As in other situations, the assistance of people in gatekeeping positions changed the course of my life.

Stable housing gave me a chance to focus on school. I finished the coursework for my M.A., moved on to the Ph.D. program, and met Dr. Enrique Trueba, an extraordinary professor and lifelong friend. Since I had no computer, he gave me the keys to his office and let me work there after hours. Every evening I brought my three children, peanut butter and jelly sandwiches for dinner, their homework and sleeping bags, and worked all night.

Another graduate student, José Cintrón, helped me get a Title VII fellowship and I was able to get off welfare, but my income remained the same. I was on a mission to save my children and to be successful, to repay the trust that my mentor and my professors had placed in me—and to prove the others wrong. I vowed that nothing would stop me. I often ran out of money; we would look for change in the cushions of the couch and eat popcorn or watermelon for dinner. I took toilet paper from the stalls in the student union, I begged friends to fix my '66 Chevy. When it seemed like everything was falling apart, the children would get lice. I became convinced that there was a scientific connection between despair and lice: a chemical must be released in hair follicles that attract lice when the human body is under extreme stress.

In spite of my difficulties, I persevered. My motivation was strong because I never saw dropping out as an option. A professor hired me to work on an evaluation for the Rockefeller Foundation, and as fate would have it, the research involved a data collection about the lives of "minority, female head of households." My research partner, Elizabeth Kirton, and myself were the only qualitative researchers on the project and the only two women. The other male researchers were incredulous about the rapport we built with the women in the study and would often disparage our work because they did not see us as "neutral." I explained that there was no neutral gear in life and that their numbers and formulas were also biased, but they were not convinced and continued to question our work.

To make matters more stressful, my adolescent niece was diagnosed with chronic depression and wanted to return to her biological mother. This was a deeply painful time for me; I let her go, but I continued moving slowly forward. I finished my dissertation and had a potluck celebration with my mentor and friends who had seen me to the end of this part of my journey; the Hmong families I interviewed; Grandpa Victor, the eldest living Chumash Indian; and my *comadres*—single mothers and their children.

My Story Part 2: Ph.D. to Professor

I applied to tenure-track positions in related fields all across the country, feeling very pressured to find a position. Although working toward my doctorate was stressful, at least the goal was clear. Looking for a university position was overwhelming, as I was in unfamiliar territory. The hiring committee of a choice university selected me, but the decision was challenged by the department chair who wanted his wife to get the position. This delayed the process substantially, and not being able to wait an additional semester, I accepted a position at another institution. I met with the dean, a woman of color, and felt positive about the job. I bought an older house through the university's incentive program, went heavily into debt, and moved my family, believing all the exciting possibilities I had been told at the interview.

Reality struck right away. My faculty load was seven one- and two-unit courses of multicultural education for early childhood, multiple subjects, and single subject. I taught every day of the week, early morning and late evening classes. The faculty did not work well together and held onto grudges from twenty years prior. Neither the university nor the town had much diversity, and children taunted my sons and made racist remarks.

I was isolated and overworked, and although getting my first tenure-track position was supposed to be a moment of success, it was one of the unhappiest times in my life because I had no support system. I tried to change the unit load of my classes so that there could be more depth to the course material, but I was blocked at every level. I did not understand the system enough to know how to win the battle. Many colleagues advised me not to leave, as it might look bad on my vitae to have only stayed one year, but I decided to resign, regardless of the professional cost.

After it became public knowledge that I was leaving, I was encouraged to re-apply to the university whose committee had previously selected me, and this time they hired me. At my new university, I met colleagues that had fought equity battles long before my arrival, and it was a progressive, welcoming environment. The School of Education was extremely diverse and had support systems built into formal and informal networks. Two colleagues outside my department became my allies and mentored me, helping me understand the politics of the institution and the tenure process.

The situation in Educational Leadership, my department, was more difficult. There was only one other woman in addition to me. The chair still resented me from the first hiring episode and it showed in the way I was treated. To make matters worse, the faculty themselves did not get along, and many meetings ended with ugly fights between some of the male faculty members. Not reflective of the larger college, the students in my classes were not diverse, and they were quite resistant to looking at things from a multicultural perspective. In my Human Resources class, one student wrote on her evaluation, "This is a class about people—what does that have to do with multicultural issues?" In addition, my school supervision assignments were all out of town. My car had been totaled in an accident; luckily a supportive colleague lent me his truck. At the end of my first semester, I was in a neck brace, in severe pain, under great stress, but still optimistic about my new situation.

Inside my department, things began to improve as faculty retired. My friend who had lent me his truck became department chair, and the faculty began to move forward in a collegial way. We worked on diversifying our student population, and I was given the opportunity to teach in the Bilingual Leadership Program, a unique Title VII program to provide bilingual administers for schools in California. Many of the students were the first in their families to attend college and were committed to protecting students from the injustices they had suffered as children. I was inspired by their dedication and gratified by their excellent work.

In the summer of my second year, I convinced my mother to come out and live with me. Her health was failing rapidly, and although there were continual emergency situations, I was thankful for the time with her. It surprised me, how secure and solid it felt to have another adult in the household who loved and cared about my children. Finally, I told my sons, we were a two-parent family.

In my third summer, the chair of my department asked if I would agree to be nominated for department chair, since he was taking an interim administrative position. I was elected by my department and appointed to the position by the president of the university, even though I did not have tenure at that time. There were approximately five women chairs amongst thirty such positions at the university, and none in the College of Education. More than once when I attended meetings with school district personnel, accompanied by a white male colleague, I was taken for the secretary and he for the chair. I had never seen my gender as a barrier, and it took one of my male colleagues to point out that some of the negative dynamics I was experiencing were sexism. As a mother of mixed heritage sons, I was always aware of issues of race. From my life experiences, I was intensely cognizant of issues of income. Recognizing sexism was new to me in my professional setting.

Eventually, my work ethic and the improvements in my department won respect for my skills. The faculty and I worked to make the department more diverse and more multicultural in its coursework. I did not worry about getting tenure, although I was relieved when the process was over. From the start, I was outspoken about my politics, my stance for access and equity, and my willingness to change rules that were gatekeeping devices. One of my mentors had a saying, "Faculty who are not willing to stand up for their beliefs when they are untenured, do not change once they have tenure." Either we fight for what we believe in regardless of job security, or we find other excuses later for not taking risks.

Even in the unusual position of working with a number of activists, human nature is unpredictable. My leadership was heavily influenced by my community work, and sometimes I expected a different kind of solidarity. I have learned now that disagreements over hiring, office space, and department funding can change relationships forever, which is exactly what came to pass. A conflict that began from a disagreement over hiring irrevocably changed alliances within the college.

While the college regrouped, I branched out to the larger university community and became active with a wider group of faculty. I helped initiate a renegade committee that gained recognition from other faculty and the administration. This group took a strong stance against the conservative propositions being passed in California—the initiatives supporting English only, anti-bilingual education, and anti-Affirmative Action. We organized lectures, debates, and demonstrations and formed a network of faculty, staff, and students that have continued to work together.

As department chair, I initiated an Urban Leadership Program, with a mission to produce well-prepared change agents for administrative positions in urban schools. In this instance, my community activist background served me well. I used my training in grassroots organizing to actualize this program without support from the university. I recruited, directed the program, and taught in the program. The success of the graduates was evidence of the hard work and sacrifices from everyone involved.

The program is comprised mainly of students and faculty of color and attracts students that are activists in their own ethnic communities. We often have to examine issues of nationalism in order to confront barriers to coalition building. Sometimes, due to issues of race or gender, general distrust is stronger than one's personal record and actions. As a woman who is identified as white on personnel forms, I have had my share of challenges around issues of identification, privilege, representation, and historical blame. Most of the time this is not a barrier, however, in certain situations it has provoked situations that require dialogue, negotiation, and soul-searching. Over time, the intensity of the program builds relationships and new alliances are formed that carry over to the public school setting and last long beyond the year of the program.

The Urban Leadership Program has enabled me to keep my passion burning. It is a vehicle for activism and an expression of commitment to urban communities. The students work to improve schooling for urban youth by creating conditions where academic achievement is expected and supported. In the cohort, we are not afraid to talk personally about issues of race, ethnicity, gender, class, and sexual orientation. My experience with these students connects us on a soul level, with an authenticity that is so powerful it reenergizes my work. I have learned new strategies, gained in understanding, and have been given access to important arenas outside of my university work. My work comes from a place of love, but I still use anger that comes from seeing injustice as a motivational force. Love doesn't preclude wrath, in fact, it sometimes demands it.

Reflection

After writing my story, I'm left to reflect upon its connection to my academic work. My narrative is grounded in my relationship with anthropological research, not only my involvement, but also my belief in the power of ethnographic inquiry. Qualitative researchers have always been drawn to the richness of the insider perspective, the life that quantitative data described in numbers and percentages. In the last decade, the use of personal narratives has gained in popularity in the field of education, perhaps due to the increased need to present a human side of life in the face of an increasingly technologically constructed world.

Presenting the human side of life is a fundamental aspect of anthropology. As stated by Miles Richardson (1989), "In the search to comprehend what it is to be human, anthropology pursues a multi-paradigmatic strategy . . . in addition to being both biological creatures and economic men [*sic*], however, we are, in the same fundamental manner, storytellers. . . . Storytelling is a fundamental quality of our everyday life. To be in a story is to be human, or better, the reverse to be human is to be in a story" (pp. 31–32). It is said that Gregory Bateson (1979) told the following story:

> A man wanted to know about mind, not in nature, but in his private large computer. He asked it, "Do you compute that you will ever think like a human being?" The machine then set to work to analyze its own computational habits. Finally, the machine printed its answer on a piece of paper, as such machines do. The man ran to get the answer and found, neatly typed, the words: That reminds me of a story. (p. 13)

Life histories, or autobiographies, have been used in the social sciences to provide specific examples of the relationships between the individual, culture and society, as well as to illustrate the process of socialization. "A biographical perspective presents a counterbalance to static perceptions of the role of sociocultural factors by contextualizing those factors within lives that undergo transitions and by presenting the informants perspectives and interpretations of the influences of those sociocultural factors" (Galindo & Escamilla, 1995, pp. 26–27).

The themes in my story are classic women's issues found in psychology, sociology, and economics. Low-income, single, head of households—most of them women—keep the family together, yet are seen as criminal, devious, lazy, dumb, and disgraceful, rather than as persevering and resilient. As one of the most powerless groups in the United States, they are the scapegoats of both political parties and the national dumping ground of blame for raising taxes, criminality, and the crux of what is wrong with America.

In order to succeed, single mothers feel they need to prove they are superhuman; any hint of vulnerability will lead to their demise. Asking for help is often equated with defeat. Yet, it is the close friends that penetrate the barrier of pride who provide the knowledge and support that make success possible. In my case, basic survival was based on the concept of extended family, peopled by other low-income, single mothers and their children. We provided for each other on a daily basis, whether it was a place to stay, food, money, a car to borrow, protection, childcare, alternative medical remedies, advice, or emotional support. At this level there was an absolute awareness that we were responsible for each other, and we could not let even one of the "sisters" give up, or else their children would have little chance of "turning out good." Returning to school proved to be divisive to the community we had established. My actions were interpreted by some as thinking I was better than others, but the friends who understood me became my intimate *comadres*. Eventually, four of my closest sisters also went back to school and completed graduate degrees.

Inside the system of academia, women no longer comprised my main support system; rather men raised in low-income families—mostly of color—were pivotal to my success. This created suspicion with some women who questioned my commitment to feminism, which pushed me to claim my own definition of being a feminist. In fact, much of the existing feminist coursework and research did not reflect the lives of low-income women, but rather to focus on white middle- and upper-class American women. In later years, women of color made a great impact on Women's Studies, but the struggle of welfare mothers was not a part of the agenda at that time. As time passed, I established strong relationships with women colleagues that support me intellectually and politically, and I have regained the feeling of sisterhood from my earlier years.

Analysis

In the complex world of academia, thoughtful analysis has been given to the different forms of storytelling and how they can be used. Goodson (1992a) makes a distinction between life stories and life histories. The former is the "story we tell about our life; the life history is a collaborative venture, reviewing a wider range of evidence. . . . The crucial focus for life history work is to locate the teacher's own life story alongside a broader contextual analysis" (p. 6). In my narrative, I have attempted to situate the struggle, the pain, and the success alongside the historical view of welfare mothers, of the challenges that are embedded in the politics of universities, and in the dynamics of personal relationships.

The complexity of the relationship between power, privilege, patronization, and true empowerment is another aspect that demands sober discussion. Goodson (1992b) articulates concerns that without contextual analysis, there exists the possibility of "valorizing the subjectivity of the powerless in the name of telling their story" (Sparkes, 1994, p. 165). Rather than contributing to expanding awareness and liberating the reading audience from unexamined beliefs or ideas, Goodson (1992b) continues, "This would be to merely record constrained consciousness—a profoundly conservative posture" (p. 240).

Sparkes (1994) describes another call for contextual analysis from Richardson (1992) who states that researchers need to engage in a self-reflexive analysis of the social categories to which they belong (race, social class, gender, age, sexual orientation, ethnicity, religion, etc.) "since these categories impact upon what we come to know and how we come to know it" (p. 166). Coe (1991) builds on the need for biographical positioning by suggesting that the researcher-as-author needs to indicate his or her positioning in relation to the research process. Acting on such advice raises the postmodern dilemma, discussed by Richardson, regarding just what to write about oneself in a research text—what parts of the biography or autobiography are salient to the text?

Gorelick (1991) adds her concern based on a feminist methodological perspective, when she notes that just "giving voice" is not sufficient. She explains, "although the telling of life stories may describe the world as perceived by the persons involved, it may also confine them within these perceptions and so provide them with little that they do not already know" (Sparkes, 1994, p. 166). Without careful examination, the unintended consequence can be a perpetuation of stereotypes.

Sparkes (1994) states, "Stories, then, can provide powerful insights into the lived experiences of others in ways that can inform, awaken, and disturb readers by illustrating their involvement in social processes about which they may not be consciously aware. Once aware, individuals may find the consequences of their involvement unacceptable and seek to change the situation. In such circumstances, the potential for individual and collective restorying is enhanced" (p. 178). The nature of making meaning from text puts the author and the reader on equal footing (Corradi, 1991) and creates the possibility of a collaborative dynamic. However, Goodson (1992a) persists in his ethical concerns and points out that collaborating on life histories does not eradicate the possibility of exploitation.

Overall, these points of view seem to address two main concerns: (1) Without contextual analysis, telling the story of one person's life (including one's own) in the context of academia may be superficial and possibly used to oversimplify issues or to make generalizations that are too broad; (2) Telling the story of another person's life may be inaccurate, patronizing, disempowering, or oppressive, depending on the awareness of the researcher.

What, then, is the role of my personal narrative, as well as the others in this edited volume? Given that the stories are autobiographical—researchers using their own lives as data—the relationship between the "teller of the story" and the "person in the story" are not distinct. However, the issues of contextual analysis, self-reflexive analysis, biographical positioning, exploitation, and ethics remain and are critically important to the task. Additionally, questions need to be answered, not necessarily agreed upon, and answers need not be standardized or prejudged. As the tellers of our own stories are we looking for self-aggrandizement or carrying out personal vendettas? Are we engaging in self-therapy, looking for emotional support? Do we fundamentally believe that there is a connection to be made with others by giving voice to our experiences? Will our story help others?

Further responding to ethical and methodological dilemmas, Sears (1992) "argues that the issue does not revolve around the ability to remain objective but the capacity to be empathetic" (Sparkes, 1994, p. 179). Barone (1992) adds a spiritual dimension in his discussion "concerning the involvement of academics in the production of honest and critical storytelling that enables both writer and reader to locate the beating and the aching of other human hearts" (Sparkes, 1994, p. 179). This is profoundly noted since empathy and compassion are not common categories for analysis in academia.

Life stories have the responsibility to speak for others who cannot speak for themselves, including ourselves when we are in the confines of our professional arenas. In autobiographical storytelling, the author is faced with issues that are normally taboo in the academic setting for reasons of politics, image, and credibility. At the same time, however, the transformative possibilities of telling our stories prevail. "Such . . . compelling stories . . . are openly political in that they have as their ultimate aim the empowerment of the powerless and the transformation of existing social inequalities and injustices . . . there is a need for researchers to move . . . toward a view of life history as an expression of solidarity with those who share their stories in the hope of creating individual and social change" (Sparkes, 1994, p. 180).

In her book, *I've Known Rivers* (1994), sociologist Sara Lawrence-Lightfoot analyzes why the subjects of her book told their story:

> In some ways, the important role memory plays in moving people forward in life (and up and out) might, at first, appear counterintuitive. That is, many believe that to move up the ladder of success and achievement, they must forget the past, repress it, and relinquish it. They worry that if they return to old memories, they may be swallowed up by them. So they avoid recalling them and deflect recollections when they make an unwelcome appearance in their reveries. But the storytellers in this volume have just the opposite view. They see old memories as a chance to reckon with the past and integrate past and present. This integration is one of the reasons for the extraordinary resilience of each person's character. (p. 615)

Telling my story is an affirmation of myself, as well as an act of solidarity with so many others; others who are also struggling to keep their core identity as the situations and circumstances of their lives change.

> Verily all things move within your being in constant half embrace, the desired and the dreaded, the repugnant and the cherished, the pursued and that which you would escape.
> These things move within you as lights and shadows in pairs that cling.
> And when the shadow fades and is no more, the light that lingers becomes a shadow to another light.
> And thus your freedom when it loses its fetters becomes itself the fetter of a greater freedom.
> —Kahlil Gibran (1923, pp. 43–44)

Chapter Two

From Slaveship to Scholarship: A Narrative of the Political and Social Transformation of an African American Educator

Cecil E. Canton

Introduction: In the Beginning

Cannot the nation that has absorbed ten million foreigners into its political life without catastrophe absorb ten million Negro Americans into that same political life at less cost than their unjust and illegal exclusion will involve?
—W. E. B. Du Bois, "What Would You Do?" *The Crisis*, Nov. 1925

One thing White immigrant groups could do in America was to believe that they were moving upward because the Blacks were always there: down below.
—Dr. Kenneth B. Clark, Overview III (as cited in Terkel, 1992, p. 334)

The ultimate expression of power, indeed of freedom, is the ability to define and describe oneself. This narrative is not the beginning of the freedom or power to define or describe myself, but the culmination of that freedom and power in an effort to express myself about who I am and who I have been, within the context of my journey through the puzzle of American higher education.

The history of higher education in this country has reflected, though not mirrored, the African American's tortuous journey from perceived nonentity, or what Ellison (*Invisible Man*, 1952, p. 1980) called invisibility, to the present conception of the all too visible and misunderstood "victim." Indeed, the current obsessive mewling heard in academe concerning the evil attacks on the canon and the ills of "political correctness" are the cacophony caused by an American society desperate to avoid facing the paradox between its dream and its history.

The reality of America's racial and ethnic history has not been one of inclusivity. Indeed, it has witnessed the virtual elimination of some aboriginal societies and the emasculation and disempowerment of nonwhite ethnic and cultural groups. The political doctrines which supported this ethnic and racial genocide were supported by the idea of a single cultural stream, a western European mainstream, which could simultaneously explain the lack of contribution to civilization of any other group, and manifest the rationale for maintaining a tight rein on diversity. If Western civilization is the end product of all history, then it stands to reason that anything or anybody not included in that history is unimportant! How advantageous it is to be able to avoid having to explain the inconsistencies between your public pronouncements, such as contained in the Constitution, and your private (or sometimes very public) actions, such as are embodied in slavery or "Jim Crow" segregation. Those of us who witnessed the revolutionary and evolutionary actions of the 1950s through the 1970s, had our identities fired by self-determination and forged in "Black Power." We would use and control the power of self-definition and description. No more would we accept someone else's version of who we were, nor would we allow ourselves to be co-opted by a system which we believed was now compelled to accept us as equals. It is within the context of this past that I define and describe who I have been and who I have become, both as an African American male and an African American educator.

Not the "New Deal," Just the "Raw Deal"

> Only in the case of the Negro has the Melting pot failed to bring a minority into the full stream of American life.
> —John F. Kennedy, *A Nation of Immigrants*, 1958

As a child, I heard and joined in with children as they chanted and sang a shortened version of that song, and reinforced and internalized that warning, which defined and described the political and social reality of African Americans in the United States:

> IF YOU'RE WHITE, YOU'RE ALRIGHT,
> IF YOU'RE BROWN, STICK AROUND,
> IF YOU'RE BLACK, GET BACK!
>
> —a folk saying

I was born part of a couple in the hamlet of Harlem, in the borough of Manhattan, in the city of New York on December 18, 1946. Big bands and their sounds were grudgingly giving way to Miles, Diz, and Bird and the rhythmic sounds of be-bop. The other half of the couple was my identical twin brother, with whom I would share life's bitter and better experiences. An older brother and my West Indian parents would round out the family and provide the first lessons for lives full of lessons. Reflecting back on that time I realize that for whites, being born in the United States is a statement of pride and a matter of privilege. For browns (or coloreds, in our own apartheidic language), it is a wish or rebirth embodying aspirations for a new life. But to others of a darker hue, the blacks in society, it represents a sense of desperation, a feeling of hopelessness and a state of powerlessness, the like of which no other group has ever known.

Double Consciousness: Learning about the Politics of Race and Racism 1950s Style

One ever feels his two-ness, an American, a Negro:
two souls, two thoughts, two unreconciled strivings;
two warring ideals in one dark body whose dogged
strength alone keeps it from being torn asunder.
                    —W. E. B. Dubois, *The Souls of Black Folk*, 1903

In the end, as any successful teacher will tell you,
you can only teach the things that you are. If we
practice racism then it is racism that we teach.
                    —Max Lerner, "We Teach What We Are," *Actions and Passions*, 1949

When I think about the beginning of my education, I go back to the time when I was in the first grade. I was six years old at the time and the family had moved to Amityville, Long Island, N.Y., where my parents thought they would have a better atmosphere in which to raise their children. The year was 1952 and my twin brother and I were enrolled in first grade. It was not our first experience with "integrated" schools, since our initial educational experience (kindergarten and the first half of first grade) had been in Harlem schools where all of the students were black, while all of the administrators, teachers, and staff were white. This was New York's interpretation of integration, and prior to 1954 it was an acceptable one. One day, perhaps a day after arriving in the middle of the term, while I sat in my classroom aware that I was the object of a great deal of curiosity from my white classmates, my mother appeared at the classroom door. Her intention was to look in on her children (my brother was in the other first grade class), but she unintentionally caused a great stir, culminating with a classmate to my right shouting to the teacher and the rest of the class: "Oh look, there's a chocolate lady at the door!" The next questions came in rapid-fire succession: Why are you different from us? Why do you talk funny? Why does your mother look like that? Why did you come here? Where do you come from? and so on. Like children everywhere, it was an opportunity to have raw curiosity satisfied. It was for me, however, a mortifying experience which caused me to look at myself and my mother in a way that would never be the same. We were the "other." For the first time in my life I was conscious of being different because of the color of my skin. W. E. B. Dubois described this state as "double-consciousness, this sense of always looking at one's self through the eyes of others, of measuring one's soul by the tape of a world that looks on in amused contempt and pity" (Dubois 1903, p. 5). Perhaps it was significant that this signal experience occurred in a school, because it represented an educational experience that would prologue the future and would be repeated in many different forms throughout my life.

Shortly thereafter, several events occurring in rapid succession would shock the country and send our whole world spinning dizzyingly off of the axis whose gravity had our feet rooted in second-class citizenship: the Supreme Court would rule in *Brown v. Board of Education* that segregation in public schooling was unconstitutional (1954); Emmet Till, a fourteen-year-old "Negro" boy would be murdered in Mississippi exposing the brutal face of America's racial segregation to the world (1955); and the Montgomery, Alabama, bus boycott, led by Rev. Dr. Martin Luther King would initiate the "Second American Revolution," the Civil Rights movement (1956).

Fast forward to 1964, my senior and final year in high school. It is January, and I have been scheduled to speak with my guidance counselor, a man whose name I cannot now recall. At that meeting I would be informed that I was not considered college material and therefore should not burden myself with any aspirations for higher learning. In fact, I was advised to choose and enlist in a branch of the military so as to simultaneously be able to learn a trade and to serve my country. Later, I would learn from my twin brother and other black students, that this "special" advice was provided to all of us. Ten years after *Brown,* sharing the American Dream would still be difficult, for there was still a reluctance on the part of educators to allow us access to and through education. If it were not for my mother's insistence that all of her children would attend college, I would never have challenged the commonly held belief that we were inferior and not equipped to compete with whites for a piece of the rock. The socialization process that was to prepare us for second-class citizenship had apparently not worked very well on my mother, for she refused to let our "education" limit our dreams.

It became clear during this time that being born black in the United States, was a political act, whether you were prepared to accept or deal with it or not. It is difficult to convey to someone who has never experienced this reality, the utter confusion and frustration involved. Growing up black in America is to experience both constant desperation and continuous guerilla warfare. You are always the enemy, never the ally. No one wants to be like you and sometimes that even goes for you. You are despised and ignored and after a while despair of ever finding peace. Eventually, you settle for and into the role of the embattled "other."

Resolution, Revolution, and Repudiation:
The Sleeping Giant Awakens

The American economy, the American society, the American unconscious are all racist.

—Michael Harrington, *The Other America,* 1962

Being Black in America is like being forced to wear ill-fitting shoes. Some people adjust to it. It's always uncomfortable on your feet, but you've got to wear it because it's the only shoe you've got. Some people can bear the uncomfort more than others. Some people can block it from their minds, some can't.

When you see some acting docile and some acting militant, they have one thing
in common: the shoe is uncomfortable.

—Terkel, 1992, p. 9–10

The awakening of my desire to define and describe myself, and therefore to manifest the ultimate power, was not an overnight occurrence, nor did it happen by
itself. My college days began in the context of the Vietnam War, the Harlem, Detroit, Watts, and other urban riots, and the Civil Rights struggles of the 1960s. It
would forever be marked in my life as the time of "resolution, revolution and re-
pudiation." As a people we would: (1) resolve to get off of our knees and to stand
up for our inalienable rights as full citizens in the nation of our birth; (2) revolt
against second-class citizenship and inferior treatment by whites; and, (3) repudiate the image which had defined and stifled us for hundreds of years, an image we
had accepted, but which we had neither created nor to which we had agreed. This
was the beginning of Black pride, and the shedding of old skins and sobriquets.
We would be Negroes no more! Behold the evolution of a revolutionary ideology:
"Power to the People!" Surely, America would never be the same. Or would it?

In spite of, or perhaps because of, my guidance counselor's assessment of
my potential to succeed in the academy, I enrolled in and graduated from Suf-
folk County Community College (1964–66) and then enrolled in the State University of New York at Stony Brook. The significance of this achievement was
that it was done in spite of my white counselors' continuing advice for me to
lower my sights and aspirations. SUNY Stony Brook, I was told, was too great a
jump for my intellect and abilities. Perhaps there were some other institutions
which would better suit me. Had I thought about some of the Negro colleges in
the South? Surely, Howard, Hampton, Fisk, or some other fine private institution would be within my reach. I thanked them for their time and consideration
and set my sights on Stony Brook, the only school I wanted to attend and the
only one to which I applied. I have often wondered, since that time, what would
have happened if I had heeded their advice and looked south toward Howard,
Hampton, Fisk, or some other historically black institution. But in 1966, I was in
no position to assume the financial burdens of attending an out-of-state college,
nor was I in the mood to accept another's limitations of my dreams. For the first
time in my life I had a dream that involved higher education!

The Evolution of a Revolutionary Ideology:
Power to the People

For the White man to ask the Black man if he
Hates him is just like the rapist asking the raped,
Or the wolf asking the sheep, "Do you hate me?"
The White man is in no moral position to accuse
Anyone else of hate!

—Malcolm X, *Autobiography of Malcolm X*, 1965

Unless you go back to the roots and begin to tell the truth about the past, we'll get nowhere. If someone would rape my daughter in front of my eyes and sold my daughter and I'd never see her again, sure I'd go crazy. And if I don't get any help to raise another child, with my insanity, I'd pass that along.

—Terkel, 1992, p. 10

My time at SUSB (as Stony Brook University was called) was for me a marvelous opportunity for personal growth and development. I learned much about myself, had the opportunity to work with a number of fellow students in creating the first black student organization on the campus, Black Students United, better known as BSU. It was also at SUSB that I learned that my true ambition was to become a teacher. There were in 1966, however, many inequities which were too obvious to ignore. First of all, when I arrived there were only nine black students enrolled in the entire university. Second, all of the professors were white and apparently unprepared to deal with an evolving black consciousness. Finally, student life was designed to ignore, if not offend, the sensibilities of the few black students on the campus.

It would be easy for me to relegate this time in my life as a totally negative experience, but that would be far from true. It is said that leaders are not so much born, as they are found among the ranks of ordinary people during extraordinary circumstances. The conditions at Stony Brook provided me with the opportunity to develop my own leadership skills and gave me my first leadership role. The development of the BSU in the usually benign, but sometimes hostile, environment of Stony Brook required the acquisition of both political acuity as well as organizational development ability. Those skills would be of great value to me later when I found myself in other hostile environments.

The assassination of Rev. Dr. Martin Luther King in 1968 would lend truth to the belief that "if you're Black, stay back!" Our political perceptions and realities would be altered forever by that event, and we were forged into a militant collective of outraged Black Power advocates, no matter what our previous political positions may have been. We were made painfully aware of two very important points: first, we needed to expand the numbers of black students on campus (by that time we numbered about twenty-seven); and two, we needed to be connected with the black community. The second point proved almost as daunting to achieve as the first. We were located on a part of Long Island which was isolated from any significant enclave of black people. In order to raise the black community's level of awareness regarding our existence, we would need to do something strategic, if not dramatic.

We were able to do this by taking advantage of the shock and revulsion which most people felt at the cold-blooded murder of Dr. King. The Educational Opportunity Program (EOP), sponsored by the State Education Department, became our vehicle for change and allowed us to use recruitment as a political empowerment tool. Through that program initiative we were able to simultaneously triple the enrollment of black students and call attention to our existence within black communities, from whence came our new recruits. Those new black students were recruited, if not admitted, with the understanding that they had a vital role to play in the empowerment of black people at the university and elsewhere. To paraphrase Frederick Douglass's brilliant observation, our demands for change were power's concessions.

We did not realize, or perhaps didn't know, that as we struggled for equality and the uplifting and empowerment of our race through racial identification and pride, we would unwittingly fuel white America's own racial insecurity and fears and ignite their need to both reclaim their ethnicity and reassert their collective power over and ownership of the country. Looking back perhaps we should have been prepared for this reaction. After all, hadn't we forced white Americans to face the shallowness of their commitment to equality and the emptiness of their promises for universal justice? And we were insistent that we should not lose ourselves, our own identity, in the process. In January 1969, when Richard M. Nixon took office as the president of the United States, I had just completed my matriculation and graduated from the SUSB. From that day forward, neither I nor the country would ever be the same. But at the time neither of us knew it.

College is a transitional experience. One is never completely the same person when the deed is done. Yet, there is a certain expectation on the part of family and friends that while you have changed in some ways, you are still fundamentally the same person you always were. Others in society do not share that expectation. In fact, as a black college graduate you are expected to take on a new persona, one much more acceptable and less threatening to whites in society. There is an expectation that you will repudiate long held values and beliefs, even loved ones, in order to be accepted into a society which will not accept you any other way; or any way! I felt a deep sense of frustration at the knowledge that I was forced to make choices which others were not expected to make. This nagging frustration and unease followed me into my first professional teaching job. By the time I enrolled in graduate school, I was convinced that while being white didn't require any adjustments, being black and having any professional aspirations required one to repudiate one's identity and to adopt the definitive social standard against which all success would be measured. I was not yet ready, however, to become a black white man! If America were truly serious regarding its pronouncements about and commitment to equality, making this choice would not have been necessary. As I looked forward to the decade of the '70s, I was not sure what lay before me, but I was convinced that my past would be its prologue. Attending Columbia University did not disappoint or surprise me.

Racism, Classism and Higher (Mis)education

Advocates of capitalism are very apt to appeal to the sacred principles of liberty, which are embodied in one maxim. The fortunate must not be restrained in the exercise of tyranny over the unfortunate.
—Bertrand Russell, "Freedom in Society," *Skeptical Essays*, 1928

> When you control a man's thinking, you do not have to worry about his actions.
> You do not have to tell him not to stand here or go yonder. He will find his
> "proper place and will stay in it." You do not need to send him to the back
> door, he will go without being told. In fact, if there is no back door, he will cut
> one for his own special benefit. His education makes it necessary.
> —Carter G. Woodson, *The Mis-education of the Negro*, 1933

I received a full scholarship to attend Teachers College, Columbia University. Attending was like going on a Freedom Ride. The journey took you into uncharted territory and you knew you would be changed by it, but you never knew whether you would make it back alive. Perhaps there was less physical danger, but the potential for psychological trauma was just as great. Nowhere was the message of white power and privilege more evident than at Columbia University. When I was a child growing up in Harlem, Columbia University was known as that place up on the hillside where black folk were not welcome. What I didn't know then was how much of the city Columbia University owned and how much we lived in its thrall. The university, on the other hand, was perceived to have little or no commitment to the Harlem community except as an "absentee landlord."

The struggle for control of black America has been waged around both the vagueness and vicissitudes of educational opportunity. Education has been viewed as society's great equalizer and leveler of all playing fields. In my own family, education was viewed as the key to making it in American society. This view was widely reflected and was certainly the basis for both the legal strategy employed by the NAACP and the Supreme Court's decision in *Brown*. However, education and its concomitant opportunities have always been defined and controlled by whites. A fact noted by African American scholar and educator Horace Mann Bond who observed that:

> Strictly speaking, the school has never built a new social order. It has been the
> product and the interpreter of the existing system, sustaining and being sus-
> tained by the social complex. (Bond, 1934, p. 13)

Education has been perceived as a privilege when it comes to black America. The relationship between race, class, and education has been the source of much consternation in the black community. Most of the time the discussion centered around "how much" education a person has or "where" a person got their education. Are you a Hampton, Howard, or a Harvard man? Do you have a B.S., M.S., or Ph.D.? (It is neither coincidental nor inconsequential that some members of the black community refer to them as Bull Shit, More Shit, Piled Higher and Deeper.) Those questions are easy to address and often prevent consideration and discussion of the more serious questions such as "who provides" or "what beliefs control" the educational experience. Because education is perceived as a privilege in the black community, those who receive it are often both revered and reviled. Obviously you must be a sellout to the community if you accept the white man's education. On the other hand, some would argue what other education is there? In the '70s we realized that one of the most significant results of the 1954 *Brown* decision was the elimination of separate (and unequal) black-controlled community schools and the reduction in the number of black principal and headmaster positions as those schools were more or less merged with existing ones headed by white administrators. The animating philosophy and belief underlying education in the black community is that without it we can never hope to compete for a piece of the American pie. How much of the pie we want and at what cost are questions which resonate in our communities today. However, in the optimistic 1970s our heads were filled with visions of freedom and hopes for a better future. We were ready to fight for our right to economic justice through equal educational opportunity. In order to accomplish that, we were (in the words of the great abolitionist and freedom fighter Fredrick Douglass) ready to "Agitate! Agitate! Agitate!"

Looking back, I find it interesting that my graduate school experience began very much like my undergraduate one ended: joining and leading a black student organization. BRO (Black Representation Organization) was more than a black student's organization. It aspired to represent even the voiceless and unrepresented black working class of the university: the staff and faculty. It was clear to us that race was both a social construction and a political contention. Broadening the political base had been a significant lesson from my undergraduate days and was both conceptually comfortable and politically pragmatic. Student deaths in Ohio, Georgia, and Florida merely gave us the poignant issue around which to galvanize our nascent power and emerging political identity. Ultimately, the issues of power, privilege, and respect, and who has and gets it, forced a confrontation with the administration of the university. As the president of BRO, I was deeply involved in this controversy and found myself facing a dilemma: was I here for a commitment to a cause or for my education and a degree; a reason or a season? This self-interrogation became for me a defining moment—a moment of truth! Was this merely a rhetorical and/or a dialectical inquiry? Could this question be answered by choosing one over the other? Or, was the appropriate response directed at both concerns? I had to consider that confronting the administration, biting the hand that fed me, as it were, was probably not wise with respect to my scholarship. I was close to finishing the work on my M.A. and had to consider whether some flaw would be found in my work, rendering me ineligible to receive the degree. It was in a very real sense a choice between maintaining my self-identity and my values or accepting inclusion into mainstream society on its terms. In the end, I decided that maintaining my identity and values was preferable to what some would call "selling out" I had to believe (and I did) that standing up for what I thought was right would ultimately leave me in better shape than a masters degree. Anyway, now I knew that I could do the work, I could do it somewhere else if necessary. In making my decision I relied on a philosophy which my mother instilled in each of her sons: "If what you believe isn't worth dying for, then it isn't worth living for," and "If you stand for nothing, you'll fall for everything."

In the end, we survived our confrontation with the administration, but only after organizing a demonstration which effectively shut down Teachers College and led to an unprecedented meeting with the trustees to negotiate changes in policy and practice. We came to the realization that without a racial identification, we would have no identity at all. This lesson would stay with me and influence my subsequent interactions with students, administrators, and faculty alike. Later that year, I received my masters in arts degree and realized that I had seen my reflection in both sides of higher education's mirror: empowerment and co-optation.

Certainly, not everyone believes in education as an empowerment tool. According to Rothenberg (1998), American society constructs differences in class as well as race and gender, which "impact directly on the life chances of everyone, and reflect and perpetuate the cycle of racism, sexism and class inequality that constitutes both their cause and their effect" (p.188–189). Education is the tool by which these constructions are inculcated and perpetuated. Given the hegemony that the notion of education as the great equalizer enjoys in American society, one has to question its apparent lack of success in the black community where jobs which do not require education beyond a high school diploma are the rule rather than the exception. While outsiders can afford the luxury of discussing whether racism or classism is suffocating the black community, to those in that community it represents a difference with little distinction. The work of researcher David Mantsios, indicates "that the class position of one's family is probably the single most significant determinant of future success, quite apart from intelligence, determination, or hard work" (as cited in Rothenberg, p. 189). Does race play a significant part in this apparent class struggle? According to Rothenberg, it is virtually "impossible to separate issues of class from issues of race and ethnicity" (p. 189). In the face of these institutional forces, beyond any one individual's control and power, we found it necessary to focus our collective power through political means.

Political struggle has been the basis for the transformation of the understanding of race in America. When Stokley Carmichael introduced the term "Black Power" as a means of defining, focusing, and steering the collective efforts of black people to influence the political and economic realms of American society, whites saw it as a real threat to their well-being and status. The concept of race overflows all known boundaries and serves to delimit both efforts and results by its very presence. We seem to dance to the tune and operate by the rules shaped by our understanding and perception of race. Indeed, it has been suggested by Omi and Winant that "the presence of a system of racial meanings and stereotypes, of racial ideology, seems to be a permanent feature of U.S. culture" (as cited in Rothenberg p. 17). If this is true, it would certainly help to explain why everything we do and think about is couched in racial terms, and why discussions about American culture and its institutions inevitably result in discussions of race.

I came to understand that "Black Power" could also be defined as teaching teachers. When I started graduate school, my aim was to get a masters degree in remedial reading and the psychology of the school subjects in order to be the best fourth-grade teacher the world had ever known. It was also to meet the requirements for securing my permanent certification to teach in New York State. It was Professor Ann McKillop who first suggested to me that I could have a greater impact if I taught the teachers themselves. At first I could not fathom going any further in higher education. After all, I had only come to get the all important masters for certification purposes. Yet, here was a scholar of some renown suggesting that not only did I have the ability to teach, but even the ability to teach teachers! I must admit that it gave me a certain ego satisfaction. After all, I had been socialized years before in high school to believe in my inability rather than my ability. The implications of the possibilities did not sink in until Professor McKillop informed me that she wanted me to pursue a doctorate in her department. Not only that, but she wanted me to begin getting some experience, as well as means of supporting my new family, by teaching at a local college. Professor McKillop indicated that she had spoken to someone at nearby Marymount Manhattan College who was looking for a lecturer in developmental reading. She made the initial contacts and it was set for me to interview for the position with her support. I went to the interview and was subsequently offered my first academic position in higher education.

Teaching at Marymount was not what I expected working in the academy to be. First, Marymount was a woman's college, whereas coeducation had been my only experience. Second, my job was to remediate their reading difficulties, which translated into helping them to increase their reading speed rather than "teach" developmental reading. Finally, I was the only black male teacher and the few black female students were increasingly being directed to me for developmental work, which required a much more significant time commitment than other instructors, for example, my white counterparts. I was too new at this whole thing to read anything into this condition at the time. It would be years before I realized that more was expected of me than others, though we were all being paid equally. During this time I continued to take on a full-time load of graduate courses since Professor McKillop had invited me to study with her in the doctoral program. Juggling the responsibilities of full-time graduate studies, full-time work, and a full-time family kept me on the run. I took courses at night and studied with my infant son on my lap after dinner. Looking back on those times, I often wonder how I made it through. People would often tell me that it was not possible to handle all of those responsibilities effectively. My response was always the same: I have no choice! I was surprised when Dr. McKillop approached me about the residency requirement. She informed me that although I was registered for full-time coursework and was meeting the intent of residency as a result of it, I was violating the "spirit" of residency by not being available as a full-time student. I reminded Professor McKillop that she had advised me to take the job at Marymount and that she knew it was a full-time job. Further, I reminded her that I had to be a full-time student in order to qualify for the tuition waiver scholarship which I had secured, as well as my apartment in the married students residence hall. I was caught between the proverbial rock and a hard place. I had gotten a taste of the good life and I was reluctant to have anybody take it away. All I had to do was work harder than anyone else and I, too, could make it! Or so I thought.

The hardest thing for black people to accept in American society is watching others with less ability and, in most cases, less motivation make it to the top, while we have to settle for second best. And so it was for me. Professor McKillop did not, could not, know that she had brought me to the doors of a theater which opened my eyes to new vistas and then told me that I could not afford the price of admission. The issues I had to deal with were the same as my contemporaries in the graduate program but our historical and present social reality made how we addressed them very different. I was not in a position, nor was my family, to request a loan or some other support while I met the residency requirement "spirit and intent." The reality of my urban upbringing was simple: work as hard as you can to make your way and don't look back home for financial support. You are on your own. Being at Columbia University, working as an academician at Marymount, and living on the "West Side" were seductive lures. It was easy most of the time to forget who I really was in the scheme of things and to lose my identity as a black man in white America. The price of admission to that good life, however, was cultural amnesia; total and irreversible. Did I really have to be white to be alright? I believed that inclusion of my voice and my culture and my reality could influence the epochal struggle for change being waged in higher education and beyond. Ultimately, I believed in the role I was playing in the struggle for equality and freedom.

In retrospect, going for the doctorate represented the definitive power struggle. I realized that I could not afford to subject myself to the stress of keeping up three (three) full-time responsibilities, and with Dr. McKillop's blessing I looked to more financially favorable programs of study. Someone brought to my attention a fellowship program in the Department of Educational Administration and suggested that I apply. The Program for Educational Leadership (PEL) was a fellowship program funded by the Ford Foundation designed to train the next generation of educational leaders. It was a program being run simultaneously at the University of Massachusetts (Amherst), the University of Chicago, Claremont College, Atlanta University, and of course Columbia University. At the time of my application, it was an elite program which could choose from a vast field of experienced supplicants, and which had admitted only two or three "minority" students in all of its previous cohorts. The graduates of the program were all expected to take their place as leaders in public education, either at the local district, state, or federal level. Admission to the program was a coveted prize for anyone fortunate enough to be accepted, since it provided a healthy stipend for living costs in addition to tuition, books, and travel expenses. Only fifteen students were admitted as part of the cohort each year from a pool of several hundred, if not a thousand, applicants. It was in the face of that level of competition that I applied and was accepted into this prestigious program.

My three years in the PEL flew by swiftly. The members of my cohort were the first nontraditional educators the program had ever accepted. In addition, that cohort was the first which had a majority of "minority" students. Of the fifteen accepted, eight were either black, Latino or female. Why the program had made such a radical change in its admissions policy was never fully explained. We were, however, expected to be "agents of change" in the world of public education. Given our diverse backgrounds, we knew that we would represent a change wherever we went. The Ford Foundation would fund the program for one more year after our cohort and then it was institutionalized as part of the Educational Administration Department. Whether it was restored to its original elitist position or not, I don't know. I do know that there were many students who were anxious to become PELers, with or without the stipend. I was not able to finish my dissertation during my three years of support in the program. In January 1976, my mother was stricken with an illness diagnosed as lung cancer and which would ultimately take her life in November of that same year. During the time of her illness I put completion of the dissertation very low on the list of things to do. When my mother died, I lost all motivation to finish the thesis project and decided that I would just be ABD. After all, are you any different once you get it? I was determined to show everyone who mattered that I could make it without the doctorate.

There have been several significant events that we use as a social reality check. The Supreme Court decision in *Brown*, the murder of Emmett Till, and the beginning of the Civil Rights movement, have been alluded to earlier. Several other significant events qualify as defining social moments, even though I have not given them attention in this work: the murders of Malcolm X, President John F. Kennedy, Reverend Martin Luther King, Senator Bobby Kennedy; and the prisoner rebellion at Attica State Prison in New York. This last event warrants some discussion because it would shape the public discourse about civil rights, including education, in inconceivable ways.

In September 1971, in the remote upstate New York State Prison at Attica, several hundred incarcerated black men would focus the world's attention on America's Civil Rights movement and its prisoner's rights position. The Attica Prisoner Revolt would redefine the Civil Rights movement being waged by blacks for human dignity and would thrust the role of race and education back into the forefront of America's body politic. For those of us laboring in the academy, it brought into stark relief the questions surrounding our education: were we slaves in an unjust system that would rather make us "free dumb" rather than facilitate our freedom? Once again we had to determine our role in the larger struggle being waged for dignity on behalf of black people everywhere. The actions of the prisoners at Attica forced us, like nothing else had before or has since, to face the bond and connection which we all shared as black people in America, no matter our status. In 1970, white students were murdered by white National Guardsmen at Kent State (Ohio) because they demanded changes in the existing social order. Clearly we were advocating a revolutionary change in society. We demanded to be treated with respect and to have accorded to us all the rights and at least some of the privileges of United States citizenship. What would stop the authorities from doing the same to any of us; black prisoners or students? In 1971, we were confident in neither the answer nor our continued preservation. Attica only confirmed our lack of stature in American society and our lack of confidence in the American way.

The challenge facing most blacks in whatever walks of life that they pursue is being able to work within a system and to maintain their values, culture, and ideals. The higher a black person moves up, the more he or she is expected to forget who they are and become mainstream. The problem with that position is that it is based upon an assumption that since we have been in this country so long we have and know no other culture but an American, for example, white European one. This fallacious assumption also exists in the black community which, as a result of the dehumanizing effects of slavery, has had imbedded in its collective consciousness negative images and stereotypes about who we are and who we have been: Dubois' concept of "double-consciousness." In fact, while other early immigrant groups have used their race, culture, and ethnicity to make progress, blacks are accused of making trouble when they attempt to do the same, placing more pressure upon them to forget their racial identity. From 1976 through 1994, I was employed in several state agencies: the NYS Division for Youth, The NYS Office of Mental Health and the NYS Department of Correctional Services. Although any of these experiences could be written about individually as object lessons in institutionalized racism, I will discuss the latter, since it was my longest stay in state government. Two significant things happened to me in 1980. I finished and successfully defended my dissertation, and I was hired by Correctional Services as an assistant deputy commissioner for Program Services. I now had a new job and new "status," or so I thought. I was given the charge by the commissioner of the department to change the structure, delivery, and curricula of educational services in the state prison system. Although I was qualified to carry out this assignment, by virtue of previous training and experience, I was perceived by several high level, but subordinate staff, to have been hired as a result of some "affirmative action" mandate. Although they never directly expressed it, they were not happy to be subordinate to a black person. In the prison systems of most states and the federal government, black men are generally the inmates, not the staff, middle management, or boss. For white men, especially those used to giving orders to blacks (inmates), it is particularly difficult to recognize and defer to power when it is in the hands of blacks.

In addition, there were many things that were done under the guise of accepted practice which had negative consequences for the families of inmates, the majority of whom were black or Latino. It is not that these things had never been questioned before but there was not much success in changing them. There are times when all that is needed is to be present in the room when decisions are being made in order to have an effect on those decisions. Sometimes I didn't even have to ask why certain things were being done in order to have them changed, simply because my presence called attention to the unfairness of the policy or practice to blacks and Latinos. Whenever I challenged policy or questioned practice too hard, I was called difficult, sensitive, and not a team player. White corrections officers (COs) and other bigots in the facilities referred to me as the "inmate in a suit," which I guess to them was the ultimate insult! It proved that in public employment, like education, we must maintain our racial identity. A fact which we would be foolish to forget. I had moved up in my status on the plantation, from the field to inside the house, but to them I was still just another "nigger." There was particular antipathy in the penal system to blacks with advanced degrees. It was my belief, however, that probably no one with higher education behind them was ever truly accepted. Perhaps it reflects a culture which only recently began to respect higher education as a valid contributor to progress in the system. Corrections is one of the last areas of employment in criminal justice where you can be hired with only a high school diploma or GED and make a decent living. In that culture one advances, not because of additional formal education or advanced degrees, but typically by working oneself up through the security hierarchy from corrections officer to warden (or superintendent), although there have been exceptions to that rule. For the time that I spent working in the penal system, I felt like I was involved in guerilla warfare where I was always the enemy. I came to believe the old folks' saying that the more things change, the more they stay the same. There is a popular phrase that is used in corrections systems all over the country: "talking the talk and walking the walk." The saying basically means being true to oneself and others at all times; being straight. People working in state penal systems pride themselves on living that motto. It is unfortunate that they don't think it applies to Black employees or "inmates in a suit!"

A Dream Deferred:
California, Academia, Race, and Racism

Give a hungry man a stone and tell him what beautiful houses are made of it; give ice to a freezing man and tell him of its good properties in hot weather; throw a drowning man a dollar, as a mark of your good will; but do not mock the bondman in his misery by giving him a Bible when he can't read it.
—Frederick Douglass, "Bibles for the Slaves"

Injustice which lasts for three long centuries and which exists among millions of people over thousands of square miles of territory, is injustice no longer; it is an accomplished fact of life.
—Richard Wright, *Native Son*

In 1991, I was recruited to join the criminal justice faculty at California State University, Sacramento (CSUS). My California adventure began with my acceptance of the state as the "promised land" of racial and ethnic diversity. It turned out that I was only California "dreaming." What I found was a state embroiled in a struggle to prevent racial and ethnic polarization from tearing itself apart. Here was the great American dilemma being played out in microcosm in one of the nation's most important racial bellwether states. It became immediately apparent to me that those who enjoyed privilege were reluctant to part with or share it. I was surprised to find out that diversity was not really considered important or necessary. There was an important drama being played out on a statewide scale that later would have significant implications for the nation.

Acceptance of the faculty position would not be without its share of controversy and drama for me. In the period leading up to the offer of the tenure-track position, I was able to negotiate the rank of professor (full) as a trade-off for the significant cut in pay I would experience having decided to take the position. Unfortunately, I was not able to negotiate tenure, which would become a problem for me later. Joining the faculty under the following circumstances was very difficult for me and all concerned. First, the university was involved in a hiring phase that was attempting to provide for more ethnic, racial, and gender diversity. Second, I didn't realize that the current chair of the division, the same person who had recruited me, was involved in a power struggle with his colleagues in the division over bringing in more women and people of color. Third, my faculty peers did not perceive me to have met the qualifications for the position, thus I was a dreaded affirmative action hire. Finally, for those who had, in their own opinion, labored long and hard to climb the ranks of the professorate, my coming in at the top of the scale was perceived as a slap in their face and wholly inappropriate. Given those conditions, I felt isolated and completely at risk in a hostile environment. The only people who would interact with me, in any significant manner were either the office clerical staff, the new faculty hired with me or those established faculty members who had some understanding of what I was going through. Even some of the senior black faculty, who I thought should have extended their support, were noticeably conservative.

In spite of my best efforts to avoid it, I found myself hearing a familiar refrain: If you're white, you're alright! If you're brown, stick around! But if you're black, get back! Unless you have come face-to-face with blatant individual prejudice, it is often difficult to recognize it when it presents itself in "hidden, sometimes unintentional ways" (Rothenberg, 1998, p. 136). Only once did the prejudice, that I felt was always there, break through the surface. Given the law enforcement backgrounds of many of my colleagues on the faculty, I was amazed that I wasn't exposed to it more often. Perhaps it was too subtle for me to recognize and respond to. Whatever the reason, what I found was much more organizational discrimination and institutional racism than the individual variety. If you were to ask any of these faculty whether they considered themselves racist, they would probably answer in the negative. They would no doubt further elucidate their positions by speaking of "affirmative action," "color-blind society" and "gender neutral" policies, which make individual racism and discrimination difficult, if not impossible, to carry out. It is conceivable that you might hear terms like "reverse discrimination," "reverse racism," and "illegal quotas" bandied about with righteous indignation. What you wouldn't hear from my colleagues would be a level of consciousness about their use of the unofficial and official rules, policies and practices that protect and promote the status quo arising from past racist and sexist actions, and continue to give them the privileged status which they believe they have earned and deserve. Perhaps because these actions are so often considered part of the "normal" way of doing things, they would have difficulty recognizing that they are discriminating and as a result would resist abandoning these practices despite their clearly discriminatory results.

Rothenberg (1998) describes the discrimination against minorities and women as an "interlocking process," which ties together individual attitudes, organizational structures, and past events into a self-fulfilling prophecy of failure and inter-generational and perpetual frustration.

> Discrimination must now be viewed as an interlocking process involving the attitudes and actions of individuals and the organizations and social structures that guide individual behavior. That process, started by past events, now routinely bestows privilege, favors, and advantages on White males and imposes penalties on minorities and women. This process is also self-perpetuating. Many normal, seemingly neutral, operations of our society create stereotyped expectations that justify unequal results; unequal results in one area foster inequalities in opportunity and accomplishment in others; the lack of opportunity and accomplishment confirm the original prejudices or engender new ones that fuel the normal operations generating unequal results. (p. 142)

The reality of my situation was that I had to make a choice about how I was to respond to the circumstances in which I found myself. I could allow my peers and the academy's racist structure to shut me up, swallow me up, grind me up, and spit me out. Or I could find other ways to maintain my values and prove my value as a bona fide member of the university. In a state whose voters approved ballot initiatives such as Three Strikes and You're Out! (Proposition 154), Denial of Services to Undocumented Immigrants (Proposition 187), and the so-called Civil Rights Initiative (Proposition 209: Anti-Affirmative Action), it appears that Californians want a return to "separate as the fingers of the hand" (the legal standard developed and applied by the U.S. Supreme Court in *Plessey v. Ferguson*), as the means for dealing with race and class issues. A social digression of that magnitude would clearly provide liberty and justice for some, but not all, and would go a long way toward protecting all important advantages and privileges maintained by the status quo. It is significant that Governor Pete Wilson attempted to use some of these "wedge" issues in his effort to win the Republican Party's nomination for president in the 1996 national election. His lack of success appeared to result more from his lackluster personality than the fact that Americans deplore the use of such issues and strategies in their politics. In the end I chose to deploy a strategy which allowed me to interact with a greater number of people in a wider array of venues and issues. This actually was beneficial from two perspectives. First, it allowed me to get to know people (both staff and faculty) and issues in other areas of the university. Second, it kept me from focusing on the hostile environment created by my colleagues and drowning in their negativity. While they thought that I was accepting "busy" work on school and university-wide committees and work groups, I was carefully and deliberately developing positive working relationships with other faculty, staff, and administrators. Rather than having to request information from departmental colleagues, whom I could not trust, I was able to go directly to the source whenever I needed information or required some action. Developing positive relationships with my students, by being interested in their issues and being available to them when they need assistance, has also allowed me to reduce the conflict and stress levels in my environment.

Is it possible to keep your identity and values while you work in the system? My experience says "Yes!" But there are important things which must be accomplished in order to make sure the value is mutual:

1. You must have confidence that you are a worthwhile and valued person, above and beyond your value to the university. Insist on being accepted as you are.
2. Find role models that you can follow and emulate. If they are available where you are, so much the better. If they aren't, find someone somewhere who can serve as a mentor to you. I have never forgotten my father's advice: When you're walking through a minefield, try and follow someone else.
3. It is important that you determine what you need to change, if change is needed. While others may seem to have your best interests at heart, you and you alone have to live with the consequences of your decisions.
4. Keep reframing issues "up" not "down." In other words, try to keep a positive spin on what you do and what happens.
5. Find the principle and stick to it.
6. Find others of like mind who can support you and support them as well. We all need support sometimes!
7. Remember that the interests and principles you have are enduring, but allies come and go depending upon the issue.
8. If you truly believe that you are right, you must be willing to sometimes stand alone.
9. Always be positive and as the late congressman Adam Clayton Powell, from New York, reminded us, "Keep the faith, baby!"

Chapter Three

Hanging In: The Journey to Good Enough

Eugenia D. Cowan

Daddy always said, "You'll never be Good Enough. You're going to have to be better." For most of my adolescence, I thought he was just criticizing me, urging me to strive for excellence. It wasn't until I had left home for college that I began to understand that "good enough" wasn't Good Enough. All these years later, I feel that I am finally "getting it."

Many times, I feel like I'm faking it, just to be where I am. What will I do when someone finds out? What will I lose? Have I been the impostor, posing as acceptable so I can "fit in?" Has the joke really been on me since I have fooled no one? Have I simply been tolerated, while all the time I thought I was really "making it?" While I've been making my way toward Good Enough, have I just been pretending so that they'd think I already arrived? Reality has it that the dynamics of the academy are such that it is easier for me to doubt myself than to disparage the institution. It is designed that way. It is a mainstream, dominant-culture institution, to which no minority cultures have historically had equal access. The point is to keep it that way. Getting in and surviving is usually a complex process of moving forward and jumping back, of demanding entry and pleading for acceptance. It usually requires that the member of the non-dominant culture who wants in meets certain standards for entry that go beyond academics and experience. And then once I was in, I wasn't sure I was welcome. I'm still not sure that I am.

The major issues I have struggled with have to do not only with the members of the dominant culture in the academy but also with members of oppressed minority groups who have been successful in their efforts to "make it." It is not simply a matter of white against the rainbow. It is more that getting in and staying in requires constant repainting.

Working in community-based organizations with people of all colors, ages, sexual orientations, religions, and both genders led me to believe that anyone could succeed as long as he or she worked hard and did his or her best. Higher education was my lesson for life, I guess. What I know now is that Daddy was right. Being skilled as an educator was not enough to get hired. Having an impressive resume wasn't enough. I began to understand the importance of knowing the "right" people. In my experience, "right" proved to be white.

Getting hired was a struggle in itself. The many years I spent honing my skills as an educator and seeking opportunities are probably not unusual among most educators, if not all. There was a brief moment of exhilaration the day I received the letter offering me a full-time, tenure-track position on the faculty. And thus my "Good Enough" journey is in full swing.

My experiences and interpretations do not speak for everyone like me. Yet individual journeys can have a profound impact on groups, communities, institutions, and their policies and practices. Higher education and professional status are not passports to privilege, contrary to popular belief. For into each arena goes all of who I am, regardless of its packaging or presentation.

Prologue

Born and raised in Carson City, Nevada, I have always been cognizant of the whiteness of the world. My mother worked for the federal government doing clerical work in my early days. My father worked for them, too, as a teacher in an American Indian boarding school. I knew the world as a place where white people ruled. Indians were kept from sight in boarding schools, and black people, well, there were so few that we could move freely between the white mainstream and the Indian hideaway. I went to school with the white kids and lived among the Indians on the campus of the boarding school. The only prejudice I knew was leveled at the Indians. I didn't understand it because my experience with Indians was positive. And aside from the way they treated the Indians, I remember positive experiences with white people, too.

I went to Bible school in Los Angeles where I got a real dose of prejudice against anyone with dark skin. It was the 1970s and the Ku Klux Klan was active to the point of burning crosses near the school. I know the intent was to frighten the black students, of which there were a handful, but the school took steps to protect us, restricting our movement to the campus. It didn't occur to me at the time to wonder why my movement should be restricted instead of theirs. So great was my fear of being safe in the white world that I elected to work on campus after I graduated, following a brief (three months) stint working for a finance company in Fullerton.

I went on to pursue a master's degree in San Diego and landed in Santa Barbara in 1983. I worked there as the executive director of the Gay and Lesbian Resource Center for seven years, during which time I attended the University of California, Santa Barbara (UCSB) for my doctorate. That came after

I heard a news report that the university had too few black professors. Not knowing anything about higher education, I assumed that I could just go there with my master's degree and apply to teach. The affirmative-action officer informed me that I needed a doctorate to teach and helped me enroll in a unique confluent education program. Finally, I felt safe. I believed I had found a "home" among academics who believed as I did about education, the processes of teaching and learning, and a host of other worldviews. I looked forward to moving into a teaching position and making my home permanently in Santa Barbara, which was, not surprisingly, much like Carson City in its overwhelming whiteness. Imagine my surprise when I learned that the university would not hire me to teach until I had gained substantial experience elsewhere! But having had no professional teaching experience, I was at a loss as to how I would get that experience. I was accomplished as an administrator, in organizational development and management, in leadership and public policy—everything, it seemed, except for teaching. At the same time, my tenure at the Resource Center was coming to an end. There was no teaching position waiting for me, no job anywhere. I knew I had to leave but where to go? How would I find another niche to fit in? I saw myself wandering as I felt I had before coming to UCSB.

I was lucky enough, because of my work experience and reputation, to secure a new position, but it was not in Santa Barbara. I left, and moved to Petaluma, where I lived with my sister, and commuted daily to my new job in Sacramento. I worked as the executive director for a statewide HIV/AIDS public policy advocacy and community organizing organization. During that time, I also began teaching part-time at California State University, Sacramento (CSUS). Eventually, I moved to Sacramento, taught full-time/part-time at CSUS, and pursued a career in higher education in earnest.

It was at UCSB that I had the unbelievable good fortune to meet professors who would profoundly impact my life and my career. One of them, a Jewish woman, would later be a mentor and colleague. It was her guidance and intervention that brought me to my current position.

The Good Little Black Girl

The politics of the academy boil down to who you know and who you "hang with," from what I can tell. I often find myself in a quandary about when to speak to whom about what and when to stay silent. On the surface I feel the most secure when I keep silent. In my waking nightmares I am the "good little black girl," one who "doesn't make trouble." In my center I am ashamed that I do not speak up, ashamed of my fear and sense of insecurity. That has meant checking myself to see that I don't say the "wrong" thing, regardless of its veracity. It has meant that I keep quiet when I feel the need to speak out. It has meant that I've done as instructed, whether I've wanted to or not. Upon reflection, I find that such individual choices are not unknown to my ancestors:

> Slaves often told "lies" to [W]hite oppressors to keep from being brutally punished or murdered. They learned that the art of hiding behind a false appearance could be useful when dealing with the [W]hite master and mistress. Skillful lying could protect one's safety, could help one gain access to greater resources, or make resistance possible. Slave narratives testify that the ability to deceive was a requirement for survival (hooks, 1993, p. 20).

Does the instinct for survival excuse what to me is so contrary to what I believe to be right? Or is this really just about appropriate judgment? I feel pressure to keep quiet or "water down" my opinions, from not only the white people in charge but from my colleagues of color as well. More than once, I have compromised my sense of truth and integrity to ensure my survival in this climate.

With the Dominant Culture

I had been at the university as a part-time lecturer for three years, following which I began my first year there in a tenure-track position. It was at that time that I was invited to participate in an effort to organize and implement collaborative efforts between the school and the local community. The group struggled to organize itself and found itself struggling with questions about the role of the school, instructional strategies, curriculum regarding collaboration, and so much more. What was clear from the beginning was that collaboration was not something prioritized in our school among either faculty or students. Because of my experience working with community groups, I agreed to work with my colleagues. Quickly I discovered that there was an unspoken assumption that I would somehow connect the group with other people of color, both in the school and in the community. All by myself! I also found that I was constantly the "voice of diversity," always the one to raise the issue of inclusion. The response I received, fairly regularly, was some annoyance. On one occasion, I raised concern that the meeting being planned did not include on its agenda addressing school-site problems centered on issues of diversity. Remarks like, "well, then, you come up with a scenario! After all, if anybody should know what that's like, you should, right?" demonstrated to me what was expected of the color of my skin, and, by association, of me. Not atypically, it was somehow up to me to speak on behalf of all people who look even remotely like me. As long as their skin color was tinted or their primary language was not English, I was the lucky spokeswoman.

Eventually I learned that the environment was not safe for discussion of diversity, so I kept quiet. Having now had time to reflect, I understand the situation as evidence of my mainstream colleagues' discomfort with people who are different. I also believe that as educators, we have the responsibility to be leaders in facilitating opportunity for all. Perhaps some of their discomfort could be traced to facing their failure to do so.

I learned two things from that experience. First, I discovered a more hostile environment than I had expected. Most of my white colleagues prefer to believe that we are somehow above the "isms"; that no one we know is in the least uncomfortable regarding issues of difference. They would rather think that they are sensitive and respectful and that they have healed all manner of racism, sexism, and homophobia that they spent most of their lives unconsciously learning. My presence seems to be initially for the purpose of proving that. That I'm invited to participate, or that I'm included, comes off like a gesture to demonstrate how together they are. But the second edge of the sword is that I serve as a somewhat thorny reminder, if I speak up, of all that has not been dealt with properly, of the racism, sexism and homophobia that still exist in their worldviews. Raising these issues and concerns triggers the discomfort of the people in power; they are forced to face the fact that people who look like me are still not completely welcomed or embraced in the academy. To the extent that they tolerate the silencing of voices like mine or fail to confront the "isms" when they pop up, they must acknowledge the "isms" they still hold. After a meeting in which racism and sexism became issues, the comment was made, "I didn't realize that these issues bothered me so much. I really thought I had it licked. I mean, I know I'm not racist, but, wow, I guess I've got some thinking to do."

The comment came as part of an apology, an act which received great respect and admiration from me. It's one of those deeply held goals for me to be so consistent and courageous that I can acknowledge truth regardless of how uncomfortable it makes me. Of course, when it comes to surviving in the academic environment, that goal becomes that much more difficult to reach. I was not invited to return to a regular meeting of another group, that included some students, and I believe that speaking up truthfully was part of the reason, if not all of it. I had commented that an activity the group was planning for Indigenous People's Day could not just be a food festival with Indians dancing at noon. It had to be an honest effort to address the meaning of the events of 500 years ago. To do any less would be insulting to those of us whose ancestral lands had been taken from us forcefully by the invading white conquerors. A sampling of the responses I received:

"Hey, it wasn't our fault! We weren't even there!"
"Well, we can't be insulting white people either."
"We don't know what else to do! How are we supposed to do all that? It would be way too much work."
"If we do that, white students won't come."

Then imagine my surprise when I was not notified about the follow-up meeting, nor further included in other activities. When I asked about it later, I was told by a friend, "I think it's because you said the truth." And that addresses the second thing I learned. I quickly became known, at least among that group, as the one who always brings up diversity. I know that there are other colleagues of mine who share a similar reputation on campus. Sometimes it gets us excluded from places we believe we should be, and we have to take purposeful and concrete action to be included. In terms of justice, of all things right and good, I believe my constant voicing of multicultural issues to be a good thing. In terms of my continued survival in the academy, I don't know.

In addition to the dominant majority culture, in general, there are pressures from the all-powerful administration. I can never be absolutely sure of the motivation, especially in cases where the administration is represented by people with skin color similar to mine. In my younger years, I heard stories from other black professional educators about how they were forcibly grouped together by having to share offices or being located in one building or part of a building. I remember thinking it absurd that these professionals would perceive that as somehow negative and racist on the part of the university administration. I thought, "Geez, that'd be great! To be all together with people who are just like me! I couldn't ask for a better arrangement."

I somehow thought that I'd experience the camaraderie of likeness in such a situation, as opposed to the loneliness of isolation and fear of the Other, when placed among so many of the dominant majority (translate: me among so many white people!). I've since learned that the color of one's skin is not a whole lot of common ground since most people are extraordinarily complex beings. There must be more for people to share. Certainly, it is part of building relationships to discover what that ground is. But for the assumption to be made that like ethnicities attract is absurd. It appears to be an effort of control when the only apparent reason for such locale assignments is race/ethnicity. It is the same thing as attempting to mandate relationships of any kind among people. It hearkens me back to the days before the Civil Rights movement when interracial marriage was illegal. By law, intimacy was only allowed among people of like ethnicity. Maybe this is not marriage but the reminders that come with it are frightening.

In other similar situations, I have asked what the motivation really was. I have never ceased to be surprised at the insistence of those whites in power that they thought I'd like to have a black person close by. Pressed further, I heard responses like, "Well, I thought you'd like to have the support. . ." or, "Don't you think it works better for you folks to be together?" and, "It just makes sense." My questioning mind has me wondering who it "works better" for. It reminds me of putting all the blacks together in one part of the plantation away from the main house. Where, I wonder, is the demonstration of support for plurality that is such a watchword these days? If, indeed, our colleges and universities are concerned about the diversity of our campuses and if we, as an academic community, really do believe in, and support, the value of diversity, should we not make every effort to facilitate its meaning? Should we not strive to introduce people of every ethnic origin to each other to enhance the growth of knowledge, ideas, and acceptance? To me, assigning people of like ethnicities to each other, for no other reason than that, directly contradicts everything I've heard about how evident our support for diversity is.

With Faculty of Color

Early in my tenure at the institution where I currently work, I was invited to meet with faculty members of color who had established themselves as an ongoing group monitoring the school's policies and actions regarding multicultural issues. The group was (is) made up of faculty of color and white faculty whose sensitivities and concerns were consistent with the mission of the group. Most faculty of color in my school are Latino; black faculty make up less than 5 percent of our school's faculty; I was one of three. Aside from myself, there was one Native American Indian on the faculty. While I agreed with the group on most issues, I found myself hesitant to speak up when I did not agree.

The sticking point for me was that most of the multicultural issues discussed (at that time) had to do with bilingual education. My interest, and concern, was in the absence of black faculty and low percentages of black students. Yet, when the bilingual issues were discussed, I was urged, rather strongly, to speak out in support of the creation of an organized resource to address them (i.e., an academic center of some sort). What about the barriers and issues facing black students? I pondered the question and asked other black faculty members how black students would figure into this department, since so much focus was placed on students for whom English was a second language. This was before the Ebonics discussion came into vogue. The overall response was, "We can't make too much noise about that. We have to go along with it or there won't be any department to address these things. Besides, we can't afford to say too much, or they'll think we're trying to take over or something."

So I stayed silent on the issue of black students in the school. A department was created and there remains minimal black faculty represented there. Most of the black students I see in the school come through that department; I wonder who they look to for guidance. I wonder what they feel when they are discussed as part of the "bilingual problem." I wonder how they feel when the public's resistance to bilingual education translates into resistance to the success of other oppressed students. It is not at all uncommon for the issue of educating language minority students to become a barrier to education for all minorities. The issues seem to get mixed up under the umbrella of multiculturalism.

What I understood from that experience was the struggle to be included and recognized, when the power structure would rather pit ethnicities against each other. It was my "responsibility" to support the cause led by Latinos at the expense of my concerns relative to my own, or any other, ethnic group. If we are unable to agree and present a unified effort, the power structure does not have to act. We empower the power structure with our fragmentation.

I also understood my own internal struggle to be viewed as a "good" person, as doing the "right" thing, by my peers. To avoid the appearance of being reactionary, or uninformed, I played the part I was expected to play at tremendous expense to my sense of integrity. Doing so has had a profound effect on my sense of self. Where I come from, the truth is what defines one's reality. And one's sense of reality is what defines the truth. In my former career, speaking out was expected, and, to some degree, celebrated—by someone. Here, speaking out is risky. Without tenure, without status, I am vulnerable. Belonging demands a price in this environment; it means I can't afford to "offend" anyone, especially not the majority in charge. My continued existence here feels tenuous, precarious. It's hard to be the good little black girl; I've never done it before.

And in the Classroom?

My primary areas of expertise are research and curriculum. Those are typically the courses I teach each semester. Every so often, though, I am called on to teach one of the diversity-related courses offered by the school. Each time I approach the course with some timidity. My experience has taught me that, regardless of the disclaimers, students tend to see me as representing the whole of diverse cultures. Some expect me, on sight, to be angry and prejudiced against white people, men, and nongay women. One student actually told me, "I wanted to take your course, because one of my friends who had you for another course said you were prejudiced against white women, and I wanted to see for myself."

And that was for a research course! Comments like that cause me to have to take another look at how I present myself and course material on bias. When teaching the school's required course designed to introduce issues of diversity in the classroom, I know I am going into the classroom complete with all my baggage, emotional and psychological, related to my many experiences of oppression.

My most recent experience with this had me before a class of twenty-two white people, including two women of mixed racial heritage and two men. The experience was actually very powerful as my presence brought up lots of emotional baggage for the students. Throughout the course, I got comments like, "I feel like dropping this course. It's painful to be reminded of how hateful people have been to me. Sometimes, it's just too much," from a woman of color; and, "I guess I never really thought about how the kids in my classes must be experiencing the world," from a white woman; and, "And what about the children? I'll bet they hurt as much as I do," also from a white woman. The students were, without a doubt, sincere. But initially they were skeptical. They weren't sure what, if anything, they could learn from the course. One student said, "We've been through this stuff a million times before. Now what?"

I see these courses as opportunities for both personal and professional growth. I try to present material in ways that are nonconfrontational but matters of objective truth; by "objective," I mean open to perception and interpretation.

My own history and experiences influence my presentation, but I try to stay mindful of that. The hard part is to manage my own emotional responses to memories or even current experiences and to pin the blame on its rightful target. It never fails, though, that my white students, or the men in my class, take very personally whatever they perceive to be criticism or blame. I try to make very clear that, individually, each of them can only be held responsible for their participation in, and perpetuation of, systems of oppression. To the extent that they benefit from the legacy of discrimination against women and people of color is the extent to which I, their teacher, expect them to check themselves and choose to act to facilitate change. What I usually get in response is, "But it's such a huge problem! How can I change the whole school district? The only thing I'd get is losing my job."

I understand, perhaps better than most, the danger that exists in standing against a power structure that controls one's financial and professional well-being. I just don't see that as a good enough reason to take no action in the face of how much damage that structure is doing. I encourage my students to take an assessment of themselves to find out how they are participating in the perpetuation of what is actually just simple hatred. That's the part of the process that, when engaged, is the most painful for them. The following came from a white male student's final journal entry for the class.

> I didn't expect to find out the things I found out about myself. I feel ashamed, and I want to ignore it. I want my life to go back to what it was before this class started. I was comfortable. Now I understand that I actually did take my power over my students in the name of what was good for them. I took away their voices. I wonder how many times I've done that throughout my life.

It got painful for me when students vocalized their objections to bell hooks's (1994) work, *Teaching to Transgress*. I assigned the Introduction, and asked for a three-page response paper and participation in class discussion. The discussion began slowly and then it picked up some serious steam. One passage, in particular, seemed to draw indignant responses:

> That shift from beloved, all-black schools to white schools where black students were always seen as interlopers, as not really belonging, taught me the difference between education as the practice of freedom and education that merely strives to reinforce domination. (p. 4)

Over and over, students kept saying, "We don't teach domination!" and, "That's a very prejudiced statement. Maybe thirty years ago, but it isn't like that now." Most of them saw hooks as a serious radical activist who simply didn't understand them as teachers or students in mainstream public schools. In response papers, students often spoke of how oppressed people should "take the bull by the horns," and make their own acceptance and potential for success. So many of them just could not accept that oppression is institutionalized in hierarchies of power to which each of us pays homage. It was only the two students of mixed racial heritage who understood that, and who, by the end of the course, were galvanized to be authentic with their classmates about their own experiences.

I found it interesting that these students had studied together for two years, were nearing the end of their program, and these two students had not shared themselves, their pain, their experiences, their journeys of discovery and triumph. They talked about being afraid, as some of their classmates were also in positions of power over them. One, a woman of color, said,

> It's too risky to talk about that stuff. I am a woman, I am of mixed ethnicities, and I am vulnerable. If I talk about the oppression I've faced and how angry it makes me, I could be putting my job in jeopardy. My superiors might see me as a radical or something, and it could mean trouble.

I must admit to some surprise. I began to think of the times I had put myself in that kind of jeopardy with my attitudes and outbursts. I wondered if my supervisors had ever considered terminating me because of my teaching about racism and sexism and homophobia. Reminds me of the days of "yes, massa." And I thought of how far I had journeyed, to be able to speak out with relative comfort, despite my untenured status.

It was a difficult course for me to teach, primarily because I struggled with the denial and defensiveness displayed by the students. I wanted them to "get it," to understand and take responsibility for their own behavior and decisions, unconscious or otherwise. I wanted them to take responsibility for the implications of their teaching practices and to act to make change in their classrooms and schools. I wanted them to say, "Oh! I see. That's true, ya know. We *are* in positions of power by virtue of our skin color, some of us our gender, and then by our professions. We can make a difference." I chalk that up to my idealism. What I actually saw reflected hooks's (1994) comments:

> Noncomformity on our [students'] part was viewed with suspicion, as empty gestures of defiance aimed at masking inferiority or substandard work. In those days, those of us from marginal groups who were allowed to enter prestigious, predominantly white colleges were made to feel that we were there not to learn but to prove that we were the equal of whites. We were there to prove this by showing how well we could become clones of our peers. As we constantly confronted biases, and undercurrent of stress diminished our learning experience. (p. 5)

I was glad when the course ended. Hearing, and dealing with their denial brought pain and fear to me. If that's how they responded to assignments and lectures and class discussions, what would they say on course evaluations?

I find these courses difficult to teach, primarily because I feel I have to prove myself and win white students', straight students', and male students' approval. I'm acutely aware of not being Good Enough. I'm aware of representing something to students of color. So many have told me, "I've never had a class with a black professor before." For once I get to be in a class where the person in power looks like me.

My educational experience was the same. But now I'm the professor, not the student. The power of my position seems to only complicate the issue because white and male students expect that I will use the power of my position to punish them, "I'm not sure what to say here, 'cos you're giving out the grades. I don't want you mad at me or anything, so I have to say what you want me to."

My experience of the students in these classes brings back yet another of hooks's (1994) comments:

> The unwillingness to approach teaching from a standpoint that includes awareness of race, sex, and class is often rooted in the fear that classrooms will be uncontrollable, that emotions and passions will not be contained. . . . Many professors have conveyed to me their feeling that the classroom should be a "safe" place. . . . (p. 39)

The emotions and passions that usually arise in these classes sometimes bring conflict with them. I'm not afraid of that. It's the perception that my presence indicates to so many of my students that my classroom is not a "safe" place for them. If only they knew that it doesn't feel very safe to me, either. "Students of color and some white women express fear that they will be judged as intellectually inadequate by [their] peers" (hooks, 1994, p. 39). The difference is that expressing my fear is perceived as weakness at first. If I am successful, that perception gradually morphs into some kind of respect for my willingness to be vulnerable and human. I want to be modeling humanness for my students. I want to be teaching them courage, especially in the face of the very real threat that oppression is. Sometimes, I do:

> You know, when you told us the first night that you didn't care if we agreed with you or not, or if we changed at all, I thought you were just being defensive. When you talked about how scary it is for you to be up in front of so many white people, I thought, "oh great! This class is gonna be a bust." Now, though, I think you do care if we grow as humans. You showed me what it is to be human and have the courage to be authentically human, even when you perceive yourself to be in danger.

Another final journal entry. Sometimes I am unsuccessful and I hurt, "This course would have been better if the professor had not talked so much about herself. That doesn't help me teach better. She seems weak and afraid of being the teacher," and, "You're a successful Black woman. You should hold your head up and be proud of that. You shouldn't be afraid of anything, because you've made it. I think you say those things to make us feel sorry for you."

I feel the pain of failing to be Good Enough more intensely than I feel the pride and joy of having proven myself. It seems that it doesn't really matter how often I am successful, or how much positive impact I make, I fear the failing and the pain it brings more. I also know that it gets in my way, that it holds me back sometimes. I can only imagine that it's another piece of the lifelong journey that I'm on to arrive at Good Enough.

It doesn't seem to matter how often I remind students that they are not graded on their opinions only on their knowledge used to arrive at them. I'm sunk if a student does substandard work and happens to be white and/or male. If I give the grade I believe is deserved, I run the risk of being targeted and punished by the system in power. If my students of color do substandard work and I give the grade I believe is deserved, I am attacked for being a "race traitor." It's a double bind that I live through, take the risks, and look to my allies in the academy to support me in managing. It's a challenge I face in every class. I'm determined to maintain my integrity and give the grade I feel is deserved, regardless. I try to mitigate my own sense of insecurity by giving those students extra feedback and support in improving so they can earn the grade they want. So, on reflection, I see that I am acting to protect myself and furthering my commitment to my students at the same time. It is sadly true that I feel it necessary to protect myself, a priority over addressing the learning needs of my students. Ouch.

I find this to be true in all my classes. Even when diversity is not the subject matter, it gets in the way of me being the best teacher I can. There is some research that indicates that the teacher's gender has an effect on how students evaluate teacher performance (reference). I believe the same could be said about the teacher's ethnicity. It's certainly been my experience. I had a black male student in one of my research classes who said, "You're the best teacher I've ever had. I wish there were more like you." That was on the course evaluation. I knew it was him because he signed his evaluation and came to my office later and repeated it to me. Since he was the only black student in class, I knew that the other comments were not from him:

"The instructor was not very consistent. She gave too much work."
"The instructor did not explain things very well. I didn't learn very much."
"I think the professor might be against Whites."

Sometimes I am amused by statements like that. Sometimes I am hurt. Fortunately for me, they are in the minority. Regardless of my performance as a professor, I know I'm not at Good Enough yet. I just don't know how long it's gonna take me to get there.

Where Do I Belong?

I am constantly struggling to maintain a sense of pride and confidence in my abilities. For the first time in a very long time, I doubt my abilities. I doubt myself. I work hard convinced that I must prove myself even though my experience is that no amount of proving will make a difference.

I came into the school with an expertise in research—particularly community-based research and evaluation—among other areas. On the basis of student evaluations and student outcomes, I demonstrated repeatedly that I had the skill and knowledge to teach research courses and chair thesis committees. Yet, when an opportunity came up to take on coordination of the master's thesis/project function, I was passed over for a Latino colleague with tenure and more experience. I felt that I was appropriate for the task and could have carried it off. Other than being asked if I would "mind" doing it, I was not further involved in the decision making. One day I had an exciting opportunity, the potential to finally "fit in." The next, I was still looking for a "niche." Why was that? I can only surmise that I wasn't Good Enough. But what does it take? Two other Latino members of our faculty have been showcased, by the department. Both are new hires in the past three years. Our department typically spotlights their experience and expertise. Sometimes I feel that I am being kept hidden from view. Or maybe the department doesn't feel I have anything in particular to show off. While I am supportive, my struggle to maintain confidence in myself grows. I am coming closer to believing that I honestly am not "as good," that I would not be a positive reflection on the department. I spend a lot of energy fighting the shame.

Expectations

What complicates my "black-ness" further are the expectations of black colleagues, who, until recently, were all black men in my school. A dispute among colleagues of color has the potential to divide even the closest of friends, as I learned. It became clear to me rather quickly that in case of disagreement, there is an unconscious expectation by some that those of color will unite against those perceived to be of the majority culture. It happened, and the efforts to force me to establish my allegiance against the majority culture became less and less covert. Comments like, "She turned on me, so I know she'll turn on you. Better watch your back!" and,

> I thought you were on my side. I mean, we [black faculty] got to stick together, you know.
> There's just so few of us [black faculty], especially in this department. They keep bringing in more Latinos and whites. We're gonna have to be real tight, you know, as a group, if there's really going to be a black presence on this faculty.
> Well, I thought you were on this side. "If you ain't *fer* us, then you're *agin* us."

What I find difficult, and almost insulting, is the assumption that I will take a stand of any kind solely on the basis of my ethnicity! I find it further troublesome that I am expected to maintain allegiance to my ethnicity over any and all other relationships. To do otherwise leaves me under some kind of suspicion and often excluded.

These assumptions are evident in other ways. I am expected to support colleagues of color, particularly those who are black, regardless of their professional performance. Such was the case with a black colleague. Among his students, he had developed a reputation for being unreliable, not showing up for appointments, and not following through with advisory duties. Many times students who had been assigned to him, for thesis or project work, came to me. We were in different departments so there wasn't much I could do for them but help them with their work until they could catch up with him. Interestingly, the students who came to me were all black! Finally, when one student's situation turned dire, as a result of the faculty member's failure to appear, something had to be done. Someone remarked, "You're really sticking your neck out here. Someone could make an issue of you buttin' in like this." That was difficult for me to understand, since I felt that our priority was our students and that we should do whatever we could to assist them. Later protestations from the faculty member involved gave me pause. What about things like professionalism, responsibility, commitment? What about following through to get a job done and done well? While I completely understand the use of flexible work standards to oppress people of color, I do not condone the use of ethnicity to build a case for what is actually poor work performance. But if I don't support my black colleagues when their work performance is not up to standard, will I survive this environment? And does support mean not speaking what, to me, is truth? It's a similar dilemma to grading students of color on substandard work. Where *is* that line?

I'm Black and I'm . . .

Survival as a woman of color in higher education means compromise and threats to my integrity. My daily struggle is to maintain my beliefs, my sense of myself. I feel that I'm walking a very fine line all of the time and that any misstep will mean my demise in the institution. As a new assistant professor, I must be very careful not to violate the political sensitivities of the institution. I think the politics of academia is a minefield, and I am stranded in the middle of it.

I've claimed my black heritage at the behest of colleagues of color because it is "good for the cause." I've sidestepped my Choctaw-Chickasaw heritage (which I learned about in the last decade) because "they" say it's more important for me to be black in the academy. This to me is kind of a paradox, because my experience has been that identifying as Indian is usually more popular than being black. As was said to me by a black friend, paraphrasing something he had read:

> He says he can always find [W]hite people who claim that their great-grandmother was a Cherokee princess, not many dare brag about their more

likely [B]lack relations. But you hardly ever hear a [W]hite person say, "My great-great grandmother was [B]lack," or "One of my ancestors had a family with his [B]lack housekeeper, so we're thinking of inviting those cousins to our next family reunion." Although I'd love to see it! (personal communication, Vernon Odom, 1996)

I've probably bought into some of that myself over the years. It's not easy to live with the experience of yourself as just barely acceptable because of the color of your skin. It wasn't easy to learn to like myself when I got the same messages that my white peers did, that to be black was the worst thing to be. Being Indian was better. Since I didn't know of my Indian heritage in childhood, I only learned how awful it was to be me. Where I've come to now is the knowledge that being both black and Indian is rich and full and life-affirming. To deny either is to engage, maybe even affirm, the comfort preferences of the dominant culture; to support the unspoken contention that black is bad, except in politics.

My fear is that to identify myself, officially, as Indian, would most certainly spell my downfall at the institution. I'd be left to fend for myself in an environment that is, in a word, dangerous. My dark skin suggests my ethnicity on the surface. Those cultural traits from my Native American Indian relatives and ancestors are also present but only serve to attract interest in some exotic perception of my background. Beyond that I'm told it is "not as important." To whom? And why is it that I must deny part of my identity to serve the interests of the other part? Sometimes I am confused. Sometimes I am angry. Mostly it leaves me sad beyond description. It feeds my anxiety about being an outsider. I am not "in step" with the mainstream of multicultural interests in the academy. Being included seems to depend on being black.

To identify with, and participate in, that part of my heritage that is Native American Indian is somehow discounted most of the time. That reflects, to me, how native people are usually discounted in general. The history of Indians in our school seems pretty bleak upon reflection. It seems to me that we have important contributions to make, particularly in the area of raising awareness of diverse worldviews and ways of learning. But these contributions seem to be unwanted or somehow not important to anyone else. There are important political issues for Indians that are not even discussed among faculty of color that I would think would be relevant to all of us. Issues of sovereignty, self-determination, economic self-sufficiency, and acculturation vs. assimilation seem critical to the ongoing discussion of affirmative action. The idea of cultural relevance should be considered in all levels of education, particularly by educators. To the extent that Indians are active participants in this country's educational system, there must be some attention to diverse learning and teaching needs. To be discounted in higher education suggests to me that Indian students are discounted throughout the educational system. And the beat goes on.

A student was referred to me who was a teacher in a local continuation school. He was concerned about future opportunities for his Indian students, particularly in the area of higher education. He came to ask if there were colleges or college programs that served the interests and needs of Indians and how his students could get access to them. As we talked, he described what he believed to be the situation facing Indian students:

> It's like there's no place for them to go after high school. I mean, they've been mistreated all along. They're in my class, because the mainstream classrooms didn't meet their learning or social needs, and this is all that's left for them in public school. It's not that they can't learn, or that they are "bad" kids. They just have different needs. But the mainstream school doesn't make provision for them. So they get labeled, and told that they can't succeed. I *know* that's not true! They are so talented, and have so much to offer! But where will they go, where they can be respected and treated like capable, productive, equal members of society?

How sad for me to have to say that it's not really that much different for Indian professionals who have managed to somehow "get in" to mainstream institutions. It doesn't feel like respect when someone, upon learning that I have Indian ancestry and heritage, says, "Oh, really? Yeah, I can kinda see the Indian in your face. Did you grow up on a reservation? Do you go to powwows? Can I go with you sometime?"

It feels even less like respect when a suggestion made by an Indian faculty member is ignored until it is made again by a non-Indian faculty member. I have seen that happen countless times. It's funny how I can make a statement or comment after identifying myself as Indian, only to be essentially ignored. Then, if I make the same comment, in the context of being black, someone takes notice!

Sometimes I think they like me more if I am the exotic Native American woman. They appear to fear me if I am the "big, bad Black mama." They smile at me when I am obedient. They use me when they need to look politically correct. What does it take to be Good Enough? Knowing when to be what.

> That's kind of hard to do when you are gifted with so many identities: For the mixed-blood American Indian, acceptance in either [any] world can be difficult. They must know who they are from both [or all] perspectives and be able to deal with rejection from both [all] worlds. (Cleary & Peacock, 1998, p. 112)

Just from the place of ethnicity, the potential for rejection outweighs the potential for acceptance. The possibilities for reaching Good Enough seem somewhat dim. "You catch more flies with honey than with vinegar." So says Mom. And she was certainly right. Thank God, I'm not trying to catch flies! Unless, of course, flies will ensure my survival in this institution. But the more honey I use, the stickier the environment. I may attract those flies, but they think I'm nothing but honey. God help me! How will I survive?

In Addition to Ethnicity, There's Sexual Orientation

Sometimes, the sadness is overwhelming because who I am is met by great potential for rejection at just about every turn. If I am the good little black girl, they still might turn away because I am not the good little *straight* black girl.

My further struggle is to function in the institution as an open lesbian, when the apparent requirements for success include indications of heterosexual "normality." I find it amusing, almost, that the explicit standards do not match the implicit reality. It is another one of those situations where my sexual orientation is supposed to have nothing to do with my role as an instructor. Oh, to be so subdivided! My truth is that I am lesbian in all areas of my life. There is something of a demand on the part of students that I stay in the closet, that I not mention what they consider my personal life. How ironic that it is expected and considered quite normal for them and for nongay colleagues to speak freely of their partners and families! How important it is to understand the difference between my partner and family and theirs. Even as a single woman, I struggle with when and how to talk about the people that are family, of the nonbiological sort to me.

On the "Comments" section of an evaluation for one of my classes, a student wrote:

> It would have been a good class if she had not mentioned that she was Gay. How dare she assume we need to know! And what did that have to do with the class, anyway? It ruined the class for me. Too bad. There was a lot for me to learn.

And what of my integrity? Given the heterosexist nature of the society we live in, I am met with the assumption that I have a husband and children. What people assume about me is their business not mine, until it limits my ability to express myself, to interact honestly with them. While I do not feel the need to make an announcement to each class, I also do not succumb to the expectation to uphold the heterosexual assumption. I made a decision twenty years ago not to live my life as a lie as a pretense of what was generally expected of me. Yet each day I must make that decision again. I do not believe that I should have to justify my openness, nor my sexual orientation. I do believe I am responsible for their knowledge of my truth. If students misperceive me or carry untrue assumptions about me, only I can deliver to them the truth. But these were responses I received in a class on multicultural education and educational administration; "No, you just need to meet the right guy. How can you be gay, and still work with children and youths [sic]? What kind of role model are you?" and, "You shouldn't tell anybody. I mean, I don't tell anyone that I'm straight!" and, "Being gay is not the same as being a person of color. You don't know how much we struggle, how hard it is for us. You haven't had our struggle. Black folk have it harder than gays. At least we belong in schools!" and from a colleague, "You can't call being gay a matter of diversity. It's not the same. Besides, if you come out to everybody, and you are a part of the multicultural faculty, you weaken the position of people of color."

Well, I can't say that those comments have had particular meaning for me in terms of inspiring me! And just as I cannot change and need not justify the color of my skin, I cannot betray myself for the sake of the comfort of my colleagues or my students. The truth, as I know it, is that my sexual orientation has no negative or particularly positive impact on my skills or expertise. But it does hold the potential of opening up new awareness for my students and colleagues that can result in more creative learning experiences. The comments of another professor at a southern university resonate with me:

> At some point, just allowing people to know I was a lesbian from what they may have gathered during their observations was not enough. . . . I realized that passively allowing people to conclude that I may be a lesbian was not the same thing as actively making sure they did not think I was heterosexual. . . . It isn't a matter of "flaunting it," but rather, of making sure incorrect assumptions are not made. (Bennett-Alexander, 1997, p. 17)

Being pressured to change, or at least to lie, has resulted in a constant struggle for me with myself. I believe that students and colleagues do not understand how important it is to me to come out. Consider Gonzalez' (1997) discussion:

> One of the first striking differences between women of color and lesbians is the decision to come out. This preoccupation cannot be shared by straight women of color. Ethnicity—very often, at least—is a public designation and not one that can be hidden. Consistently, however, whether to come out preoccupies many lesbians in the academy. Obviously this is the overwhelming first decision for white lesbians. A woman of color who is a lesbian faces a different dilemma. She will probably appear in the academy as a woman of color first. She, too, must decide whether to come out, and in many instances it is easier for her not to do so. The pressure of being a representative of a racial or ethnic community can pull the woman of color in many different directions. Adding the issue of sexuality complicates an already convoluted relationship with the academy. . . . The key here is visibility. Women of color often have no choice in their visibility and hence are expected both to represent their group[s] and attempt to include [them] in the curriculum. Lesbians can choose not to be representative. The pull to represent specific populations on a campus [and in the curriculum] requires making choices about what does not get represented. (p. 236)

It's kind of like a *Sophie's Choice* dilemma. In addition to concerns about representation, I have my own concerns about my personal integrity. Therefore, it is my decision to be out; a decision renewed daily in the midst of struggle.

Twenty years ago, in the midst of my graduation from and subsequent employment at Bible college, I chose to openly acknowledge my sexual orientation. Not to my parents, but certainly to anyone else I knew who could not threaten my job or future. However, not long after that I was forced to confront the choice of coming out to my family. I was preparing to participate in Gay Pride activities and knew they would be televised. I stole a moment with my father at the end of a family visit, while he was packing the car.

I said to him, "Dad, I have something to tell you." He responded in his customary way, "Yep?" "Umm, Dad, umm, well, I guess, well, Dad?" "Yep?" "I guess what I'm trying to say is, well, you know that woman I live with?" "Yep." "Well, she's, umm, she, well, we're kinda like lovers." I waited. "Yep." Well, what was that supposed to mean?! So, I went a little further. I said, "Dad, I guess what I'm trying to say is, umm, umm, Dad, I'm, umm, I'm gay."

Every fiber of my being was tense beyond imagination. I was waiting for the expected rejection. But all I got was, "Well, just don't tell Mom." I was so excited, that I said, "Oh, sure! 'Course not! Absolutely!" I went away feeling as though I now shared a wonderful secret with my father and that the world would now love me just like he did. Not too many months later, when my family was again visiting, I had to go to an office I shared with a colleague at the local gay center. My mother insisted on going with me. I thought she'd just stay in the car and wait. But not my mother! She followed me into the building, and she looked around in silence. I swallowed hard and started picking up what I had come for. A few minutes later we left, I locked the door and we returned to the car. My legs were trembling because Mom hadn't said a word. After we were settled in the car, she spoke. "So, I guess _____ must be gay, huh?" "Yes, Mom, umm, he is." "So, I guess that means you are, too?" "Well, okay, yes, I am." I couldn't meet her eyes. I had done the unthinkable. I had told Mom! Now, I could only wait for her to condemn me to eternal damnation and banish me from my family. Finally, after thirty seconds of slow, agonizing silence, she spoke. "Well, you're still my daughter. You're not in jail, you're not drunk in a gutter somewhere, and I still love you." My breath of relief must have been heard around the world. But before I could respond, she said, "Just don't tell your father!" Such is the struggle I engage daily. It's okay to be openly gay with my colleagues but just don't tell my students? Or is it vice versa? Who did I tell? Who doesn't know yet? Who shouldn't I tell? It feels unfair that I should have to make it known at all. But if I don't, I, and I alone, am responsible for the perpetuation of the heterosexual assumption.

I spent my first professional career as a gay/lesbian and HIV/AIDS organizer and activist. The politics in those communities, I've learned, are not so different from the politics in the academy. Racism and sexism are alive and well among gay men and lesbians. I was called on then, as now, to represent my race(s) and my gender. I experienced oppression from white lesbians, especially in terms of relationships. I struggle with loneliness on a grand scale; it's hard to find an acceptable place to belong *any*where with anyone. My ethnicities and my sexual orientation have been barriers everywhere. Being lesbian does not guarantee me a seat at the table of gay/lesbian politics. Being black and Indian sometimes keeps that seat empty. And, conversely, it is that very combination of identities that sometimes gets me invited to the table, "to expand the presence of diversity on our board and in our organization," or so they say. Am I there to silence the critics who object to the unilateral white, male-dominated voice that calls itself speaking for all? Or do "they" want to hear and learn from a single voice of diversity? Whether this be the table of gay/lesbian/bisexual/transgender politics or the table of the academy, it is the same effort to appear inclusive: "Unfortunately at too many places multiculturalism is seen as adding an African American to a committee, or a book by a woman to a reading list, or adding the gender variable to a case study" (Gonzalez, 1997, p. 238).

The positive side is that my openness has brought the issue to the center of the discussion table more than once. My presence among the multicultural faculty has forced the introduction of gay and lesbian concerns into the light of day. I enjoy the support of some of them for which I am grateful. We must address it as a matter of justice. We can not claim to promote justice for everyone except. . . . If we exclude, we are doing the very thing we are fighting. I am often asked about my experiences. Many students want to know "what it's like," and how I deal with religion and family. Most are supportive at best and curious at worst. But it only takes the false accusations or errant interpretations of one or two to put me at risk because of who I am.

As if the struggle to retain my integrity and to fit in were not enough, white colleagues who are also gay have made it *my* mission to carry the issue of sexual orientation into the diversity fray. I did not volunteer! They expect that being gay is the more important of the multicultural identities with which I am blessed, that it is primary among my interests and commitments. They seem to overlook my ethnic identities in favor of my sexual orientation, particularly when it comes to multiculturalism. As one said to me, "We've got to get more focus on gay issues! They [referring to the multicultural faculty organization] seem to forget that you and I are discriminated against, too!" I wonder who is forgetting what.

The hesitation of my colleagues of color to take up the issue of sexual orientation puzzles me at times. I have carefully studied the historical struggles of gay men and lesbians, of black Americans, and of Native American Indians. I have found similarities across the three groups. Who's to say whose oppression is the worst? And what pride is there to be found in being more oppressed than someone else? I refuse to engage that battle. I have also found that there are differences in the ways different groups are oppressed. Since I have the gift of being identified with all three, I have had the good fortune to experience oppression in a variety of ways. It's all still oppression! It all smacks of prejudice and hate. Want to hate me or exclude me? Pick a reason! Want to make me less than you? Anybody can do it! I also understand the need to establish an agenda, and that there are way too many issues to be included on one agenda. I'm one that can agree to prioritization as long as I know that all of these issues will in some way, at some time, be addressed. And I also know that the issue of sexual orientation crosses all ethnic lines both in terms of its expression and in terms of its acceptance. And I know, finally, that none of my identities can be left at the door. Where I go, they go. How is it that I should slice off my sexual orientation in favor of my ethnicity? And which of my ethnic identities should I keep, and which should I toss out? How about my gender? Should I become asexual in the struggle for ethnic identity? How do I cease being anything that I am in an effort to be all of who I am?

Maria C. Gonzalez (1997), a professor in the Department of English at the University of Houston, writes:

> We can and do recognize the narrowly defined stereotype and its reflection in a straight, white, male-dominated curriculum, but the full panorama of experience escapes our vision of the academy and, hence, the curriculum. The academy is now the domain of the "other," which can include class, sexuality, culture, and any number of "differences. (p. 235)

It's that "full panorama of experience" that leads me to a recognition that all of the concerns that I face, due to my multiple identities, are important. Whether it is hate crimes, employment protections, the right to marry, or poverty, I am touched by each and more. I recognize the relative diversity that now permeates the academy struggling for recognition and validity. I recognize my role in bringing diverse voices forward in the curriculum and in professional practice. I cannot in good conscience ignore any of the multitude of issues brought about by oppression any more than I can ignore any of my several treasured identities. It is a sense of wholeness I have about myself that I bring to all the tables at which I am invited to sit, including my classrooms (Bennett-Alexander, 1997). It is my experience of living in the margins (personal communication, Dr. George Nishida, Professor of Sociology, Biola University, 1975) that helps me to acknowledge the importance of addressing all the parts of the whole. The arena in which I now do that is the academy. And it is the perception—which I believe to be accurate—of threat that makes my heart beat in triple time when, as Bennett-Alexander (1997) writes, "This wholeness spills over into the classroom" (p. 21).

The current climate of hate and intolerance reinforces my fear. I know I am not safe in the academy. But is any place safer than any other? Many believe that my fear is unfounded:

> "It may not be comfortable, but you know nothing's going to happen to you here."
>
> "You're just being paranoid. Things like that don't happen here" [reference to the murder of Matthew Shepard].
>
> Well, you know, if you don't do stupid things like flirt with a colleague or something, nobody's gonna care.
>
> "Relax! You're in California, remember?!"

As if that was enough! I'd been foolish not to be a bit concerned. Perhaps I need not be too concerned about my safety as a lesbian. Perhaps I need not concern myself with fears about my safety as a black Indian. But here, nearing the end of the century, hatred and intolerance still lead to violence and death. Witness the reported hate crimes in 1998. How many go unreported? Is it really unreasonable for me to be a little scared?

Slavery and racism are two important factors in the history of African Americans in the United States that have dramatically shaped the social and psychological development of this group over time (Paniagua, 1994). I think it's actually fairly healthy to have a little paranoia given the histories of all my ancestors in this country. Whether it is based on my ethnicities, my sexual orientation, or my gender, the threat is there and very real. I just choose not to live my life by it. But sometimes I have to wonder, how long until this voice, too, is silenced? Hatred, intolerance, and violence manifest as behaviors and attitudes. So, if someone doesn't tie me to the back of a truck and drag me to my death, am I safe? Or will it be tying my career to the back of a powerful movement by the religious Right that will silence me? Or will it be the suffocating fear of these possibilities that will lead me to silence myself?

And So It Goes

So, what does it all mean? First, I understand that I have a great deal of healing to do, a process that is likely to last for the rest of my journey on Earth. Our efforts to make change and bring healing to the academy seem to stumble, and I believe that is because we—white, black, Latino, Indian, Asian, and the mixed-bloods—are wounded individuals committed to change. "When wounded individuals come together in groups to make change, our collective struggle is often undermined by all that has not been dealt with emotionally" (hooks, 1993, p. 5). The academy is not immune from the pain and degradation created by oppression. For all its lofty ideals, it is an institution of a macroculture structured to exclude some from participation and to promote the power and prestige of others. What draws members of oppressed groups together is our collective struggle; in the academy, it is our collective struggle first to survive and then to make change.

Current efforts to transform the institution into a corporate model seem to me to be efforts to perpetuate, and even embed, the very processes and structures of oppression that we struggle against. Corporate America has demonstrated its allegiance to the dominant power group. Why would I expect that the academy will be any different if, indeed, it operates like a corporation?

I've also learned that as the academy is not immune, no individual is immune. The social and political environments created so long ago have damaged the human spirit, "Irrespective of our access to material privilege, we are all wounded by White supremacy, racism, sexism, and a capitalist economic system that dooms us collectively to an underclass position" (hooks, 1993, p. 11). It doesn't matter whether I have tenure or not. It doesn't matter how many promotions I get or whether or not I get any. I know firsthand what it feels like to be disrespected, to be discounted, to be rejected. I also know firsthand what it feels like to be included, though my experiences of inclusion are fewer. What I must first address is my own woundedness and what that means on the journey to Good Enough.

To me it reaffirms what I have learned about the struggle of Americans who are different, to be included in mainstream society, to be treated with respect and equal consideration, "What is important is that all humans be allowed feelings of integrity and pride connected with who they are, with how they identify" (Cleary & Peacock, 1998, p. 58). I don't have any predictions about my survival in the great American academy. The future remains to be seen. But I do know that with each reinvention of myself, I have become more of who I am. When I make honorable declarations about my unwillingness to lie, or my commitment to integrity, I accept that there are likely to be consequences, not all of them positive. But in the end, with whom must I live?

I sometimes feel that I may not be Good Enough to keep my job without the intervention of the right people, without playing the politics. The only thing that will make a difference is the intervention of the right people. Surviving means keeping the white people happy, especially if they are male, and/or tenured. Surviving means proving myself to my colleagues of color who are tenured and are leaders.

The more I learn about human behavior and the influence of culture on everything else in life, the better I understand the dynamics, the politics of the academy. My task is to challenge them without sacrificing myself. I know now that full commitment to what I do will not get me to Good Enough. I know that my love for my profession is not nearly enough to keep me safe in it. I know that my only real hope for survival is my full commitment to who I am, and the struggle of equality and acceptance.

As for being found out, well, word is out. This is who I am and that doesn't change regardless of the political climate in which I operate. There isn't anything to find out; there are no secrets. But there is a lot to learn about me, about people like me, and about how we survive in an environment bent on our failure. All of these experiences lead me to believe that I will, eventually, get to Good Enough. In fact, I'm already there. The paradox of the journey being its own end just means that it's all process. I cannot pretend to be Good Enough, when, in fact, I am.

Chapter Four

Disabling Institutions

Concha Delgado-Gaitan

Journaling has been an integral part of my ethnographic research process, a practice which actually began during my high school days. In those days it was a means of maintaining a private identity apart from my parents, siblings, and friends. Later, journalism provided a strategy to gain critical insights about my community fieldwork activities. In my academic research, reflective journaling is an integral part of the data collection and tracking where my personal feelings intersected. Little did I know that as a senior professor at the University of California, I would become afflicted with a disabling illness and once again my daily journaling would be the instrument to assist me in making sense of my experience.

Gradually, my physical strength and ability to remain active as a professor diminished. Writing personal reflective narratives enhanced my understanding of the power relations between myself and the university which shaped my identities as a learner and educator. With my journal as my companion, I recognized how my subjective and objective realities became one. Fundamentally, I learned that while I relied on the support of my family, friends, and cultural values to strengthen me and to overcome the illness and retain my position as a professor at UC, the university did not consider my needs; instead it dealt with my situation only according to its interpretation of the Americans with Disability Act—the bureaucratic law. This was not the first time I had experienced discontinuity between myself and the one institution I trusted.

Schools have played a central part in every aspect of my life. It has been a bittersweet relationship of finding independence, achievement, and a place to learn. At every stage of playing school, the power of knowledge left its imprint on my identity first as an immigrant child eager to embrace everything that education offered, then as an immigrant woman working in the ranks of educational institutions. Boundaries between school and the rest of my life became nearly impossible to discern.

57

A School of Opportunity

My parents were international migrants from Mexico and had no opportunity to attend school in either country. As a young school-age child, my parents impressed upon me and my sisters the value of schooling and education in general.[1] I both feared and loved school: Although I faced unjust ridicule for not speaking English, the school also provided novelty. Memories still haunt me of spending almost my first year at Victoria Elementary School with my head down on my desk at recess because the teacher believed in punishing me for not speaking English.[2] My parents instructed me in ways to overcome adversity, they taught me to appreciate the support of family and friends, to work hard, and to learn all that I could. I relied on these pearls and internalized them as my inner strength—my cultural law. Initial ridicule and prejudice for belonging to a different culture and language group gave way to serious work and commitment to learn everything I could, in and out of school.

With that determination, at the age of nineteen, I walked through the doors of a second-grade classroom at Boggs Track Elementary School in Stockton; this time, as a new elementary teacher. Then, moving to the Bay Area where I continued working in schools and communities maintaining my identity as learner. My relationship to my students and the communities where I taught changed me just as much as I'm sure I influenced them. Political consciousness was inevitable for anyone teaching in the early '70s in inner cities. Teaching became a platform to protest segregation, poverty, and the Vietnam War. Schools were both friends and enemies of the communities and as a teacher I worked for the children and their families.[3] Poor communities were beginning to find their voice and express their disquiet about the failure of schools to teach their children. As a teacher whose professional training underscored that I was the change agent, I joined with the families who proposed complete change to demand the quality of education their children deserved.

My disenchantment with schools and administrators became reason enough to join the leadership ranks. At the age of twenty-eight, I became an elementary school principal, the first woman hired in the south Bay Area district of twenty-six schools. I made it my goal to become the kind of leader that would increase the educational opportunities for poor children. Once again, although my professional role and title changed, my identity as an educator remained unquestioned. My leadership style was democratic but aggressive, and in a few short years I yearned for more time to reflect on the myriad of questions which crossed my mind daily and had no time to research while I was a principal.

Thirsty for critical reflection, I returned to Stanford for my Ph.D. A career in academia had never been a lifelong dream. In fact, as a doctoral student at Stanford, I adamantly rejected the idea of becoming a professor. But my passion for solving a good mystery led to a pursuit of scholarly agendas in research, opportunities typically housed in the bastion of a university.

A New Learning Emerges

I was a senior professor at UC Davis, moving fast in my ethnographic field research, publication, teaching, and thick in the university politics. A sudden onset of a debilitating illness which was diagnosed as systemic lupus gradually rendered me physically disabled to the point where I could no longer remain active as a senior professor. In spite of the objective evidence of my health condition, I forged ahead with an insatiable tenacity, attempting to accommodate the physical restrictions visible from the beginning of the illness. My situation was reminiscent of the one-eyed man in the valley of the blind—a story by H. G. Wells which I assigned my class to read in a graduate seminar. *The Country of the Blind* is a story about a community that had been blind for fourteen generations.[4] They had been cut off from all the sighted world. Names for all the things people could see faded and changed. They created a new culture, a new language with new imagination through other senses that became more sensitive. A partially sighted man was lost and found himself in the country of the blind. He believed that he was superior to them because he was sighted, but in time, he learned to appreciate their life as they convinced him that their lives were just as complete without sight. In my newly unfolding experience, I had become part of the blind community and attempting to learn to perform my work as a disabled person. I attempted to convince the university that although I had become physically disabled, I was still a capable professor. My circumstances required specific modifications at the university in the scheduling and the size of my classes, transportation to buildings on campus.

Away from the university, I conducted fieldwork in Mexican immigrant and Russian refugee communities in northern and southern California. Other research collaborations and invited speaking engagements in Alaska and Mexico and Spain also kept me traveling, but transporting myself to my research sites was a tremendous effort. Even with good research assistants, I begin to feel the strain of traveling, conducting interviews, making demanding observations, and writing. I tried to keep up with the demands of the university but the fatigue and pain increased, which required more and more time to recuperate after every activity. Canceling research trips and invited lectures became common practice.

Traveling to communities around the country to conduct research decreased, while chasing after miracle therapies and cures accelerated. I experimented with chiropractics, mega-vitamin therapies, macrobiotic diet, KM nutritional supplemental diet, yoga, hands-on psychic healing, faith healers, mineral baths, *curanderismo*, visual imagery, and inspirational lectures. Loved ones gave me ample ideas and suggestions as my abundant tenacity pursued them. However, except for superficial benefits, all endeavors had limited effects.

The implacable reality of my physical identity mirrored my work at the university. A person's ordinary social roles, all become temporarily suspended when he or she falls ill.[5] In my case, each passing day required more time for me to get ready to go to work and demanded new energy determined by the changing nature of every new activity. Before I became ill, my fast-paced daily routine could outrun the best of them. I could jump out of bed, wash up, throw on my jogging suit, run out the door, do my power walk, run home, jump in the shower, dress, grab a nutritional bar, and drive to work all in the span of an hour. Now, the pace was drastically impeded: I woke up two-and-a-half hours before leaving just to fit in my meditation, physical stretch, and strengthening workout, boil my herbs, shower, and eat a hot breakfast only to feel like I wanted to return to bed, instead I forced myself out the door.

My uncharacteristic late arrival to meetings became a pattern. Mentally, I still operated under the time frame I knew in my former "normal" body identity.[6] I relied on the vanpool for transportation to campus; the van stop was a few blocks from my home. It departed at 7:45 a.m. Riding the vanpool worked for a while, on days I could get out the door in time.

Stubbornly, I insisted on maintaining my full-time teaching load, advising students, conducting field research, writing proposals, attending meetings, and publishing. I felt smug. I could defy the illness like I could other physical adversities in the past. It had not defeated me in spite of the medical complications and time delays I faced daily. Everyone encouraged me to keep fighting. I interpreted this as meaning that if I stopped working hard, both at the university and on my healing, I'd be a failure. Fearing that I would never get up again, I maintained my frantic pace. My fear kept my drive alive. I resisted learning how and why I should possibly concern myself with the body. I harbored a fantasy that soon a miracle would materialize.

In January 1992 my symptoms intensified. Dr. Brown, my rheumatologist, had warned me that an aggravation of my condition would mean an increase in medications. My reluctance to submit to increased medical treatment kept me focused on getting stronger. All the while I feared the side effects which medications caused. I was in my office at the university on the day the doctor called me to recommend stronger dosages of steroids and immune suppressants (chemotherapy). What did this mean now? When would all of this end? I wanted my good health restored without chemical intervention. Nervous and scared, I attempted to read my mail but the phone rang and interrupted. It was Dr. Castaño from Granada, Spain. He and other scholars from the Laboratory of Anthropology at the University of Granada read my books. They invited me to lecture in their summer institute in September that year. I loved lecturing abroad. I explained to them that I could not commit myself to much these days due to serious health problems. They empathized and assured me that the pace would be comfortable for the two weeks. I would teach the topic of international migration with four other international scholars from European universities who would coteach the seminar with me. Without further deliberation, I agreed to go to Granada late summer. A soft voice within me assured me that this was a good omen.

"Great, that gives us a goal to work with. We'll get you stronger by September," exclaimed Dr. Brown. This encouraged me. I was now proficient in asking questions about medications and other therapies. My greatest curiosity was how and why immune suppressant worked differently for lupus patients as compared to cancer patients. About the time I began chemotherapy, Lukeran, and increased dosages of steroids, a friend had a mastectomy. She received the same drugs. Lukeran and other immune suppressants are sometimes administered to some lupus patients when steroids alone are ineffective. Immune suppressants helped to control the inflammation by shutting down the immune system. In effect, the system can cease producing antibodies and strengthen itself. The heavy dosages administered to cancer patients were divided into daily dosages. Along with the daily oral chemo, I took steroids, other nonsteroid drugs, and handfuls of herbs.

A chemical taste camped in my mouth day and night. Even the tastiest foods failed to eliminate the taste of medications. Thank goodness the Bay Area has a great selection of different international food restaurants—all near my house. The taste of flat chemical in my mouth suppressed my appetite. This sent me on a daily hunt for food with strong distinct tastes in hopes of erasing the metal taste in my mouth. On my way home from campus, doctors' appointments, lab work, or hydrotherapy, I stopped at a Vietnamese restaurant,

"An order of sautéed chicken with garlic sauce."
"White rice?"
"No thanks."
The next day I went Mexican, "*Chile verde* and extra *salsa* for the beans."
"No rice?"
"No rice thanks."
Another day I wanted Indian cuisine, "Hot curry chicken and *roti*, please."
"It comes with white rice."
"No rice, thanks."
A special favorite was Szechwan and garlic eggplant.
"You get rice too."
"No, thanks."

Rice muted the spices and I couldn't allow anything to interfere with my antidote for the metal taste of medications.

Committed to feeling well, I welcomed each morning with hopeful anticipation that today would bring a miraculous remission. Morning rituals now included longer prayers before leaving for campus and every night after my writing. I prayed that I get well just like I did as a child: "I need to feel good, I want my health. Release me from this hell! Give me the money to pay the pile of medical bills that are mounting by the day totaling hundreds of dollars each month." Expenses related to medical care exceeded hundreds of dollars monthly with no relief in sight. Chronic conditions are a financial nightmare with constant doctor visits, lab work, physical, herbal, and hydra therapy.[7] I want my life back the way it was, *now*! These demanding outbursts expected this God or a goddess to remove my pain. My supplications went unanswered—the problem persisted with a vengeance.

Something was wrong. What good did faith do me? Even prayer failed. I, nevertheless appreciated more than ever the little things family and friends did for me.

Adjusting

Contrary to the caring gestures from loved ones, the bureaucratic obstacles on campuses were most unfriendly. My ability to walk long distances at the university to teach my classes became increasingly impaired. The quarter when I first fell ill I didn't need a ride to my class from my office because the registrar's office assigned me to classrooms adjacent to the building where I had an office. I could walk with my cane and pace myself to arrive on time for class. However, the subsequent quarter I was assigned to a classroom across from the campus where it took me almost half an hour of fast rigorous walking to get to my classroom. I called the office in charge of transporting students with physical injuries to class. Evidently the small carts that transported students with temporary physical injuries was a student service governed by an office financed from student fees and unavailable to professors. I was informed that I had to supply my own transportation to class no matter how disabled I was.

> The administrator in that transportation office informed me, "We can give you a ride to your class for a couple of times but we can't do it for a long term."
> "I may need it for an indefinite time."
> "Well, when will you be well?" she asked.
> "I wish I could answer that question for you, but even my doctors don't know. Meanwhile, I have to teach my class which is a twenty minute brisk walk from my office."
> She responded, "Well, have your administrator send us a letter. I'll present it to our director and we'll get back to you."

Lengthy letters from my division administrators finally persuaded the Office of Disability Transportation to provide services for the remainder of that winter quarter, conditioned on my calling their office each morning before 9:00 a.m. to confirm my ride. Special permission to get handicapped transportation ended with the quarter. Their policy no longer permitted me to get a ride to class. The situation worsened the following quarter when the transportation service refused to transport me to class and claimed that my insurance company was responsible for paying for transporting me from my office to my classroom. The university had no answer for this complaint except to tell me that my insurance company had to provide for my transportation. When I conveyed this to my insurance company, they laughed as they reminded me that the university was responsible for making the necessary accommodations so that I could successfully conduct my work. Not only was I burdened with taking care of my health, but I was forced to make my own arrangements in order to perform my work. I found it increasingly inconvenient to take the vanpool to the university because I was too fatigued to remain on campus a full day as was their schedule. This forced me to get on my forearm crutches and drive myself to the different buildings on campus where I had meetings and where I was assigned to teach. This was only the beginning of the turmoil about classes that ensued every subsequent quarter. Inevitably, I was always assigned to teach in classrooms that were located long distances from my office and designated class hours impossible to meet because I felt too debilitated to get up very early in the mornings or stay late enough in the day on campus to teach. Most quarters I fought with the administration about appropriate scheduling of my classes up to the last minute before class began. This impeded students from taking my course since time and place were often undetermined until the first week of class.

It baffled me that the bureaucratic wheels of the university expected me to find my own transportation to class and forced me to fight for a convenient location and class time. Part of the university's hypocrisy that hurt me during this period was the designation of a special week to call attention to people with disabilities.[8] During that week, they held daily activities including noontime competitions where people who weren't necessarily disabled held wheelchair races. "No experience necessary" read the notice inviting participants. A student on the staff of the university student paper contacted me to interview me about my dealings with the university services, given my disability. Weeks passed and the student changed her appointment with me many times until she stopped calling me and stopped returning my calls. What irony! Maybe she knew that I had a rather dismal report about the university's services for disabled professors.

Once the quarter began and I got myself to the designated classroom, I also had to figure out a way to be heard. Teaching large classes of almost one hundred students posed more problems than getting transportation to the classroom. Scarcity of funds granted me only a one-quarter time reader. Except for the grading of one minor midterm exam, I ended up doing all of the teaching, grading, as well as leading the weekly discussion groups for my class. More challenges presented themselves in the classroom. Because my voice had become so weak, I had requested a microphone from the center in charge of equipment, but they couldn't provide one. They claimed that it took too long to set up and dismantle the equipment and other classes used the same classroom. And so, I stood in front of one hundred students without a microphone, trying to manage with the inadequate accommodations. Students became increasingly impatient when I became inaudible and unable to project my voice as the lung muscles debilitated more. My bronchial problems were further complicated as I strained to be heard. Too debilitated to fight the university, I sought the services of the Teacher Resource Center. A consultant, Wini, assisted me in my classes by signaling to me when my voice had dropped to the point of becoming inaudible. It was on me to put forth the extra effort to make myself heard.

I was short of breath, with diminishing strength, and finding it increasingly difficult to pace back and forth to hold my students' attention as I was accustomed to doing. Students complained that I wasn't lecturing as much as they wanted and they resented having to hold discussion groups. "This is a waste of time," students commented, "We can't learn from other students."

Feeling more frustrated than I had ever been in my teaching career, I talked with colleagues and friends at the university about ways to remedy the problems that burgeoned from every direction. At the Teacher Resource Center, Wini, one of the specialists, was a refreshing support. She helped me to review the changes I had made in order to succeed in my classroom, given my changing circumstances. We worked very systematically to put everything in writing for students since I had to conserve my voice as much as possible for the lecture. I met with her before the quarter began and we reviewed my syllabus. Wini and I planned well-organized small group discussion sessions and she attended all of my classes to monitor if my lectures were audible and if the variety of student activities were well managed.

In spite of my efforts to ensure high quality in my teaching in the face of my immobility, by the beginning of spring, students' complaints were more commonplace. They were impatient that I could not move the class at the faster pace they expected. They were right in that my voice dragged, I had to pause frequently, and I sat in front of the class since I could not walk back and forth as I had before. Nonetheless, their complaints felt cruel when they showed up in my office with comments like, "You're too disorganized and I need an 'A' in this class because I don't want this course to ruin my grade point average."

"I got a 'B+' in my midterm and I need an 'A.' You need to present the lecture in an outline form we can follow."

"My paper is an 'A' paper and you gave me an 'A–.' My mother edited it for me and if you don't change my grade, I'll make a formal complaint."

In my fifteen years of teaching university students, they had never complained so much about my teaching. I felt totally incompetent especially because a couple of colleagues made me their target just as the students had. They viciously criticized me to other students and to colleagues. They believed that I was not a good teacher. Other colleagues in the division had a more holistic perspective about my work since I continued a successful productive pace in my research and publication in spite of my affliction. Feeling more frustrated than ever, I questioned my ability to maintain my academic career along with everything else in life.

One student's visit stands out in my mind as a message that I had to keep going. A Vietnamese student from my undergraduate class, Social and Philosophical Foundations of Education, came to my office. I had little energy to sit up and talk to students by 2:00 p.m. but this student's visit was a real gift to me. He introduced himself as a senior student in engineering. He was an immigrant from Vietnam. "I came to talk with you because in class you're always talking about how important it is for students and professors to work together and break down barriers. I've never talked to any of my professors and so I came to try it and see how it feels."

"And how does it feel?"

"It's OK, I'm not nervous."

"Tell me how you got interested in engineering."

We talked for a while as he shared a moving story about his family's life in this country and their value of education. His visit eased my feelings of incompetence and restored a bit of my confidence.

Evenings at home were a battleground. Would I surrender to demanding academic work or to total collapse? Some days I did both; after a brief few minutes of rest, I forced myself to work until my concentration declined and I fell asleep at my computer.

Working was often preferable because it was a way of feeling competent. When I stopped to rest or listening to music required just as much concentration to focus away from my body. However, friends recorded favorite music which I played sometimes to transcend the pain momentarily. The various pieces affected my mood differently. "Ode to Joy" made me feel calm as did Steven Pasero's classical guitar. Mexican guitar, like that of El Mariachi del Sol, boosted my energy a bit but the boost was brief. A friend at the pool where I went for hydrotherapy gave me a tape with favorite vocals like Violeta Parra's, "Gracias a la Vida," Streisand's "Memory," Bette Midler's "Wind Beneath My Wing," and the Beatles's "There are Places I Remember," and Sara Vaughn's "Prelude to a Kiss." I was lost in song and words that for selected minutes penetrated deeper than the pain. My delightful music interlude ended with the audiotape as my consciousness returned to the familiar body fatigue, pain and distress, and the thought work.

Even a new building did not help my situation. The Division of Education was moved to a new temporary building in the 1993 academic year. The building looked like a postmodern shopping mall with all of the false signs of sensitivity to physically disabled. Specifically, the new building had signs indicating access for "disabled." And, although a ramp existed for wheelchairs to enter the building there was no access to the rest room. It took two years before the university would install a push-button door in the bathroom that enabled me to enter without further public degradation.

The frustration continued, the doors to offices in the building were fire retardant for the purpose of securing people inside during a fire and their weight was too much. Unfortunately, when I attempted to enter the bathroom I was unable to open the door. I humiliated myself by pounding on the heavy fire retardant door with my cane until a staff member came to assist me.

The mechanics of getting to do my work on campus stressed me—from getting to class, raising my voice to conduct class, to getting into the rest room. This made me appreciate my home even more. Family and friends called regularly to check on me to remind me that they loved me.

One evening the phone rang, "Concha," came the familiar child's voice, my niece Nikkie. "I got a certificate for best speller in my class today."

"That's great Nikkie, what did you spell?"

"The words I spelled were enormous and meticulous. The other kids couldn't spell them."

"Congratulations dear!"
"What do those two words mean?"
"I've got to look at my list, bye."
Nikkie's call reminded me that my loved ones were the best medicine throughout this ordeal.[9] In spite of the unconditional love which my family and friends extended, the moment-to-moment struggle was mine. At times the external challenges paled in comparison with the inner strife.

In dreams, I saw myself dancing down the same path where I once walked one hour every morning. I danced gracefully in a long flowing gown and I awakened feeling so encouraged, thinking, I will walk again. My personal journal was privileged to my excruciating pain in a way that I could not share with others because I felt too much shame to admit to how I was being devastated by my illness. My fear of admitting to having this illness was intense. If I admitted to feeling so ill I might make it real. Since there was no known cure, I felt horribly vulnerable believing that my body might be held hostage forever. My compensatory skills enabled me to maintain a semblance of a normal life as I managed to perform my work by exerting my body. I made bargains with it like agreeing to rest as much as possible on the days when I did not teach or spend more time with my loved ones. In total, I was unwilling to surrender to my body's cry.

Just keeping the body from totally collapsing required every ounce of mental and physical stamina I could evoke. So I knew that I must help myself as much as possible by getting more rest, more drugs, more physical therapy, and more hydrotherapy. My full attention was on doing whatever I could to place one foot in front of the other. The body had my full attention like never before. The unrelenting physical inconveniences made this a surreal reality unlike anything I had ever faced.[10]

Losing Perspective

Unable to rely on my memory, every meeting with students, colleagues, or research participants required me to write down each time, place, and directions to a meeting, the person's name, title, and physical characteristics. Added to the physical impairment, my increasing memory loss extended the time I spent on every piece of work. Keeping up with research and university business became an impossibility. Reading, which had once been an effortless and defining activity of my work, quickly became a grueling act. Everything required at least three to five readings to decipher the meaning. On one occasion a colleague came into my office and showed me a published article. She asked me to read it and give my opinion. She came into my office flustered and asked me to read the first page of the article, "Look at this, just read the first page and tell me if this isn't an outrageous line of thinking." I read it slowly but even then I couldn't make sense of it because meanings of words eluded me. I asked her to forgive me for the delay, I continued reading and rereading. Feeling embarrassed and confused, I asked her, "What exactly do you disagree with?" She explained it to me. I could hardly hear her, I was too preoccupied with my concentration and comprehension problem.

My once loved research and teaching became painstaking. Spontaneity was suspended as classes took the form of lectures which I had written out one word at a time. This was appalling since I had always scoffed at passive lecturing as inadequate pedagogy. When I began doing this, it didn't feel natural but I couldn't help myself. I carefully wrote out every word and armed myself to bombard the class with a recitation of words that sounded more meaningless as days passed. I felt myself becoming increasingly dependent on reading every letter verbatim from my notes. This ritual was accompanied by intense fear that overwhelmed me when I taught. When students asked questions, I feared not knowing the answer. This was totally foreign because my philosophy had always been that no right and wrong answers existed in any discourse. In my classes we critically explored issues, and suddenly my twenty-eight years of experience in the field failed me as a resource. Frustration complicated my fear, I tried to remember common facts, names, dates, and titles of common sources which I've always had at my fingertips. "Maybe there's something wrong, but I can't tell anyone." I couldn't bear to confirm that this insidious illness was complicating more areas of my body and my work. The shame was more than I could bear. I proceeded with my daily routine hoping that maybe I was just stressed. I questioned my competence but no one could know. My compensatory strategies were well in place. I consciously tried to divert attention to this new development. Friends teased me about being in a profession where absent-mindedness was just as accepted as sharp intelligence.

I remained focused on doing my work as best I could in hopes that this nightmare would pass. Work felt so distant and grueling that my desire to heal shifted in purpose. I wanted time to recreate with my loved ones. Everything else seemed more work than I'd ever done. All of my time was consumed with doctor appointments, medications, and therapies. This in addition to my academic work cramped my life with no respite.

The increasing memory loss made it more imperative to follow a predictable routine. Months after my initial diagnosis, Dr. Brown recommended that I work out in a heated pool rather than doing weight bearing exercises. Getting to the heated pool daily was necessary, although it consumed three hours of my time in the late afternoon and evening.

Recreating

By summer 1992 my desperate attempts to strengthen mentally and physically rewarded me. Granada and Madrid, Spain, were a reality. I had recovered a great deal of my ability to concentrate and recall. However, I realized that I wrote my lectures verbatim just as I had done months earlier in my university classes when I couldn't remember. This amounted to many reams of pages that I had to pack and carry overseas. I complained to a friend that I had to translate all of my lectures for Spain.

"You're creating too much work for yourself." He observed.

"I have to be prepared." I explained

"You're an expert in the field, why are you so preoccupied with these lectures?"

Fear filled my chest and suddenly the idea of forgetting something tormented me. My confidence had eroded so that it felt necessary to write out everything. Before, I actually didn't remember concepts, ideas, and names among other things. By the time I left for Spain, I felt I had regained about 70 percent of my short- and long-term memory, but I distrusted myself. I had worked rigorously to train myself to use language and memory in a concentrated way. Every moment was a test in which I would force myself to reconstruct in words. I wrote lists of words I heard around me when I did not know the meaning. It hurt that my efforts to remember on demand were still strained.

A strenuous flight, lectures, meetings, and travel weakened me considerably, but overall, I was pleased that I did not totally collapse as my loved ones dreaded. They feared I might regress and reverse the progress I had gained prior to my departure to Spain. I felt confident that maybe I had beat this illness after all.

Fall quarter classes began with new expectations in a new building where our division had been moved. We were now located almost in the outskirts of campus near the hog barns. My colleagues commiserated with me on their feeling of isolation from the rest of campus. Although this was a new building, the place resembled a large, cold, and impersonal shopping mall with long hallways and doors to offices that were designed to remain shut. My ability to stand and teach two classes was applauded by my colleagues who had seen me make great strides. According to lab tests, I was now in remission. I too wanted to remain convinced that the illness had passed. I still felt it was up to me. Maybe if I took care of myself, I could remain in complete remission. But in mid-October, a bronchial infection ended my brief week of respite. I was in trouble again and saddened by the continued uncertainty this illness brought. Unpaid bills multiplied and a routine of doctor visits, medications, and hydrotherapy consumed my day. I stubbornly continued to teach and perform full-time university work in a building that separated me from the center of campus. Just as before, I was immobile, and the university now refused to provide shuttle service for me to classes from this new building because it was not on their route. This I remembered.

Since the onset of the illness, in my dreams I always appeared dancing and walking until the prospect of using a wheelchair became real. One night my nightmare seemed lifelike. Someone pushed me into a wheelchair and told me I couldn't get out of it. After futile efforts, the chair rolled down a corridor out of control. I couldn't see where it was going. My screams went unheard. I woke up hyperventilating in panic! These feelings surprised me. I attempted to make sense of this new development. Scared and out of control described it well—feeling trapped in my fear of confinement to a wheelchair.

I held on to the prescription for a wheelchair as long as I could, wondering if I really needed it and expecting to make a miraculous recovery any minute. Ordering a wheelchair was more of an ordeal than I ever imagined. Above the $1,000 payment to the insurance company as a co-payment for hardware, the hassles of insurance paperwork required from the neurologist and me consumed complete days at every step.

The salesman in my home asked, "What color do you want your wheelchair?"

"Color? I asked. "I thought wheelchairs were all black."

"Not anymore, here's your selection."

Once we decided on the style and its measurements, the salesman spread out a leaflet of colors from which I could select a color. I saw magenta, navy blue, light blue, teal, pink, forest green, and black. Apparently most of the wheelchair was black but part of the rail could be a different color.

"Teal, of course."

"You made a very quick selection."

"You've got to understand half of my wardrobe is teal. Can I have wheelchairs in three other colors?"

"Yes, if you're willing to pay for them."

"Teal will do thanks."

My attitude strengthened with plenty of inner searching for a way to make my riding a wheel chair a comprehensible development in my healing. A trip around the long hallways in my office building at the university convinced me. I felt a great difference from having to walk the long stretches holding up my listless body on two forearm Canadian crutches. I was actually able to stay on campus an hour or so longer without collapsing.

Overwhelmed by the storm of monthly medical bills for conventional and alternative medicine made me consider that I may just stop all medical treatment. In my frustration, I sat down and began to breathe deeply and meditated for inner guidance on how to deal with this problem. How can I pay all of these bills? No one believes that a full professorship at a University of California campus cannot pay medical expenses for all of the complications related to this illness. The insurance company refused to pay for any alternative medicine, including Chinese therapies, that has helped me immensely. They paid only for a few sessions of acupuncture since they believed that acupuncture was for a short-term ailment. I found myself broke and angry about the cost of getting and staying well in this society. Although I could get around in my power wheelchair, I was still unable to work at full capacity. Remaining functional required a strict regimen of physical therapies, drugs, herbs, acupuncture, and stress management to stay well. The time-consuming routine prevented me from consulting for extra salary to pay for the added expenses that have depleted my savings.

New Approaches

Quarter after quarter I looked forward to summers and sabbaticals in hopes of replenishing my immune system with lots of deserved rest. In January 1995, I returned from my sabbatical to teach two seminars. I taught a doctoral seminar in Davis and after the first day of class, I wondered how I could manage to hang in until the end of the quarter. A surprising accolade, however, rescued that quarter. The Spencer Foundation selected me to receive one of the highest awards given to senior scholars in my field. With the money they awarded me, I was able to fund five doctoral students to pursue their research for two years. Part of the gift stipulated that I continue my mentor work with graduate students. We met regularly to discuss our respective research projects and our writing, but mostly we shared the humorous and pointed life stories which kept our ideas alive.

Winter and spring quarters I was scheduled to teach a doctoral seminar for the CSU Fresno doctoral cohort. Since I could no longer fly down to Fresno on a regular basis as before, I experimented with Interactive Television (ITV). This was a tremendous advantage that enabled me to teach my doctoral seminars at CSU Fresno without the commute. Since I became more conversant with technology, I frequently commented, "If one is disabled, this is a great time in history to have it happen. Everything we need is available on remote control." This was indicative about my attitude. For me, this meant that I could drive a couple of miles to UC Berkeley and sit in a large room with a square screen the size of a ten-foot wall. The technician instructed me how to work the buttons for focus and volume. My students appeared life-size on the screen. They sat around a table and I could see the full group together. They received the reverse. My big face bigger than life on their screen. By the second week of class, students had adjusted to the slight intimidation they felt in having to talk through a camera. I, on the other hand, appreciated the technology of the ITV medium. I wasn't nearly as stressed after an hour of class as I always was when I drove one hour to campus and taught a room full of students. Unfortunately, too many problems existed between UC Davis and UC Berkeley technology which prevented me from teaching my UC Davis classes through ITV.

Experimenting with ITV spurred me to attempt a new physical therapy. In this third phase of my healing I noticed an inclination to move slower. I felt more comfortable with quietness around me than ever before, in fact, I preferred to be in serene settings than in large groups.

At this point, my bimonthly appointments with Dr. Brown consisted of an examination and a report I made on how I managed my daily activities from physical to metaphysical to help myself. My written report to Dr. Brown consisted of a list of activities, which comprised my healing program.

1. Daily—REST LOTS OF IT—reduced teaching load and working more time at home than office
2. Daily—hydrotherapy/pool

3. Daily—meditation
4. Daily—Chinese herbs
5. Daily—nutrition—mostly vegetarian
6. Weekly—physical therapy
7. Weekly—Chinese acupuncture

Beyond Empowerment

In summer 1995, I returned from one of my summer trips to research and lecture in Alaska. My thoughts were no longer on worrying about what would happen to me or who would take care of me if I remained ill. Alaska always had a calming affect on me. A new potential crisis now claimed my attention. While I was trying to take care of myself so that I could continue performing my academic work, some unsupportive circumstances began stirring at the workplace, which admittedly upset me. I was outraged at some university colleagues who circulated a report stating that my leaves as a result of being ill contributed to people having to teach more than their official load in the division. I retorted with a well-crafted letter, not so much in defense but as an explanation of the errors of the committee, to consider my side of the problems in the division. They'd failed to consult me with their concerns and neglected to mention my many efforts to continue performing my teaching and research, as well as service to the university. By the time the report was issued, I had only taken one quarter of medical leave in five years and the rest of the time my leaves had been sabbatical leaves to conduct my research and academic writing. Furthermore, even throughout my illness, I had taught full-time with the additional burden of reinventing my classes to accommodate my disability, against all the odds that the university's obstacles had presented me with. And the truth was that no one had ever taught my doctoral classes during any of my sabbatical leaves. I sent thirty letters to various colleagues across campus who were related to the design and distribution of that committee report. Not one person ever responded to my concerns and questions. The university's silence was another form of insensitivity to my situation. Nevertheless, I felt good that I had asserted my position about the matter, it helped to put things in perspective even if no one at the university accorded me the courtesy to respond.

My fourth academic book was on family and community literacy. *Protean Literacy: Extending the Discourse on Empowerment* was published in fall 1995.[11] This represented a culmination of a decade of academic research which was at the heart of my intellectual investment. With the publication of the book I felt a sense of completion with a part of my academic career which I had loved but which had to change. I knew I had to alter my research approach. My former community-level ethnographic research which demanded laborious time and techniques with heavy equipment had to give way to projects which required more predictable and physically manageable hours and travel. The specifics of my new direction were still a mystery. Nevertheless, I welcomed the change that tugged at me. Until this point, my desire and dreams to explore were dampened. Issues for research and writing quietly intrigued me.

The publication of my new book represented a new affirmation of my accomplishments. I have always worked with families and communities out of a genuine sense of relatedness rather than from a need to change them. To observe, listen, and join with them if invited, but not to impose my ideas on them. This is the process of *empowerment* I have discussed in my research. Now I saw how genuinely possible that was on a personal level when we join with others to critically review our experience and by doing so, shift our perspective which shapes and redirects our purpose in life.[12]

In the fall quarter of that year, I intended to fully utilize every minute of my sabbatical since it would be the last one I would have for years to come. I eased into a steady pace of caring for myself while tinkering with unfinished manuscripts to submit for publication. A surge of energy emerged during the course of one week where I became obsessed about getting a new house, a new partner, and a new career. When I examined this wish list, I noticed that no mention of my health appeared. I felt more peaceful with myself each day. My health was manageable day by day, but keeping my health stable still consumed most of my time and emotional stamina. I learned to listen to my body's fatigue, pain, and multitude of complicated ailments that remain constant and require time-consuming care. Nevertheless, they have been a medicine in and of themselves because they focused my attention on one minute at a time.

I maintained a rhythm of exploration in my scholarly pursuits. Against the university's obstacles to my teaching accommodations on campus and at home, my scholarly commitment flourished in more creative ways. I incorporated personal autobiographical story in my graduate seminars. I included the students' own biographical accounts to teach culture. At the end of the seminars students wrote, "This was the most meaningful class I've ever taken." The genre proved to be such a successful teaching tool, not only for my students but for myself, that at the end of the course, students wrote, "The self-reflective writing we were assigned in this class made it the most valuable thinking I have ever been challenged to do in academia."

A piece of my writing that was not as well received by the university was a proposal for ways to modify my position. As I reviewed my health with my doctors, it became clear that my work demands including driving over two hours round-trip to teach at the university had to be adjusted long-term. I needed a way that allowed me to manage as much from home as possible. Working at home on projects like distance teaching I could pace my activity with sufficient rest periods enabling me to be productive with less stress. I proposed to the university that my position would be moved full-time to the Joint Doctorate Program at CSU Fresno that would permit me to continue the distance learning courses I had taught in the program for years with excellent results. I had been an active faculty with the program and Fresno faculty very much wanted me to continue with the program. During the six years of the health ordeal, I had managed to change the meaning of disability to "diverse abilities" in pursuit of my academic career.

Three months after I submitted the proposal, the university responded. They rejected my proposal and said that if I could not return to work full-time I had to leave the university. They claimed that the university was not responsible for helping me to perform my work from any other place except from the physical parameters of the institution. The administration claimed to be within their legal requirements of the Americans with Disabilities Act. They believed that they had helped me by allowing me to select the hours that I could teach on campus. Most sobering was the realization that the illusion of protection, which tenure once believed was a semblance of security, in actuality meant nothing during a time when I most needed it. By not allowing me to work in a manner to accommodate the limitations of the illness that physically disabled me, I was forced to leave on disability. Not yet of age to retire, I had to wait until I turned fifty to become professor emerita.

With perfect hindsight, I've learned how the culture of illness gets constructed and how healing itself is also a complex culture. My personal life history has been imperative in understanding my healing. Living with difficult health has taught me about the internal power and insights which my cultural and family values dictated. By listening to that inner wisdom, I adapted to the relentless situation. It was ultimately the act of letting go of trying to meet external laws, which gave me only a false sense of power that returned me to my true source of strength.

In Retrospect

My illustrations about academia as a place where learning and teaching were held in high regard eventually disappointed me as I struggled to remain a productive scholar while confronting serious health problems. Ironically, while my scholarly research, publishing, and teaching on empowerment thrived, I found myself in the midst of a situation at the university designed to disempower me. In spite of the circumstances, I felt that I had exhausted every means to accommodate the demands of my career and productive excellence. The university found it more efficient to behave in absolutes while life presents us mostly gray hues. The university bureaucracy failed to create a means by which I could maintain a position in a workplace that professed to be a "learning institution." Subsequently, I have read universities' promotional magazines where they attempt to convince the public of their interest in hiring and promoting ethnic, gender, and disabled minorities. But in my case, diversity was a meaningless word—in spite of the Americans with Disabilities Act.

Since leaving the university, I am committed to recovering my health and continuing to pursue learning in a way that I can maintain my health. It's almost like I have come full circle. As a child I never had a dream of "what I would be when I grew up;" rather, I only hoped to do what would allow me to learn and grow. Throughout my career in education, although I resisted school, I fully appreciated my opportunity to learn. After the many positions I have held as an elementary schoolteacher, a school principal, a curriculum director, and a professor, I am now a professor emerita and still learning.

Notes

1. More expanded description of this period of my experience appears in Concha Delgado-Gaitan, "Dismantling Borderland" in *Learning from Our Lives: Women, Research and Autobiography in Education.* Anna Neumann and Penelope L. Peterson (Eds.), pp. 37-52. New York: Teachers College, Columbia University, 1997.

2. Much has been written about the trauma inflicted on students who do not speak English by untrained teachers. One of the most recent publications addressing these issues is Carlos Ovando and Virginia Collier, *Bilingual and ESL Classrooms: Teaching in Multicultural Contexts.* Boston: McGraw Hill, 1998.

3. Delgado-Gaitan, *Learning from Our Lives.*

4. H. G. Wells, *The Country of the Blind.* London: Nelson, 1910.

5. In a serious illness that requires changes in lifestyle, a person needs to make accommodations to continue surviving for the moment. Ordinary obligations change for the person who is ill as well as does the expectations of that person by those around him or her. Two books speak to this issue: Leon Festinger, *A Theory of Cognitive Dissonance,* 1962; and John Gliedman and William Roth, *The Unexpected Minority: Handicapped Children in America,* 1979.

6. Questions of how an ill person transforms their inner perception of self are discussed by Goffman in two books: Erving Goffman, *The Presentation of Self in Everyday Life,* 1959; and *Stigma: Notes on Management and of Spoiled Identity,* 1963.

7. Accommodating one's life to cope with a persistent physical challenge requires more than changing one's attitude and identity, it's complexity engulfs every aspect of one's lifestyle as these authors' comment: Robert F. Murphy, *The Body Silent,* New York: W. W. Norton, 1990; S. K. Pitzele, *We Are Not Alone: Learning to Live with Chronic Illness,* 1985.

8. A great deal of ridicule of ill people in society stems from fear of becoming ill and incapacitated. These authors aptly deal with cases of people whose strength is tested under the social stresses that surround them as a result of their illnesses. Robert Murphy, *The Body Silent*; Erving Goffman, *Stigma*; and Jessica Scheer, They Act Like It Was Contagious in *Social Aspects of Chronic Illness, Impairment and Disability.* S. C. Hey, G. Kiger, and J. Seidel (Eds.), pp. 185–207. Salem, Ore.: Willamette University, 1984.

9. Physicians have begun researching and writing about the whole person beyond the physical symptoms and the social world that supports healing. Among the most prolific of doctors who speak to patients and their families is Bernie S. Siegel, *Love, Medicine and Miracles: Lessons Learned about Self-Healing from a Surgeon's Experience with Exceptional Patients.* New York: Harper and Row, 1986.

10. The surreal experience of people with illnesses that manifest physically are described in such caring manner by Oliver Sacks, *An Anthropologist on Mars,* New York: Alfred A. Knopf, 1995.

11. Concha Delgado-Gaitan, *Literacy for Empowerment: The Role of Parents in Their Children's Education*. London: Falmer Press, 1990.

12. Three books in which I discuss the ramifications of self, family, and community empowerment are: Concha Delgado-Gaitan, *Literacy for Empowerment*; Concha Delgado-Gaitan and Henry Trueba, *Crossing Cultural Borders: Educating Immigrant Families in America*, London: Falmer Press, 1991; Concha Delgado-Gaitan, *Protean Literacy: Extending the Discourse on Empowerment*, London: Falmer Press, 1996.

Chapter Five

Reflecting on the Games of Academia: A View from "the Porch"

Myriam N. Torres

Introduction

"We can be strangers by being in a new land; we can be strangers by virtue of any difference: physical, psychological, social, cultural, religious, political, racial, personal. One can be a stranger by remaining within oneself or by being at odds with the world" (Shabatay, 1991, p. 136). I shall add that one can feel oneself a stranger when other persons act in such a way as to make one feel doubly strange, as in the following situation I was involved in not long ago. My first encounter with the department and search committee chair of a well-known university, where I was invited for a job interview, was very revealing to me. After a brief greeting she asked me, "Well, Myriam, what can a Bolivian person bring to this university?" My immediate response was, "I don't know what a Bolivian person can bring, but as a Colombian. . . ." She apologized profusely. But meanwhile I was thinking about the question and not about the confusion of countries. Is she assuming that since I'm from *any* of those South American countries, I don't have anything to bring to this university? Do I represent my country, my race, or myself? What should I answer to this unsettling question? This conversation took place while we were walking to the dean's office for my interview with him. I was rescued by a professor we came across in the hall, who had strongly recommended me for the position. It turned out that the question was irrelevant anyway because I was only a "straw-person," used on that occasion to camouflage a decision that had already been made.

My story is about the strange becoming familiar, or at least less strange, within U.S. academia starting in 1990. It has been a continual survival struggle to overcome the multiple obstacles (as the one in the situation described above) hidden in the higher education system which a person like myself, Latina, mature woman, with a Spanish accent, must face as part of one's academic life.

Awakening from the "American dream" took me some time. Even though I was somewhat weakened by the surprise factor, I had enough determination (*ganas*) and have put in enough hard work to overcome obstacles and to continue in my pursuit of a Ph.D. and then a job as an educator in higher education. To reach the place where I find myself today would have been impossible if I had not been helped by some wonderful people who believed in my capabilities and potential, and who were able to break through their initial assumptions about me. In addition, my husband's unconditional support was indispensable.

I had three major reasons for emigrating from Colombia to the United States: the first was that I had a fiancé, now my husband, who had waited for me for nine years; the second was my desire to carry out my doctoral studies; and the third was my disillusionment with the privatization, corporatization, and the subsequent decay of the higher education system in Colombia. I had somewhat conflicting feelings; on the one hand I had the illusion that the "American Dream" had come true, but on the other I felt defeated because I was powerless to prevent the impoverishment of teacher education in my native land, which I had fought against.

The awakening from the "American Dream" was at the same time a deeper "conscientization"[1] of my identity as Latina, appreciating more my origins and cultural values regardless of how problematic that may be living in American society. I am using purposely the term "conscientization" (Freire's notion) rather than awareness because it has become clear to me that my identity as Latina tends, in some people's minds, to overshadow my intellectual work, professional aspirations, and relations, and consequently to cloud my personal life and self-confidence. It matters little how hard I have worked to build and maintain my credibility. This is the harsh reality that I experience on a daily basis. However, as Anchor and Morales (1990) found common in many Chicanas holding doctoral degrees, I also convert the negative messages and doubt-casting into self-propellers to prove the message wrong.

This chapter is an account of my experiences and perceptions from "the porch" of U.S. academia, since I have not as yet been able to enter as a permanent member of the family. Being on "the porch" of the house relates to the *outsider's* feeling generated when gatekeepers, just by looking at me and listening to my accent, decide not to let me enter, even though I show them all the credentials which prove my readiness to be part of the club. But even from the porch I have been able to observe and experience the gambits and games of the academy and to learn immensely from those experiences. Of course, as Bruner (1983) points out, any account of past experiences is reframed and interpreted within the context of what is happening to oneself at the present time. Thus, our stories are subject to continual interpretation and reinterpretation. They are, as Bruner (1994) calls them, "life-making" processes, a way of thinking.

In the same vein, O'Loughlin (1996) assures us that "by telling our stories we become conscious of the storied nature of our lives" (p. 11). From this postmodern perspective of narrative, telling one's own story is a way of knowing and understanding not only one's life, but through it the complex net of meanings and interactions of the community and society in which one is immersed. Carter (1993) conceptualizes "story" as a way of knowing and thinking about issues with which we deal, specifically in the area of teacher education. For her, a story "became a way of capturing the complexity, specificity and interconnectedness of the phenomena with which we deal" (p. 6).

In trying to make sense of my experiences in academia in the United States, I have engaged in thinking about the deeply rooted system of beliefs in this society, about cultural diversity, social interactions, social goals, systems of prejudices, and in general the social structures and patterns of social action that otherwise would not have been the focus of my inquiry. In writing about my experiences, first, I will preview what I am going to cover. This, of itself, reflects my first lesson; writings and presentations must be very focused. The organization of the story will touch upon academic discourse, dispassionate academic work, time as imperative, social relations, the culture of niceness, dealing with students and teachers, hunting for a tenure-track job, power and privilege, and my own conflicting desires to take part in the game and at the same time to resist full acculturation.

Academic Discourse

As a doctoral student, I realized that in so-called discussions, students avoided arguing; if they disagreed they did not express it. My fear of using English inappropriately often precluded me from going forward and disagreeing—although I did once in a while. Soon, I realized that this kind of behavior was not acceptable as a way to discuss issues about academic themes. I began to feel uncomfortable arguing, and it was easier for me to stay quiet and to follow the same strategy as my classmates; I had learned the lesson, yet in my mind it was simply a waste of opportunity to go more deeply into issues. The condition of being on "the porch" pulled me back from being authentic; rather I tried to accommodate the American way (white middle-class manners) of classroom discussion. Under conditions of asymmetrical power relations, accommodation became essential to survival. Furthermore, at that time I was very naive concerning the numerous sensitive points of conflict and power struggles among different racial and ethnic groups, and even more naive with respect to "political correctness" as a crucial mediator of the interaction among students and between students and the professor.

The lack of opportunities to discuss issues openly with other people pushed me to read more intensively about hot topics such as oppression, racism, critical multicultural education, and marginalization, and this helped me to articulate and understand my own situation. I was delighted with, and still continue enjoying, the easy access to bibliographic materials and other sources of information. This has been for me the best part of the U.S. academic life. Lacking live interlocutors, I found many distant mentors and authors with whom I could discuss issues which concerned me. Thus, I began to write papers with a critical and argumentative tone. This was an opportunity to argue with diverse authors and to advocate for oppressed and marginalized groups. Of course, I was also feeling oppressed and marginalized myself.

Making the best of a bad situation, I found in my frustrations the inspiration for writing. My critical and argumentative style of writing was accepted insofar as it met the academic requirements. However, it was problematic for presentations in professional conferences. To deal with presentations in the "American way" has been quite a challenge for me. To write proposals and to get approval has not been difficult but to do a successful presentation has been somewhat tricky. I have learned that the best format is the dominant type for that specific kind of conference: reading or talking. The language should be direct, very concise, and formal. It is better to avoid rhetorical, persuasive, or metaphorical style. These nuances are only allowed for people who are already well known. In brief, academic discourse should be direct, formal, and detached from the affective and personal dimensions. This American way contrasts with the kind of rhetorical type of discourse that is very common in Latin America, including my country Colombia. We have a tendency to give the background of the issue, to connect with socioeconomic and political issues, and to give a historical sense using a rhetorical type of argumentation. This Latin American style is seen in the United States as unfocused and as beating around the bush.

Dispassionate Writing, Talking, and Teaching

As I became more aware of the American style of academic discourse, I discovered how important it is to avoid taking stances on hot political issues and defending one's ideas with reason and passion. It is simply not seen as a professional style. Trying to appear as neutral was, and still is, very difficult for me, perhaps because I do not believe that neutrality can happen, rather, we dissimulate our stances. In teaching one needs to give the impression of being neutral. It is not "correct" to take a position explicitly, argue in its favor, and persuade students to embrace that orientation. This sounds like indoctrination, especially if it is oriented toward advocacy for disenfranchised groups. People need to believe in free self-determination, thus "choice" is the magic word even when the available choices are very insignificant.

In teaching I have found that trying to be neutral, and letting students choose freely the approach with which they sympathize most, is often antithetic with the development of a critical consciousness. Consequently, deeply rooted systems of beliefs, as well as sociocultural, economic, and political factors that constrain our actions, are simply left unexamined. This apparent neutrality is based on the assumption that the personal is independent from the social dimension, cognition is separate from affectivity, and theory from action. In this regard, Bruner (1986) criticizes mainstream psychology because of its individualist conception of the self, that is, the self has been divided into independent dimensions such as cognition, affect, and action. In contrast, Bruner demonstrates how stories have the power of bringing all the dimensions of the self back together, in dynamic relation with culture.

In the same vein, Maxine Greene (1986) advocates for the exercise of teaching with passion. Thus, teaching "is an undertaking oriented to empowering persons to become different, to think critically and creatively . . . to care about what they are coming to understand, to be concerned, to be fully present and alive" (p. 72). Similarly, Paulo Freire (1998), in his last book *Teachers as Cultural Workers: Letters to Those Who Dare Teach*, proclaims the holistic nature of teaching and learning:

> We must dare in order to say . . . that we study, we learn, we teach, we know with our entire body. We do all these things with feelings, with emotions, with wishes, with fear, with doubts, with passion, and also with critical reasoning. However, we never study, learn, teach and know with the last only. We must dare so as *never to dichotomize cognition and emotion.* (p. 3) [emphasis mine]

I find Greene's and Freire's claims much more human and meaningful views of writing, teaching, and learning than the cold and neutral style required in academia. As O'Loughlin (1996) remarks in his autobiography, this cold and neutral style is carefully and explicitly taught and privileged in U.S. academia, including teacher preparation:

> I was taught not to trust my instincts. I was taught that head rules over heart, knowledge rules over emotions, experts have answers . . . the message from most of my professors was to deny myself and my roots. Use the passive voice when writing, I was told. Avoid personal language and anecdotes. Don't use the Irish spelling of words because they are distracting to readers who are used to American English. Be scientific! Be rational! Don't be emotional! Don't be angry! Don't show your passions! Be detached. . . . Be silent. . . . Be invisible. . . . (p. 4)

Montero-Sieburth's (1996) study on Latinas in academia highlights similar feelings and struggles these scholars have had with the type of academic rationality that "excludes, or at least minimizes, passion and experiential insights" (p. 75). Montero-Sieburth sees this learning to write academically not simply as learning a new skill, but as "a cultural shift, a shift to a new, distinctively different and, from the Latino's point of view, a restrictive mode of experience" (p. 75). Montero-Sieburth quotes a Honduran researcher/consultant about feeling restricted while writing academically in English, "When I write in Spanish I tell my story and give it breath. When I write in English I begin to sterilize my language by the shortness of the words and the directness of meaning" (p. 75). I cannot agree more with this sentiment.

The cultural shift I have experienced required me to learn a new language with all the cultural meanings and actions constituting it. In addition, I needed to become acutely aware of how people perceive me. Being perceived as a "radical" is a terrible label by which to be distinguished in the academy. It does not mean a person who is struggling for radical changes in society in order to have more equality and social justice. It means inflexible, troublemaker, bitter, and negative. This could be unforgivable for a person such as I. When I began to realize and understand the socially constructed meanings and labels of being critical, that is, radical, I had to step back and rethink ways to deal with this, given my condition of having a temporary faculty position and being a foreign Latina searching for a full-time job. I had naively believed that I was free to talk openly on educational perspectives according to my beliefs, convictions, and commitments. This is an illustration of the myth concerning freedom of speech. Is one really free to talk and perform professionally? The answer is, it depends on who you are in terms of race, gender, class, age, national origin and first language, among other factors of discrimination.

To awaken to one's own reality is painful and overwhelming. I became overwhelmed with cautious postawakenings; it is better to be silent rather than to speak up, it is better to avoid using terms that identify one as a radical, it is better to appear cold rather than passionate. I need to avoid talking about my educational experiences prior to coming to the United States since they are always ignored; it is best to reveal to others the least possible about my work, the more secretive the better. This led me to embrace silence as the easiest way to cope with the situation—and silence is not exactly my forte! Moments of intense frustration and anger pushed me to begin a conversation with myself; to write a journal. I discovered that, to a great extent, frustration has been the inspiration of my writing in the journal. The more frustration, the more intensely and deeply I write about the situation that generates it. At the same time, writing becomes the vehicle for better understanding and for thinking of strategies to deal with future similar situations. I felt more relief when I found that Joanne Cooper (1991) attributes to writing a journal an important role in the caring of oneself, the same role I had just discovered:

> It can be a place to dump anger, guilt, or fear. . . . A place to clarify what it is we feel angry or guilty about . . . in working through that anger and guilt . . . to transform silence into language and action. (p. 105)

Time: The Implacable Constraint

The perception of time is undoubtedly different between Latinos (recent arrivals) and people of the United States in general. I am, by familial habit, punctual, so I did not have any problem with that. Indeed, I am really enjoying the punctuality of people for classes, for meetings, and for appointments. I feel that I am able to accomplish planned things on a daily basis because of punctuality. Somewhat different is the management of time in situations of severe time constraints, such as the presentation of a paper. I find it very hard to give a good sense of the essence of a paper in the time given, which usually is no more than twenty minutes. In such a compression of the paper, what usually happens is that the context, theoretical framework, and reflective accounts are left out, and data, facts, and results are what make the substance of the presentation. I become concerned when empirical data and the garnishing around them are at the center of the stage, and the historical perspective, sociopolitical context, and even a thoughtful interpretation of the data are discarded. Isn't that pure empiricism? Historically, empiricism has limited human potential by reducing the concept of valid knowledge to only that coming through the senses, thus leaving out the knowledge that is constructed beyond the perceptual realm. Shotter (1993) talks about "knowledge of the third kind," which he refers to as the meaning-making of our conversational realities.

As in professional conferences, time constraints in other areas of academia lead to shortcutting important and necessary community activities and social processes. I understand that we need to plan our activities carefully to take advantage of time allowances. But when we become obsessive about *doing things* at the expense of mutually enriching collegial conversations, we are at risk of losing the essence of academia as an inherently social system of relations. Consequently, we can easily become isolated beings surrounded by other isolated beings. Interactions with others do not go further than a greeting and a weather comment at best. Even on the telephone, I always feel pressured to state concisely the object of the call and hang up immediately. Very often, I want to continue the call but I receive signals like lower intonation or an "OK?" which I have learned to recognize as "we have to finish because I have other things to do." Now, I think for a while before I call someone. It needs to be extremely urgent. It seems as if everybody is in a race, including myself. How can I be different in such circumstances? I resist the idea that this is organization, efficiency, and progress. I feel that we are losing the true social dimension of existence and of human activity. Alienation has consequently forced me to speak and observe "from the porch."

In her life story, Martha Montero-Sieburth (1997) refers to the special meaning of time in U.S. academic life:

> I quickly learned that the implicit message in concerns with time use was that time is to be valued for personal production, publishing, and research, not necessarily for advising students. To the degree that I clocked my time, I could squeeze in more time for such production. (p. 142)

This is exactly what I observed and was affected by as a graduate student. Now, as an instructor, I am struggling to avoid falling into the same pattern. Although I am not legitimately in the academic track, I feel the pressure for publishing in order to increase the possibilities of entering into it.

Social Relations at the Personal and Academic Levels

Since I have been nourished with the works of Vygotsky, Freire, and Bakhtin, I have developed a strong basis for believing that the true origin and development of knowledge, and even of one's identity occur through interaction and dialogue with other persons with whom we are connected in any way. I come from an environment in which I had multiple connections and where it was easy to put together a group with common interests and goals. As a leader-educator, I was heard, respected, and accepted without any apprehensions by colleagues in higher education with whom I worked.

In contrast, in the college environment of my doctoral studies I could hardly develop any connection with other students and be part of a permanent group. I felt excluded, and the phantom of "outsiderness" was always my companion. I began to speculate on the reasons for that exclusion and wonder whether perhaps one of them was that those students were thinking that I was not able to contribute to the group. In my mind that was very unfair because I had shown in the whole-group discussions how I was able to contribute fundamental ideas. Of course, many students didn't hear or didn't want to hear me because of my Spanish accent in English, then I realized that this was another reason to be excluded.

I had not experienced before, in Colombia or in Mexico, being excluded by my own classmates, therefore, it was painful and disconcerting. This was the first experience of discrimination that I felt deeply in my soul for being Latina, because of my Spanish accent in English, and obviously because of my skin color. I thought this was not the type of situation to discriminate against anybody because there was no obvious competition about anything. Since the system of grading in those classes was not a zero-sum game, I could not figure out why I could possibly represent a threat. For me, the whole situation was puzzling at best, or a case of rampant discrimination at worst. Actually, it took me at least two years to realize that the strange things I was experiencing were, in reality, race discrimination. I had been conditioned by media exported to Latin America to think of racism as something of the past, not as a problem of the 90s, and even less as something that would so often happen to me.

These first experiences of discrimination of which I became aware, were for me like starting an engine. I speedily awoke to my reality as Latina. I began to understand why some professors (fortunately only a few) ignored or even denigrated my contributions in class conversations. I could understand better why some professors, and students too, were so surprised when they read my papers. It became clear to me that they were not expecting good performance on my part. Now I know that low expectations are a very generalized habit of thinking about Latinos as well as blacks and Native Americans. In this country, it is enough to have a Hispanic, black, or Native American appearance to be boxed into the category of a potential failure.

While dealing with disillusion, anger, and confusion, I searched eagerly for other Latin graduate students to talk about our experiences. I heard quite similar stories of feeling invisible and undervalued in class and of having to face the professor's low expectations. However, I did not hear stories about being excluded by classmates, so I blamed myself for not having the necessary social skills to get closer to them. This realization made me look actively at forming a group of Latino doctoral students to support one another in doing our dissertations, even though we were from different programs and departments. I found another Latina doctoral student called Nora (a pseudonym), whose focus area was close to mine and even overlapped in some dimensions. We supported each other both emotionally and intellectually, thus, I overcame the feelings of marginalization from my own classmates.

Furthermore, the library was my refuge at least in two ways. First of all I was delighted because of the easy access to a wide range of printed materials and computerized information. Undoubtedly, this accessibility kept me very busy, and in this way I could cope with the difficulties of communication and the feeling of isolation in my classes. I wanted to do each of my papers in depth since I had the bibliographic resources I had never had before. Secondly, the library was my refuge in my search for the dialogue partners I was missing. I was able to sustain a constant dialogue (in the Bakhtinian sense) with distant mentors and friends who were talking to me as if they knew what I was going through. Their insights enlightened my understanding of the gambits and games of U.S. academia.

As Nora and I advanced in our dissertations and built our friendship, the themes of social interaction, cultural differences, racism, oppression, marginalization, dialogue, and communication became central to our purposes. I was eagerly reading Paulo Freire, Henry Giroux, Peter McLaren, Mikhail Bakhtin, Jurgen Habermas, Richard Bernstein, Michel Foucault, Pierre Bourdieu, and Patti Lather, among others, who were supplying the language and the frames for a deeper and broader understanding of my own situation and that of my friend and colleague. Those theoretical frameworks were also in fact strong foundations of my dissertation. I was experiencing a turning point in my academic interests and endeavors, as it became clear to me that experiences of exclusion and marginalization are part of the life story of minority groups and especially of Latinas and Latinos who are immigrants. Reading the personal academic stories of Maxine Greene (1997) and Martha Montero-Sieburth (1996, 1997), I have found how exclusion has impacted their lives and ignited their willingness to embrace major professional and personal commitments as advocates of multiculturalism, diversity, and cultural identity.

Through the dialogues with Nora, I discovered that in her classes there were several Latino students, in contrast to my case when I was often the only Latina and often the only so-called minority in the class. That situation probably enhanced my outsiderness, and consequently the feelings of powerlessness. At that time, I was analyzing the data of my dissertation research about interactions among teachers, which led me to realize that my way of contributing to class conversations could have been interpreted as too passionate, too outspoken, too radical, and even too philosophical. Certainly, I was pretty naive concerning the practice of political correctness and the tricks of the power structure.

Growing in awareness of the cultural nuances of academic discourse and group interaction is an ongoing journey with moments of intense disappointment, confusion, and feelings of being powerless, as well as moments of insightful understandings. Group interaction has been both the focus of my inquiries and the primary source of my problems of maladaptation to American academia. On one of the first times I worked as a member of a team in the United States, I came to realize that I needed to change my way of participating, in terms of style, content, and attitude. Rather than spontaneously devoting all my knowledge, experience, and time to the goals of the team activity, it would have been better for me to make only marginal contributions. It was clear to me that my contributions, which implied a deep examination of the ideology behind some team decisions on curriculum and program orientation, were not welcome. I have no doubt in my mind that the fact of being a Latina scholar and having a Spanish accent overshadowed my genuine participation in the work in the eyes of those members of the group who felt that only their mainstream ideas were the valid ways to do things.

A self-prescribed silence became the least frustrating way to deal with the situation, and writing in my journal became the opportunity to reflect and process the anger and discouragement I was experiencing. I gradually became more and more silent and adopted for myself a slogan: *NO DIGA, ESCRIBA* (don't say, write instead). For me that means, do not say anything substantial and/or anything that can be considered as a criticism, rather write about it. At that time, I had no expectation of being able to talk about my experiences to anybody, least of all in a professional conference or to write a chapter in a book. Several Latino/a scholars (Tania Ramalho, Maria Mercado, Martha Montero-Sieburth, Henry Trueba, José Cintrón) and hearty friends of Latinos (Lila Jacobs and Cecil Canton) looked at and validated my story as something worthwhile to share publicly. After all, many others share these experiences of exclusion and discrimination as well.

Now as I reflect on my experiences in team-working situations, I continue having insightful understandings of why things happened the way they did. I realize, for example, that even when we agreed to disagree, we all adopted group collaboration and social construction of knowledge as the basic premises of the program and the teamwork. However, I was interpreting those frames very differently from the others. I had not suspected that competition could have been an important factor in many failed attempts on my part to get together with other people to work on what appeared to be shared ideologies, interests, and goals. I naively believed that if we committed ourselves to work in a collaborative group, we set aside every vestige of individualism and its companion, competition, and we were ready to work with a new perspective of education. The U.S. educational system, influenced by the political and economic system, has been the world's king of zero-sum games; that is, some gain what others lose. Standardized tests are the best way to maintain this competitive spirit. How can we expect people to get rid of competition easily if it is rooted in the way we perceive ourselves in relation to others? Actually, it would be more precise to say in opposition to others. This deep-seated individualism and competitiveness in the so-called Western civilization is metaphorically articulated by Sampson (1993), inspired by Bakhtin's dialogics, in these terms:

> We need to think of the self as a kind of bounded container, separate from other similarly bounded containers and in possession or ownership of its own capacities and abilities. In order to ensure this container's integrity, we need to think of whatever lies outside its boundaries as potentially threatening and dangerous, and whatever lies inside as sufficiently worthy to protect. These beliefs establish a possessive individualist view of the person and the assumption of a negative relation between self and other, both of which understandings permeate much of Western civilization. (p. 31)

When I became fully aware of how competition could be an important factor for classmates and even for team partners who felt threatened by my participation in the group, I became very cautious, thinking much more about how what I said was going to be taken than in the thing I was going to say. I found another reason to practice my *lema NO DIGA, ESCRIBA* (don't say, write), which was working for me in terms of avoiding conflict with the group. In addition, I came up with another *lema* for myself: *NI MUCHO, NI POCO* (neither too much [flame], nor too little). This is an abbreviated version of a popular saying which stands for balanced actions: *"Ni tanto que queme al santo, ni tan poco que no lo alumbre"* (Neither so much [flame] as to burn the saint, nor so little as not to illuminate it).

I was being conditioned to remain on "the porch" to keep others happy. The absence of discussion, challenging questions and remarks, it seemed to me, was well received by most of the other team partners, because in this way we could concentrate on the assigned task. However, I was feeling silenced and guilty. This was the second time I realized how task-oriented action as opposed to "communicative action" (Habermas, 1984) dominates social interaction, and therefore, teamwork. The first time was when I was analyzing the data of my dissertation about teachers' interactions in a small group. One of the most important insights was that personal communicative interaction, as opposed to goal-oriented interaction, led teachers to engage genuinely in coconstructing knowledge, rather than merely meeting requirements (Torres, 1995). Nonetheless, there existed several impediments at the social, institutional, and individual levels which prevented teachers (I will say also academics) from engaging in genuine coconstructive endeavors (Torres & John-Steiner, 1995). Specifically in collaborative intellectual work, cognitive individualism may be a paramount impediment (Torres, 1996).

My experience with working groups, in the context of U.S. academia, accounts for some patterns of which I am becoming harshly aware. These patterns are: predominantly task-oriented work, avoidance of disagreement, participants' contributions controlled by competition, and cognitive individualism. In addition, the fact of being a minority person in the group, in the full sense of the term, placed me in a very disadvantaged position. In this situation, it is better to work alone if there is a chance to do so. Until now, I had always preferred collaborative work to individual work. Now I am deeply reconsidering that attitude, especially when I am going to be the only minority in the group. This change in preferences does not make me happy, but given the circumstances, it is less oppressive for me to work by myself. It is not really a matter of preference, but a matter of surviving. In other words, working on the "porch" actually became a refuge.

Understanding and Resisting the Culture of "Niceness"

My desire to understand the U.S. academia led me to become a very acute observer of the cultural nuances within it. I began to see some common threads in European Americans' reactions to other people in simple social interactions, as well as their reactions to hot social issues. Although some patterns were evident to me, I was not able to articulate what they were. It was only until I read Paley's (1979) book, *White Teacher,* that I became able to see in words the "white" culture of "niceness," in contrast with the ways black children interact among themselves: "These girls [black girls] do not believe in the platitudes with which I grew up. "If you can't say something nice, don't say anything. Silence is golden" (p. 132). What I find misleading in these niceties is the difficulty of knowing what the person really thinks of the issue at hand. Such a situation is even more puzzling for a person like myself who is not automatically attuned to the subtleties embedded in this culture.

Another thing that concerns me about being nice is that it tends to compromise authenticity. It cuts off the possibility of open criticism and debate on issues, and consequently, of obtaining a wide range of reactions. When I became aware of the "golden rule of niceness," I started internalizing it quickly. I began to hear a voice saying "be nice, be nice." I began to recognize other people's strategies for framing criticisms in a nice way: "I'm having a hard time to put this in a positive way." When this class of cultural rules underlies people's work relations, I see little opportunity for critical examination of important issues. Everybody is afraid to be seen as a negative, not-nice person. Certainly, I would not like to see niceness confounded with consideration, though they may overlap. At any rate, I would still prefer an authentic comment, a constructive criticism, rather than a nice innocuous comment. How much longer can I resist assimilating this trait? I do not know for sure and that scares me. Meanwhile I have learned to become more aware of people's expectations from me.

Speaking of niceness, I really do not want to sugarcoat my story to appeal to those who refuse to see how reality is different for different people, not because of their abilities and potentialities, but because of their identity. To enter and move up in academia, some people need only push a button and the elevator door opens, while others need to take the stairs step-by-step, jumping over and through numerous hurdles and hoops on the way.

Dealing with Students and Teachers

Since my field is education, most of my students are either teachers or students preparing to be teachers. Teaching is my passion and the source of many of my intellectual inquiries and also some headaches. I have worked at all academic levels, from elementary to graduate school. In Colombia, as an insider to the Colombian culture and to the teachers' culture, reaching teachers' interests and hearts, as well as creating a classroom community, was fast and efficient. Teaching in the United States has required me to develop some new skills. All my reflections on U.S. academia have helped me in my dealings with some students, especially, but not exclusively those from a European American background. At the beginning of each semester, I usually become aware of two subgroups of students in each class I am teaching. One group consists of students (nonmainstream students including minorities and open-minded European Americans) who quickly get engaged and adapt well to my accent and teaching style. The other group consists of students (mainstream students, mostly European Americans and some minorities) who exhibit body language, verbal reactions, facial expressions, disengagement, judgmental attitudes, and a subtle resistance. I feel as if they had put up a glass wall, including low expectations, to impede my reaching them. Then, I know that I have to use all my communicative resources and teaching strategies to engage them in the course activities and gain their trust.

This process is easier and faster depending on the relative size of the easygoing group in relation to the resistant one. The easy-going group becomes my support and motivation to keep going. Reaching the second group of students demands an intense effort and time from me in addition to the preparation of the classes and the grading of papers. I must say that I have been successful with most of those resistant students. Many of them become my allies. After a few classes, they take down the glass wall and begin to see that I am not the person they thought I was. However, there have often been one or two students per class who have resisted all invitations to full engagement in the course activities and have denied themselves the power of participation and the opportunities of learning. Most of all, they have not been able to overcome their prejudices toward me and in particular their low expectations. For them, I am sure, being in my class is like being in hell. I feel sorry for their blindness and deafness, due mostly to my identity as a Latina and not really for what I do.

I have never heard anyone acknowledge how much extra effort, time, and heart are demanded of a person like myself to overcome the prejudices, and hence the low expectations and resistance from the students and from anybody else at work, in contrast to those who have the right race, gender, national origin, and first language. By acknowledging this extra work, I mean to consider it as an important part of a workload, or at least to take this into account in the performance evaluation. However, it is far from being recognized. Rodriguez' (1993) report illustrates the magnitude of the problem. He indicates that in 1991 only 2.3 percent of Latina full-time faculty were tenured, compared to 88.2 percent for white female faculty. No doubt, this triple or quadruple loading for Latinas—the need to prove themselves to everyone, their teaching and research loads and high demands, besides their commitment to fight injustices and to give back to the community—put them at risk of burning out and leaving academia for another type of work. Reyes and Halcón (1997) indicate that giving up is one of the four most common responses to racism in academia by Latinos. Considering the figures given above, this response is even more common in Latinas. Consequently, there will be few role models for Latinas who pursue higher education and even fewer for those who pursue graduate studies.

I find stories similar to mine comforting and also worrisome. They are comforting because my experiences and my understanding of them are validated intersubjectively. The feelings of empathy and connectedness are intense. It is worrisome because the problems of Latinos are more extensive and entrenched in the system than I had thought they were. When I began to write my journal, I was convinced that the problems I was facing were really only my particular problems. I thought other Latinos may have problems, but never like mine. I wrote the first draft of my story as a collection of memories of my experiences. When I began to read other stories and the conceptualizations about stories, and to connect them with my own story, I woke up to a new way of knowing, this time about the entire institution of higher education in the U.S. context. It is a way of knowing and thinking that allows me to perceive the complexities of the institution as a whole, as well as the specificities of particular situations. I also realized that knowing about U.S. academic life "from the porch" is not an individual but a collective experience. By working on my story, I became a part of a community of people with shared experiences, struggles, cultural roots, understandings, feelings, and social goals. This is true empowerment. Even though I have made only a few, yet very important connections, I see the possibility of expanding them in a fairly rapid way.

Hunting for a Tenure-Track Job

Entering into U.S. academia is difficult for most people but for a Latina like myself, it can be extremely difficult. It is already difficult to learn and deal with the nuances of academia, but it is overwhelming to overcome the barriers of race, gender, class, national origin, and first language other than English—the more so if that language happens to be Spanish. Similar things will happen if the first language is Chinese or black English. Since I obtained my Ph.D. in educational foundations in 1995, I have applied to over 110 positions. The best job I have secured so far is a one-year appointment. Each application has entailed not simply changing the address of a standard letter and mailing it. I always study the requirements carefully and if I fully meet them, I apply with an individually tailored cover letter.

The process of selection, interviewing, and hiring decisions have been very instructive for me; I have learned much about the very creative maneuvers of inclusion and exclusion in academia. However, living this reality is painful, confusing, and demanding. The cost for learning is very high and becomes even higher for me because of who I am, and not because of what I am able to do. Some stories of exclusion have been confirmed as I meet colleagues in professional conferences who say to me "Your name is familiar to me. Have you applied to my university?" Then I know that there is an interesting story to follow, "The committee was really looking for a white man," or "they were looking for a really feminist person," or "they were committed to hiring a black person." I continue discovering this kind of story in every conference I attend. It has become clear to me that institutional micropolitics plays a major role in this process of selecting and hiring new faculty in institutions of higher education. These games are unknown by the applicant outside the institution; and even inside, one never knows for sure how to play them. Unfortunately for me, I haven't been able so far to present the required qualifications along with the right gender, the right color, the right accent in English, and the right nationality. Optimistically (maybe stubbornly) I think I will one day have all these at once, in a felicitous coincidence. I feel that I am getting closer to it.

When I read Reyes and Halcón's (1997) "Racism in the Academia," I was able to relate totally to their experiences and those of other Latinos(as) they found similar. Like all of them, I had the illusion that once I got my degree I would be ready to play in the big league; that "Ph.D.'s pave the way to an egalitarian status with mutual respect among professional colleagues, where the new rules of competition will be truly based on merit" (p. 300). However, we were far off base with our expectations since discrimination on the basis of race, gender, class, language, etc. is common practice in academia. Discrimination has become very subtle, yet no less pervasive—"the old wolf in new clothing."

Another issue indicated by Reyes and Halcón (1997) with which I could relate immediately was the type of covert racism they call "typecasting syndrome." This refers to the specialization imposed on different minority groups. For example, a Latino/a-Chicano/a is expected to work in Bilingual Education or Chicano Studies. In hunting for a job, I began to explore other areas besides my strongest area of Educational Research and Foundations, given the fact that I had found nothing available in my area. I applied for some positions in Bilingual Education and I was called for interviews. Of course, I was at a disadvantage with respect to other candidates who were able to claim specialization as their major. Having gotten caught in the trap, I began taking courses in Bilingual Education, in order to extend the range of possibilities for job search. Through my continual struggle to understand the puzzle of faculty selection and hiring in higher education, it became clear to me that if I had studied Bilingual Education, it would have been easier to get a full-time, tenure-track job. I also became aware that my expertise in different types of educational research and different disciplines of foundations was neither understood nor recognized, because a great part of it was obtained previous to my coming to the United States. On my bad days, I think how difficult academic life could be for me as a Latina, if I remain on the porch of academia and if I face tremendous barriers to entering and even to working on the porch. The irony is that I have been "marginalized in the margins" by people who, rather than displaying solidarity with others in similar alienating conditions, having acquired a little more power, step over their comrades heads as a result of their own internalization of oppression. Freire (1992) indeed remarks that part of the condition of being oppressed is the internalization of oppression, so that when given the opportunity the oppressed becomes the oppressor.

On my good days, I feel privileged, successful, optimistic about getting a full-time tenure-track position and about being able to establish a complete program of participatory action research with my students/teachers and perhaps a colleague or several of them. I agree with Paulo Freire's (1994) statement: "I do not understand human existence and the struggle needed to improve it, apart from hope and dream" (p. 8). I haven't lost my hope, and I still dream of having a successful career in U.S. academia.

Power and Privilege

Is hard work needed in the pursuit of an academic career? Yes, it is. Without working hard I would not have been able even to graduate. However, I have to make clear that there are huge differences between the level of work that a person like myself needs to perform in order to succeed, in contrast with that of the person who knows the system and for whom the system works in his/her favor. I have found myself having to work two or three times as hard. In my case, this does not happen because of my lack of abilities or any significant language barriers. It happens because of the higher standards imposed on me as a result of the low expectations of those who are in the position of judging my work, abilities and potential, and which are based primarily on the obvious characteristics of my identity as Latina. I have learned to accept this unequal treatment as a given and to mitigate its discouraging effects on my work. However, this does not mean that I forego any opportunity to denounce this corrosive practice as unfair and unacceptable in a society that prides itself on having the best democracy in the world. Despite the undervaluing of my expertise and potential, I am slowly making it but at a much higher price than others pay. However, I need to recognize that even at a higher price I am privileged; other people, working even harder do not make it at all. Is this fair? Why is it happening?

To explain this unfair and unequal treatment in the academics to persons like myself, I found very enlightening the theory of "Ups and Downs" by Terry (1993). He maintains, "What makes an up an up and a down a down is that an up can do more to a down than what a down can do to an up. That's what keeps an up up and a down down" (p. 61). To move from down to up is certainly determined not only by effort and ability, but by race, socioeconomic class and gender, among other factors. Sleeter (in progress) displays the intersection of these factors in what she calls the "pyramid of power," which allows us to get in a simple image the complexity of the structure of power in this society. There are two pyramids, one, broad base down, represents the population; the other, upside down (over the first one), represents power. Along the axis which represents socioeconomic class (income/wealth), the concentration of wealth and power is in very few people's hands. The intersection among social class, color, and gender is shown by cutting the pyramids diagonally by two planes: from top-right to bottom-left for color, and from top-left to bottom-right for gender. The intersection of these three major discriminating factors determines the position of a specific person in the structure of power in this society, and therefore his/her participation in the distribution of resources and opportunities. Besides race, class, and gender, I would add two other important factors which have multiplied the number of "limit-situations" in my case—they are national origin and Spanish as a first language. For Freire (1992), "Limit-situations imply the existence of persons who are directly or indirectly served by these situations, and those who are negated and curbed by them" (p. 92). Limit-situations include for Freire those oppressing situations that not only preclude opportunities for the oppressed but also prevent them from understanding their reality, or in other words, their own alienation. Limit-situations multiply as we add more factors to the identity of the person. Hence in my case, as the limit-situations multiply the opportunities diminish significantly.

Based on Terry's parable of "Ups and Downs," Sleeter (in progress) develops a conceptual frame to explain the disparity of opportunities for "ups and downs." First of all, a widely and deeply accepted belief is that, if we want something (concerning education, income, a decent job, housing, vacation, health, safety, power, etc.), we only need to possess the required ability and to work hard and we are assured to get it in a fairly consistent way. This logic, as Sleeter points out, works quite well for the "ups," but not for the "downs," whose hard work and abilities are not correlated with their opportunities in a systematic way, or not correlated at all. The worst part is that "ups" systematically blame "downs" for the latter's own failures, rather than examining the disparate opportunities due to their disparate positioning in the structure of power and using their privileged position to make opportunities equitable for all people.

In my own journey through academia, falling automatically in the category of "downs," I need many more steps, and much more time through each step. Looking at the positive side of this journey, these experiences have made me highly aware of the academic maneuvers, have made me a stronger fighter, and a savorer of every success in moving up, in contrast with those for whom things are much easier. Reflecting on my academic experiences has made me not only an acute thinker, but also a more determined person. However, I need to recognize that I am "moving on," in the sense of Reyes and Halcón (1997), because I have been lucky to get the support, encouragement, and mentoring of open-minded people across color, gender, and nationality lines, who have come to value my experiences, expertise, and potential. Unfortunately these persons are seldom in positions of power. The insights I have gained have greatly benefited me, but I also believe they would benefit not only Latinos, but other minorities and even mainstream European-Americans. For Latinas and other minorities who may find themselves with similar experiences, the sense of sharing helps them in their daily struggles. As for mainstream European Americans, including Americanized minorities, they are going to become aware of their internalized prejudices and hopefully they are going to be more ready to understand the situation of Latinas in the academia. Meanwhile, as I am slowly moving into academia, I am learning to play the games of the academia, yet resisting the pressure of total Americanization.

Note

1. I am using "conscientization" in the sense that Paulo Freire (1992) created and used it. "Conscientization" means more than merely becoming aware; it includes a critical understanding of one's own reality concerning the power structure that dominates this society and that excludes some people because of their race, gender, national origin, first language, etc. It is a clear understanding of one's limit-situation as a person and as the group with which one is usually identified.

Chapter Six

Academic Adversity and Faculty Warriors: Prevailing amidst Trauma[1]

Chalsa M. Loo and Maria Chun

> I received a letter from the Chancellor stating that I'd been given a terminal ap-
> pointment of one year. I felt that I had a terminal disease. I had one year in
> which to live or die.
>
> —Female professor at a state university
> who overturned a negative tenure decision

Introduction

As I enter the twenty-first century, inequities for faculty of color in institutions
of higher education continue (Turner, Myers, & Creswell, 1999). Problems in
the retention of faculty of color remain, leading Turner et al. (1999) to conclude
that the academic workplace is a difficult work environment for racial minority
group members. In the interest of preparing minority faculty for the possibility
of a denied tenure or promotion at their academic institutions, and informing
majority faculty members about the difficulties facing minority faculty, this
chapter presents the cases of eight racial minority faculty who fought a denial of
tenure or promotion at their academic institutions and won. These "warriors in
an ivory tower" succeeded in overturning negative decisions or secured a large
monetary settlement.

This chapter attempts to capture the functional strategies used to overturn a
denied promotion or tenure decisions as well as the psychological reactions
stemming from an experienced assault on the person's worth. This approach
conveys the message that the battle, while external, has an emotional impact and
that the effort of academic combat is as much functional as emotional.

These cases center largely on events that were initiated in the mid to late
1980s, one of which was not resolved until the 1990s. Accordingly, these cases

might be viewed partly as a reflection of the times. To what extent the experiences of these faculty of the 1980s reflect the reality today is a mission for another study.

Before the case analyses, I include a brief description of the academic structure and promotional procedures. There are several promotional steps in the academic arena. Generally, a professor begins at the assistant professor level and is evaluated every two years (via a merit review) for each of three steps. Some institutions have mid-career evaluations, a precursor of the tenure decision. The biggest hurdle is tenure when one gains the title of associate professor. Tenure essentially means that faculty have a permanent position with that university and cannot be fired. After tenure, the process of evaluation continues. The promotion steps normally come every two years and continue for another three reviews until one attains the rank of full professor. Throughout one's academic career as a professor, accelerations are possible, which means a faculty member can be advanced to a higher step level at a quicker rate than normal.

Teaching, research, and service are generally the three areas upon which promotion and tenure are based, with the more prestigious institutions generally having higher academic standards for research and publication. The phrase "publish or perish" refers to the expectation that if professors fail to publish original research, they can expect to be denied tenure, which equates to losing one's job.

Promotion lies in the hands of those further advanced in the promotional ladder. A professor's career, determined by promotions and tenure, lies in the evaluations of faculty with higher rank. Full professors determine the academic fate for associate professors, and both full and associate professors determine the academic fate of assistant professors. Higher in the academia hierarchy are deans, the vice president or vice-chancellor, the presidents or chancellors—who have the power to consider appeals and overturn a lower decision.

The sample included Asian American professors of both genders who occupied tenured or tenure-track positions at institutions of higher education in the United States. Each of these faculty were administered a structured interview by the senior author. Excerpts are included from either interviews, written appeal material in their file, or from data contained in the structured interview schedule. A fictitious name has been given to each faculty member in order to honor anonymity and confidentiality.

Shattered Beliefs in a Meritocracy

Asian Americans have been taught to believe that academic achievement is the ticket to success. Therefore, after achieving their Ph.D. and earning coveted positions in academic institutions of higher learning, a denial of tenure or a promotion can be a shattering experience, especially for those who believe in a meritocracy. Two professors explained the crumbling of these basic beliefs:

"What you feel you have accomplished doesn't mean anything. I would have expected people to acknowledge my work and accomplishments." "I had assumed my record spoke for itself. Instead, what I had done for the university was being questioned." Dale Minami, an attorney who represented several Asian American professors in discrimination cases, made this observation:

> The academic institution is not immune from political considerations in tenure decision . . . among my Asian American clients in these situations; I have noticed a common attitude. Invariably, they believe in the merit system: If you work hard, you will be duly rewarded. When faced with an adverse decision based on something other than merit, they have difficulty accepting that reality. All too often, they never understand that politics and racism may have as much to do with a particular decision as merit. (Minami, 1990, p. 85)

The following eight cases convey various functional methods by which each professor successfully sought to overturn negative academic decisions, despite common emotional reactions of distress, anger, hurt, and shock.

The Case of Owen: Ethnic Studies, the President, and Vice President

Owen was a tenured professor and chairperson of Ethnic Studies at a state university. In the late 1980s, his promotion to full professor was denied at the level of the vice president of Academic Affairs. Owen's strategy was to convince the president, who could overturn the vice president's denial, of doing just that.

Owen saw "absolutely no [rational] justification" for his promotion to be denied. The evaluation for his promotion had been "unanimously positive all the way to the vice president of Academic Affairs." Lower level support is generally sustained at the higher administrative levels. "What was so shocking about the denial was that I thought my political bases had been covered, with my community service and all." The threat of denial generated a "sense of vulnerability . . . that what you feel you've accomplished doesn't mean anything." Owen experienced "a lot of distress, a drain of energy, and anger at the arbitrariness of academic decision making." His informal appeal to attain his promotion lasted five months. The president eventually overturned the vice president's decision. This case describes how that positive outcome was achieved.

Owen knew that his publications would be at issue, but he found the vice president's criteria for promotion to be deviant from the precedent used for Ethnic Studies. "Ethnic Studies draws on oral history and community studies, which tends to deviate from the scientific realm from which the Vice President's criteria was apparently based."

> The Vice President called research the weak link [but I] defined the standard differently . . . I had started a new curriculum, catalogue, reached a broader audience. I had a lot published but not a lot in refereed journals. Such criteria

had been drafted much earlier and the institution had already approved of these criteria. So the Vice President was going against an already existing criteria for promotion.

I discussed this with my staff. I went through this [informal appeal] because I was pissed. I felt it was unfair, arbitrary. This was a small town. I wondered—was there a personal agenda on the Vice President's part? Was I being punished for going around proper channels, getting resources from the outside, from state legislators who had previously been involved in the program, whom I had helped in many ways? Or was it retribution for my criticisms of his work?

Owen wondered whether the denial represented some antagonism toward Ethnic Studies.

"It wasn't difficult for me to imagine that other faculty on campus might be hostile to Ethnic Studies and perceive the program as overzealous. . . . After all, Ethnic Studies is a field devoted to an analysis of institutional and social discrimination." Owen sought some explanation for this shocking event.

Owen's advice on how to successfully cope with academic adversity contains significant lessons for the faculty warrior.

First, it is very important to detach emotionally and psychologically from the situation—to objectify it. To step back from it and look at what's happening. I asked myself—if this dossier came before me, how would I judge it? . . . I would sit down to consciously look at it in a detached way, which allows you to set self-doubt to rest, which then allows you to fully utilize other strategies.

Second, get an honest assessment from colleagues—make sure they believe this was unjust to turn down.

Third, take a look at the organizational chart. Where does the person who has attacked your record fit in the structure? What are his strengths or weaknesses? How vulnerable is that person? Assume that he will not change his mind. In my case, the President had the power to overturn the Vice President. . . . Go after the President, not the Vice President.

Fourth, locate those who could impact the President—my Dean, the [Board of] Regents, the Governor's office, politicians who knew our program, then know that the President or Regents would not be turned off by politicians or community groups that were in a position to talk to the President or Regents directly (such as JACL, Okinawan groups, anti-eviction groups). In the past ten years, I had developed close working relationships with the community through my community work.

Fifth, I had to convince the President that it was worth entertaining the appeal and antagonizing the Vice President under him. I had several long discussions with the President, one lasting one and a half hours. The President indicated it would be very difficult for him to overturn the Vice President. He was already having trouble with this man . . . so the President did not want to use my case to punish the Vice President. But he also knew I had good relations with state legislators. So, the President formed another [review] committee of five persons. They came back in favor of promotion, but they were divided (three to two). The President said this was difficult. What I sought to determine was—Who were these people [on the committee] and who selected them? The President would not disclose their names or who appointed them, but I inferred that the Vice President was involved. I wanted us to go through the list. I reminded the President that Ethnic Studies had made a lot of enemies. I suggested that if he could not tell me who was on the list, I will name him fifteen senior faculty who are sworn enemies of Ethnic Studies. The Tenure Promotion Review Committee (TPRC) policy allows faculty to submit such a list of persons who you believe cannot be fair in evaluating you. I stated that if any of these people are on this committee, then let me suggest that this process is tainted. I read him a dozen names, and then asked him if any of these names were on the committee. The President said, "Yes, there's one." I said to him, "I don't know what you're going to do about this." Not long after this, the President overturned the Vice President's decision. In addition, I had people, including Regents, periodically checking in to see how the case was going.

Owen noted the importance of understanding "the mechanisms of the process because it is important in showing evidence that points to bias in the process." Owen relied on emotional and political support "within Ethnic Studies, colleagues on campus, family, and parts of the administration. It was very helpful when people indicated they believed in what I was doing. People's willingness to mobilize, talk to people, organize some means of appealing—people's loyalty became very important. Emotionally, what was most supportive was my family, the program, the outrage at how they [the university] could do this, someone articulating the outrage for you, and validation, your partner needs to express this."

Owen believed that his experience was a lesson in the "continuous possibility of arbitrary injustice" that should never be underestimated, and that "this kind of thing can happen and [one must not] be prey to cynicism [because it happens]."

The Case of Marge: Three Reviews

Marge, a tenured Asian American female professor in the Department of Psychology at a state university, was denied a merit increase (promotion) for the 1978–1980 period. She was the only ethnic minority faculty member in her department. Her promotion battle began four years following the denial and ended three years later—"an incredibly long time for a pittance promotion." With no statute of limitation on appeals, Marge evaluated the prospects of obtaining a fair appeal decision, given the composition of who was in power. Until the arrival of a new vice-chancellor—four years after her department denied her promotion—she had not believed justice would prevail. Thus, there were four years of "hiding my hurt and anger followed by three more years of feeling my hurt and anger." Marge filed an appeal to the new Vice Chancellor. This case chronicles the process by which this negative decision was eventually overturned.

Over this seven-year span of time, the position of chair of her department thrice changed. "The first Chair, who was in power when my promotion was denied, would not listen to reason." The second chair put in writing material that Marge's attorney eventually used to demonstrate bias and a violation of the university's procedures. The third chair, who held this position at the time the denial was rescinded, was "perhaps the only decent man in the department."

In the process of securing material for her appeal, Marge uncovered a lengthy history of bias. Evidence that pointed to a pattern of discrimination helped her win retroactive pay, retroactive promotion, and a workers' compensation claim. What is most notable about this case is the thoroughness with which Marge challenged every procedural error, every erroneous accusation, every statement that reflected bias, and at every opportunity, presented contradictory evidence to the department's false conclusions—all of which together laid the legal foundation for a successful appeal. As her attorney once said to her: "You were your own attorney."

> [The denial] especially after I was already tenured—was very unexpected and markedly distressing. I learned that tenure does not mean you're out of the woods. My record for the period under consideration was extremely strong. It was a shock. There was no reasonable cause for a denial. I came to realize through it all that racial and gender bias is not reasonable. Prejudice is blind to reality. Racism is blind to fact.

Going into the promotion review, Marge was confident about her research and publication accomplishments. In the two-year period covered by the review, she had been awarded a large, coveted three-year research grant from the National Institute of Mental Health, a study intended to test a number of social science theories and to provide groundbreaking data relevant to public policy. In that two year span, she had published two articles in professional peer-reviewed journals, had given ten presentations at professional conventions, and was awarded fellow status by the American Psychological Association for "significant contributions to the profession of psychology." Despite this record of accomplishment, and by a mixed vote, the tenured faculty in her department denied her a step promotion.

In her efforts to overturn the denial, Marge secured an attorney and the assistance of the ombudsperson. She filed an appeal and requested her confidential personnel file. Following subsequent actions, Marge asked the second department chair to rectify the underpromotion, she secured support outside of the department and university, and ultimately filed a workers' compensation claim.

In her appeal, Marge cited sections of the *Academic Personnel Manual* that the department had violated. First, the department had failed to evaluate all the work that she had submitted. Marge submitted evidence from the department's administrative analyst demonstrating that two articles and one awarded grant proposal that had been submitted for this review had not been reviewed and had never been submitted for any previous review, contrary to the claim of the department chair. When Marge brought this matter to the chair's attention, he refused to acknowledge any error.

Second, the department had violated a section of the personnel manual by failing to establish the role of the candidate in any joint authorship. Marge had coauthored a chapter with a historian. She suspected that when the review committee stated that Marge's work was of questionable value to the field of social sciences, the department mistakenly assumed that the historical portion written by the historian had been written by Marge.

In the appeal, Marge challenged every statement by the department that was false or reflected bias. Marge had been given an authorized leave of absence (for one year and one quarter) from teaching on campus because her research grant bought out her salary for that period. "I felt that I was being punished for not being on campus when the department chair and university had approved my leave to be off-campus to conduct research."

The chair's summary stated that Marge had shown "less than expected conscientiousness in supervising students in individual study." In the appeal, Marge asserted that she had carried two students in independent study, one as a favor to the student since she was on authorized leave of absence and thus not required to take on any teaching responsibilities. Since that left only one student who could have made such a complaint, Marge argued that elevating the opinion of one student to the importance given in the chair's letter was not objective or reasonable.

Criticized for limited service to her university and department, Marge provided evidence to prove the statement false while pointing to disparate treatment based on race and gender in regard to departmental service. A white male professor, who had performed no service for the department, had not been penalized for nonservice when he came up for promotion.

The department chair's summary asserted that Marge "had irregular attendance at department meetings." In her appeal, Marge provided evidence that when she was not on authorized leave, she had attended all department meetings. Being punished for not attending department meetings while on authorized leave was "entirely unreasonable." The coordinator of academic personnel wrote in response to Marge's request for information on this matter:

> The Privilege and Tenure Committee assumes that if a [department] has demonstrated their support of a faculty member's grant by giving them a leave that they cannot expect that faculty member to serve the department during that time. If, in fact it is felt that a faculty member is not carrying his/her weight in the department then the department should not have granted a leave in the first place.

The vice-chancellor concluded that procedural errors had been made, and he instructed the department to conduct a rereview. In the meantime, Marge read through her confidential personnel file and discovered what she and her attorney perceived to be a pattern of discrimination beginning from her first hire. When Marge was hired, she had a Ph.D. and two publications; yet she was hired at a

rank and salary less than a white woman in the department who had had no publications and who had not yet attained her Ph.D. In the next review after Marge
was hired, the department had apparently recognized Marge for her achievements
in securing a large research grant from the National Institute of Child Health and
Human Development by recommending an acceleration, but the recommendation
was disapproved at the chancellor's level. The chancellor's reason for the disap-
proval was because an acceleration would result in a "premature consideration for
tenure. . . ." Marge argued to the vice-chancellor that: "This line of reasoning
would make accelerations impossible to attain—obviously, an acceleration results
in earlier considerations in future reviews, but if this is to be avoided, then no one
should be granted an acceleration." Clearly the university was granting accelerations to others in the department "but only to white males."

> The *Academic Personnel Manual* states that a committee should not hesitate to
> endorse a recommendation of accelerated advancement when there is evidence
> of unusual achievement and exceptional promise of continued growth.

As part of the appeal, Marge collected data on publications, research grant
awards, number of citations to publications in the Social Science Citation Index
(the most objective reflection of the quality of scholarly research), length of employment, and current step, comparing her record with the white and male faculty
in the department. Marge's number of publications and grant awards were comparable to those of white males who had been accelerated above her. The number
of citations to her work in the Social Science Citation Index far exceeded those of
two other faculty who had been promoted above her and was comparable to a
faculty member who had been promoted three years ahead of her. Thus, she argued that by the most widely used academic index of scholarly work, the data
revealed that Marge had been substantially underpromoted and underpaid.

The department completed the first of what would become three rereviews
and voted unanimously against granting Marge a merit increase. "My belief in a
meritocracy, fairness, and justice had been shattered. I just couldn't believe it."
The department offered two reasons for denying the merit increase. First, they
argued that Marge "could some time later request an accelerated merit increase
or promotion when the research carried out under the current grant proposal
produces its findings and she publishes them in a book or journals." Marge had
demonstrated her scholarly worth for the two years in review; she felt there was
no reasonable justification for delaying her promotion with no guarantee of future remedy. Second, the department claimed that new ground had not been bro-
ken by her research grant proposal, a criteria that had never been applied to the
promotion of white faculty for a merit increase promotion.

Marge and her supporters took exception to the department's rationale. The
director of Chinese for Affirmative Action, Henry Der, wrote to the university,
specifically offering the argument that Marge's research was groundbreaking.
Moreover, he questioned whether the department had unfairly penalized her
because of her research in an ethnic minority community and her involvement in

university affairs that promote ethnic minority student participation. To this last point, the department chair had previously advised Marge that harm would come to her if she served on the division's Affirmative Action Committee whose goal was the hiring of more minority faculty. Marge served on the committee, never believing the threat was real.

Marge's attorney brought the case to the attention of a member of the Board of Regents and an assistant to the speaker of the state assembly. He wrote: "Her fight revolves around both the unfair treatment accorded her and the granting of merit increases and in the insensitive perceptions of Asian Americans. She has been denied merit increases with qualifications much greater than white males who have received such increases. . . ."

Meanwhile, back at the department, another white male replaced the first as chair. Hoping to head off more conflict, Marge met with him to provide him with the comparative data and requested that the department accelerate her in order to rectify past underpromotions. Marge had also been offered a job elsewhere and she so informed the chair. The chair indicated that he personally felt she was a valuable colleague but that he needed to consult other senior faculty. Having consulted them, he then advised Marge to respond to a solid offer from elsewhere and stated that he could not recommend an acceleration because of the "feelings" of some faculty. Marge's attorney suggested that she ask the chair to put this in writing, and he complied. Marge's attorney used this document as evidence to demonstrate bias on the part of the department.

> The Chair's remark that while Professor X has been "very valuable to the [department] and campus in teaching and service" but that it would be "good for you to respond to a solid offer from elsewhere because some . . . faculty have feelings impairing full colleagueship" violates personnel policies. "Feelings," as emotional reactions and subjective sentiments should have no place in an "informed and objective judgment of qualifications and performance" [Academic Personnel Manual—160 (1a)]. By not restricting its judgment to criteria indicated in the APM—teaching, research, and service—the department had violated the Faculty Code of conduct... which states that "it is unacceptable conduct to evaluate the professional competence of faculty members by criteria not directly reflective of professional performance" or to discriminate against a faculty member for reasons of race, religion, sex, or ethnic origin or for other arbitrary or personal reasons.

Marge's attorney concluded: "Under the circumstances, I seriously question whether the Psychology [department] can be objective and non-biased in judging Marge's performance."

Marge believed that the chair of her merit review committee inappropriately penalized her for having secured a job offer from another academic institution. Marge had been asked how long she planned to remain and whether she would accept another job. "If I had been a white male and had received a job offer from another university, my value to the other faculty would have been enhanced. Instead, as a minority woman, a job offer was viewed as infidelity, thereby decreasing my value." Marge consulted the coordinator of academic personnel about this matter. The coordinator responded by writing to the chair, citing the policies: "The policy for merit increases does not address future intentions to commitment . . . [only] demonstrated evidence of what a faculty member has done in the last two years is applicable for merit increases."

Marge's advice to others is to "solicit letters of support from scholars from universities considered equal to or superior to your university. They add credibility to your case and make more questionable the criteria used by your department." For example, a letter sent to the vice-chancellor from the director of the Survey Research Center at the University of Michigan (who knew the quality of Marge's work over the two years in question better than anyone in her department) referred to the department's actions as "strange and unbelievable," "by most standards I would regard Marge as having achieved distinction, national recognition and scholarly accomplishment that year. . . . She deserves very real congratulations." Such letters lay the foundation for suspicion about the standards used by Marge's department.

Due to the distress Marge was experiencing, she was advised by her attorney to file a workers' compensation claim. Three university administrators sent letters to her, alleging that she had breached her contract by not continuing to teach there. Marge's attorney wrote to the vice-chancellor stating that if such a contract existed, the university had failed in its responsibilities to Marge and had breached the implied covenant of good faith and fair dealing. From the number of reviews, the nature and extent of the irregularities and prior actions taken against her, her attorney maintained that the university's treatment of Marge deprived her of rights under state and federal laws. The failure of the university to properly process and review her grievances was a sufficient basis alone to conclude that a breach has occurred. But significantly, there is a direct relationship between her inability to teach in the upcoming academic year and the irregularities in the review process. In other words, the university itself, through errors made in the process of review, had caused the very situation it is now claiming as a breach of contract. By alleging breaches of contract as well, the university was only aggravating her condition.

The second rereview vote was positive by a majority of the faculty.

Finally, the promotion due me was recommended, seven years later, but even this victory was bittersweet. The summary contained inaccurate statements, prejudicial omissions, discriminatory criteria, and biased tone, terminology, and biased weighting of evidence. Those faculty who refused to alter their vote admitted to imposing a more rigorous standard than the psychology profession itself uses for acceptance of an original article for publication. They also ignored the evaluations of external reviewers who were experts in her field.

Marge received a merit increase, retroactive pay, and retroactive promotion. Her workers' compensation case was found compensable, and the university made a monetary settlement.

The Case of Holly: "Mommy, You Beat the Bullies"

Mommy, you tell me who's bad to you, and I'll go kick them.

Holly was an Asian American woman, a differential psychologist employed at a state university, the only Asian American in her department. Her tenure had been denied. The quote, which introduces this chapter, was hers. The "terminal illness" she refers to involved the emotional impact of "anger, depression, and anxiety" over the "loss of my career and professional identity."

Holly described her case, which lasted a year and affected her husband and eight-year-old son, besides herself, as "markedly distressing." Her son's desire to protect and comfort his mother was reflected in his statements to her: "Mommy, I don't know if you should go to school if they don't like you. They just don't know you."

Holly saw "no justification" for the denial of her tenure. Just as Owen had done, she searched for explanations for the denial. Politically, she reasoned that she "was not part of the departmental network." Her office, physically separated from the psychology department in another building, was a metaphor for her psychological separation from the rest of the department.

Holly was the only differential psychologist in her department. She based her appeal to the chancellor on grounds of "discrimination within the profession—one group of specialists within her profession discriminated against and misunderstood the work of another group of specialists." Holly argued that the denial of her tenure had nothing to do with her accomplishments but everything to do with reviewers who were incompetent to judge her work and antagonistic to differential psychology. She also argued that the tenure committee had not followed the procedures of the university's personnel manual.

One, the strengths for which I was hired are now evaluated as weaknesses;

Two, my research was evaluated from the viewpoint of experimental psychology rather than from the viewpoint of my field (differential psychology) wherein APM [Academic Personnel Manual] 210-1 specifies that "promotion to tenure positions should be based on consideration of comparable work in the candidate's own field or in closely related fields," there is considerable evidence that this was not followed in my case. The evaluation of my promotion to tenure was not based on criteria appropriate to the field in which I was hired. In a department composed almost entirely on experimental psychologists, I am the only behavioral geneticist and am also a differential psychologist. Differential psychology, with its focus on individual differences, is one subdiscipline of psychology; the other is experimental psychology, which focuses on general laws underlying behavior. The long-standing differences with respect to philosophical foundations, theories, methods, goals, and substantive concerns between these two orientations are well documented. These differences were set forth in a presidential address as well as a keynote address to the American Psychological Association by the Stanford psychologist Lee Cronbach, "The Two Disciplines of Scientific Psychology" (1957) and "Beyond the Two Disciplines of Scientific

Psychology" (1975). I will briefly cite some of Cronbach's points because they show that the most important criticisms of my research are criticisms by experimentalists of differential psychology in general and hence are not criticisms of my work from the viewpoint of my field;

Three, despite positive external reviews, departmental criticisms reflected the experimental bias;

Four, my primary research focus and its implications for method and theory in my field were virtually ignored; and

Five, after the letters were received, an important safeguard procedure was violated—the department failed to provide me with a summary of the extramural letter or the opportunity to respond to them after the department's first vote, which was damaging because my department had no specialist in my field to interpret the external letters. While a second meeting was convened in an attempt to correct this violation, I am concerned that the second meeting was viewed by some members as pro forma. The extent to which such an error can be corrected by a second vote is far from obvious. My colleagues' own research shows that impressions once formed are difficult to change.

Holly argued that "the department failed to conduct a fair and procedurally proper review." She framed her argument academically, using citations to scholarly works to inform the chancellor about discrimination within her field. Holly also expressed cynicism that her case would be treated with fairness when the original parties who were biased initially were being asked to correct their own error; she cites research to show that "impressions once formed" are "difficult to change" in her challenge to the department.

Pointing to an entrenchment of bias in her department, Holly noted an increasing discrepancy between the majority's opinion on the one hand and the opinion of external reviewers on the other hand.

A serious discrepancy exists between the departmental majority opinion and the opinion of the external reviewers, a discrepancy that grew even larger this year with further external letters solicited.

Where there existed a discrepancy between the opinions of external reviewers and that of one's department, she argued that the external reviewers who were experts in her field, should be given more credence.

I believe that the judgments of experts within my specialty should be given more weight than appears to have been the case.

Her response points to pertinent teaching evaluations missing from the department's evaluation. "The chair's letter includes ratings for all my undergraduate courses except the course of my area of expertise in which I received the highest ratings." She argued that its absence precluded a fair review.

A rereview was conducted and a new set of [external] letters solicited. In her letter to the vice-chancellor, Holly pointed out the flaws in the rereview.

Despite further evidence of productivity and further positive assessments of the quality of my research, the vote of the department remains split, with a narrow majority against my promotion to tenure. The following are problems in the department's re-review of my case:

1. While a re-review may correct procedural errors, it does not, however, provide a new jury to examine the case with a clean slate, it may be particularly difficult to change the mindset of some departmental colleagues when the candidate's specialty is unique to the department, the academic philosophies, methods, and goals of the candidate's subdiscipline differ significantly from those of her departmental colleagues and when traditionalists of the two subdisciplines have historically tended to strongly devalue each other's work, and when the departmental program in which the candidate was hired has formally been eliminated and the recruitment strategy in the department has changed.
2. In spite of the effort to correct several procedural errors in the re-review, there is no attempt to correct the specific conceptual error that my research continues to be evaluated from the viewpoint of experimental psychology rather than from the viewpoint of my field and my primary research focus and its implications for method and theory in my field are still virtually ignored. Thus, the evaluation of my promotion to tenure continues to be based upon criteria inappropriate to the field in which I was hired.

Holly reiterated the point that a rereview does not guarantee fairness. In fact, it can provide the department with an opportunity to "clean up" its procedural errors, thus affording the faculty of color fewer flaws upon which to argue that bias or discrimination occurred. Minority faculty are well advised to be vigilant to the possibility that a re-review may not lead to a reversal of a previous decision. In this case, the procedural error was corrected. Holly continued to point to inappropriate criteria used in both reviews that had not been corrected.

Writing to the vice-chancellor at her campus, this Asian American criticized the manner in which her chair handled the matter: "The Chair's discussions with me about the department's review were intimidating, insulting, and abusive." She attacked the competence of the committee and noted its damaging impact: "the Committee misinterprets its promotion policy to my detriment by denigrating my professional and scholarly achievements."

At a conference, a legislative aid, who knew of Marge's successful effort to overturn a negative promotion decision, advised Marge of Holly's tenure denial. Both women spoke. Following Marge's advice, Holly sought the help of Chinese for Affirmative Action. Henry Der's letter in support of Holly praised her record, noted the apparent flaws in the review, and reminded the department of their commitment to ethnic diversity.

It appears from our examination of the record that the department by its own admission was ill-equipped to evaluate the quality of Holly's work . . . after soliciting an unusually large number of letters from experts in her subfield, departmental critics ignored the overwhelmingly positive assessment of [her] work. . . . Given Holly's outstanding record and the questionable practices in the tenure review process, CAA is puzzled and bothered that the Department of Psychology has voted twice to deny her tenure. CAA takes notice that Holly is the only ethnic minority professor and one of very few females in the department. . . . In response to President Z's call to all Chancellors to reaffirm the University's commitment to achieving racial and ethnic diversity on each campus . . . you have the opportunity to fulfill the commitment to faculty ethnic diversity. Holly deserves to be granted tenure not because she is an Asian American but because she has been an outstanding Asian American professor with a strong record of publication, research, and excellence in teaching.

Even though Holly felt she did not need legal representation, she viewed an attorney's presence as "psychological insurance," akin to securing flight insurance before embarking on a potentially hazardous plane trip.

One year later, Holly was awarded tenure. Her son greeted her with glee in his voice:

Mommy, Mommy, you won! I'm so proud of you. You won at a game where the bullies treated you bad!

This experience taught Holly "much about systems, how they work and don't work, about the importance of networking, about being aware of important networks, about being a political person, and about subtle as well as overt discrimination."

The Case of Dave: The Misinterpretation of Criteria

Dave was the program coordinator of Asian American Studies at a large state college. Facing a denial of promotion to full professor, this Vietnam veteran felt "attacked" by a different "enemy" on a different battlefield. His experience in academic warfare was "considerably distressing" as "it constitutes an attack on your integrity. It is "an illegitimate attack," reflecting "a lack of integrity" on the institution or committee's part.

The denial was "very unexpected" because "I qualified for promotion and my record was quite good," Dave stated. Angered and stressed by having his "record and credentials questioned, he appealed the decision within the requisite seven days."

Like the others, Dave felt "absolutely no justification" for being denied a promotion. "In my opinion, my record was far better than anyone else on the committee." However, his record was not a traditional one and those judging him were from traditional departments.

Being an administrator of an Ethnic Studies unit, none of those responsibilities were appreciated by this [review] committee. It is very easy for Asian American Studies faculty to presume that others think as I do—that what I do has value because I value what I do—but one must be cognizant that others often do not see things as I do.

In retrospect, Dave reflected on preventative measures he could have taken—market yourself.

I could have done a better job making more alliances. They [the traditional departments] have no idea what I [Asian American Studies] do. You have to market yourself. Get out there as a professional and educate people to inform them of what you are doing, how it serves [the university], how you're making contributions, and how these contributions are different. I am different, and that's why I exist, but I don't want to be seen differently. [Our outcomes and responsibilities are] manifested differently. It's complex, and no one has explored these questions.

Dave reminds us that the composition of the review committee: "is a crap shoot. Had I a strong advocate on that committee, this [outcome] would be different."

The Academic world is supposed to be collegial. Consequently, it is easy to think that things operate by justness and fairness, but they don't. People act out of self-interest. Although there is some integrity, but what someone else defines as integrity may not match your definition of integrity.

Dave was "pleasantly surprised at the steadfastness and strength of support" from colleagues and administrators on campus in light of the denied promotion. Others communicated their beliefs that "You were unfairly treated. We're going to help you." One colleague, who helped him revise his appeal, "knew the standards quite well [and] helped [him to] discover the improper application of standards."

Citing the RTP standards at his university, Dave's rebuttal argued that the review committee had misinterpreted the criteria for promotion.

This letter appeals the decisions by the School's Personnel Committee and the Dean to not recommend me for promotion to professor. My appeal rests on the argument that they seriously misinterpret and improperly apply the University Retention, Tenure, and Promotion Standards. . . . There are two basic criteria for evaluation: "(1) effectiveness in academic assignment, and (2) scholarly or artistic or professional achievement." The committee's basic concern of "scholarship and the related professional activity" ignores the criteria which does not state that a candidate must demonstrate achievement in scholarship and professional activity but that he or she must demonstrate achievement in scholarly or professional activity.

One word—"or"—was pivotal to Dave's evidence that improper criteria had been used. In addition, he reiterated his record of accomplishments in professional activities (as the alternative to scholarly achievement), a record not mentioned in the committee's report.

> In 1985, I organized a session and presented a paper to the prestigious American Historical Association. I have been invited to present a paper at the meeting of the Organization of American Historians, the leading organization in the field of American History. Since 1984, I have presented four other papers, with another scheduled for March, and been a discussant at three other sessions. . . . Have my contributions been acknowledged? My work has been recognized by election as Director of four professional organizations, five consultantships, and numerous lecture invitations. I chair the Outstanding Book Award Committee for a professional association. I participated in an NEH Summer Seminar, and won an MPPPA Award from [this university.] The School Committee did not see fit to mention any of these in their report.

Dave delineated how he met the other criteria—effectiveness in academic assignment—and how the committee ignored mentioning his achievements in their evaluation.

> "Teaching is primary" states Academic Senate Policy F87-1. . . . The School committee entirely disregards this guideline. I ask the committee to take a close look at my student evaluations, which consistently place me above university norms. Please note the high proportion of GE courses I teach, a category generally more difficult in which to score well. Look closely at . . . the very large number of different courses that I teach—and take note of the fact that every semester I teach an overload! Please look carefully at my record of service to students and this university. . . . I have been a faculty sponsor for four student organizations. . . . I took a leading role in the committee which established the Division of Cultural Pluralism in the School of Social Sciences and was the prime mover in developing its first course, Cultural Pluralism 1, approved by the Board of General Studies for next fall. I served on seven University committees over the past five years. . . . Upon the Dean's request, I created the School's Student Affirmative Action Task Force. To characterize my performance in this category as "more than adequate" is to damn with faint praise. A more appropriate characterization of my accomplishments in Academic Assignment might be "exemplary."
>
> I find the failure of the Committee and Dean to follow university policies most disturbing. Are they implying that my professional achievements as well as my performance in teaching and my services to the Asian American Studies Program, the School of Social Sciences, the University, and the larger society are not worth considering? I hope not. It appears to me, however, that the School Committee and the Dean have arbitrarily constructed their own set of criteria for promotion.

Dave's rebuttal concluded in this manner.

> It is evident, as this appeal will show, that under any reasonable interpretation of standards for publications, public service and international reputation, I have

met such standards. Rejection on these grounds indicates that the TPRC has not understood the nature of my contribution to the University.

Two months later, the denial was overturned.

This was a big growing experience for me . . . I cannot assume that the piece of work speaks for itself. I have to lay the groundwork. . . . This was a reality check of the political world. No matter how good I am professionally, I still have to pay particular attention to the politics of the matter. You have to make firm alliances with those around you.

Dave advises other faculty of color who battle academic adversity to "repeat to [yourself] over and over again—the expertise in your field lies with you. Lean on your authority. You know what you're talking about. Then you need to communicate in a language they will understand."

I have to gain those alliances. . . . I still live in a society where our performance is not good enough. People reward those they have an affinity for . . . I do not live in a world governed solely or principally by meritocracy. . . . While this applies to everyone, it is more manifest for ethnic minorities and women in non-traditional fields. You have to persuade them that you're one of them. That you're just as much of a scholar. You have to convince them that you're advancing the field, that you are at the cutting edge. You must do this in their way. [Present it as a] common goal rather than that you are at odds. You are redefining their world.

Dave galvanized his anger toward his objectives:

In order to do something, you really have to be angry. I wanted to humiliate these people just as they had humiliated me. I came to the conclusion that these were incompetent yo-yos. . . . What motivated me was realizing how stupid and ignorant these people were. I imagined I had an ax in my hand [as I wrote the appeal]. I had to be very focused in writing the appeal, and blank everything else out. I went on the attack.

Dave's advice for life thereafter: " The best revenge is to live a good life."

The Case of Joe: The Sword of Damocles

Joe is a professor in a marginalized department—an interdisciplinary program called Comparative Cultures. He was denied a promotion during his midcareer review. His approach to overturning the negative decision lay in appealing to the top administrator at his university and providing rebuttal to the committee's criticisms of his work. Joe's case lasted two months before the denial was overturned. Although not lengthy in duration, its effects were "markedly distressing." The denial was "very unexpected. My publications were low but my teaching evaluations were excellent. Basically, their evaluation was saying—'You suck! You're not doing anything right.' . . . I didn't expect it would be all negative!"

Joe refuted the committee's "woefully understated evaluation" of his teaching.

> Besides student evaluations, there are other indications of my teaching effectiveness, such as the increasing size of my Introduction to Asian American Studies course (from 21 to more than 80), the number of graduate students from other departments that have enrolled in my seminars or in independent studies, and the times I have been invited by honor students to participate in the Honors Convocation . . . in short, I contend that my teaching is much better than "slightly above average."
>
> The decision to deny me a promotion is neither constructive nor a positive inducement. Instead, the decision is punitive in that it diminishes the work I have done thus far. . . . The only message I get from this tentative decision is to drop dead since refusal of promotion at this stage is tantamount to early denial of tenure.
>
> Instead of being given an opportunity to resolve this matter in a timely and orderly manner during the academic year, I must now probably wait several months with the sword of Damocles dangling over me, before a final decision is reached.

Joe identified stages to his emotional reactions: first, "shock; second, anger and shame; third, the desire for revenge and mobilization to action."

> First, I believed that if you worked hard, it would get recognized. That went right out the window. Second, I believed that there is an objective standard of fairness. That was shattered. Third, I thought my colleagues were trustworthy, but I came to realize that I was better off arguing this myself. One side says, "You're shit." The other side says, "You're doing a good job." It destroyed my belief in collegiality with Ethnic Studies professors. These colleagues never said, "I'll fight it." It was, "You fight it." Fourth, this denial shattered my belief in myself as an agent of change; it left me feeling powerless, impotent. I felt alienation in the Marxian sense. An estrangement from others and myself.

His sense of security also "Went right out the window. I knew as a kid there was no justice, but it isn't until it hits you personally that it really sinks in." Joe's analysis was that "the institution has standards that do not reflect what people in Ethnic Studies should be doing." As he judged it, the standards were "antagonistic."

Joe experienced similar reactions to the trauma of a midcareer denial.

> The parallels [of my experience in academia] to the combat soldier are perhaps much stronger than you think. While the physical integrity of professors denied merit increases or tenure is not endangered, their responses can simulate the

physical reactions of a combat soldier. In my case, the immediate desire after learning of my merit denial was to physically hit someone, preferably a person involved in the tenure process. During the first few days, I was verbally abusive in the hopes that if obnoxious enough, someone would hit me, then I could physically wreak vengeance. It didn't really matter whether I won or lost this fight, although in my head there was little doubt that total annihilating victory would be mine. All that counted was that I could sink my fist into something tangible. This was similar to my brother's behavior when he returned from Vietnam. He would often provoke people, daring them to hit him, even his brothers.

This points to a second parallel . . . which for me was the most negative effect of this incident. Until this mess, I believed in the integrity of most of my colleagues, inside and outside of the department. Afterwards, I trusted very few of them, even those who professed strong support for me. I felt, and still do, that most of them couldn't be counted upon in a crunch. That's how my brother felt about many of his fellow troops. . . . With regard to my brother, many a time I maintained silence because I felt any questioning of his action would be misconstrued as a sign of disloyalty. With the merit denial, [my wife] occupied that unenviable position. I was reaching the point that I believed that perhaps she thought the denial was in some way justified because of something I had or hadn't done. This had to be bordering on paranoia.

Writing the appeal diffused Joe's anger.

Writing the rebuttal redirected my energy away from physical acts of violence and questioning the loyalty of those closest to me, but it never restored my faith in the integrity of my colleagues or the institution. Trust is fragile under the best of circumstances. With stress, it becomes paper-thin. Ironically, although the rebuttal positively directed my emotions and psychic energies, it also made me more fatalistic. First, the time and energy I used to compose the rebuttal distracted and discouraged me from doing research beneficial to my case. Second I believe the rebuttal forever labels me as a "bitcher," as someone who whines when the game isn't played my way. For many, I was probably also seen as a potential troublemaker. What was crucial to the rebuttal as a means of dealing with trauma was the belief that you are fighting back. Even if you lose, there is a certain amount of satisfaction that you didn't take it lying down.

"The vice-chancellor from Heaven" overturned the denied promotion. But "the attack on the self, the humiliation, the loss of integrity" lead to fears of going up for future review: "I didn't want to go through it again," but three years later, Joe came up for tenure. Anticipating that there would be difficulties, he spoke with Owen at the Association for Asian American Studies (AAAS) annual meeting. "For me, the incident shows the importance of professional ties and having top ranked Asian American administrators in the system." In addition, Joe obtained copies of the appeals of other Asian American faculty in order to assess "different tactics to fight back." He did achieve tenure, but the university eliminated Joe's department, and he now works as a faculty-at-large.

The Case of Marie: A Million Dollar Settlement

Marie was an Asian American woman on the faculty in the School of Architecture
at one of the top universities in the country. Her ten-year tenure battle required "an
army of attorneys." Of all eight cases described in this chapter, Marie's case was
the longest and financially the most costly. Looking back, she reflected:

> The bizarre behaviors that [I] a 28-year-old, female Asian Assistant Professor
> elicited from her older white male colleagues ranged from cool isolation to un-
> welcome attentions. It was a no-win situation, and I resolved to ignore this pe-
> culiar environment and concentrate on my work. As an untenured Assistant Pro-
> fessor, I was aware but uncertain of the potential impact that my differential
> treatment in the Department of Architecture would have on my eventual tenure
> bid. Although the tenure process did seem to be a pretty cut and dry system of
> "publish or perish," at a gut level, I sensed I would probably perish despite pub-
> lishing. At a logical level, I was aware that there were the loudly trumpeted, so
> called "safeguards" and "checks and balances" and "personnel manual proce-
> dures" that supposedly would protect the outcome of the tenure review from race
> or gender-based bias. Supporting the notion that there were safeguards, was the
> idealistic Mandarin Chinese chant that had been drummed into all of us kids
> which went something like—"work hard, don't complain, and you will suc-
> ceed." However, due to my sixth sense, by now well developed by the relentless
> belittlements of academic racism, if I had to bet my life, I'd bet that I would be
> denied tenure. Still, I was curious to know on what basis they could deny me
> tenure since relative to my peers, I had ostensibly fulfilled the requirements.

In 1985, Marie was denied tenure. Concurrently, she received information
from the Campus Title IX officer that the contents of her file were those of a
person who normally gets tenure. Marie found that all referee letters were positive and that the departmental ad hoc committee's report unanimously recommended tenure. She saw no [legitimate] reason for the university to have denied
her tenure. Marie filed a grievance with the Campus Committee on Privilege and
Tenure (P&T), wherein she argued:

1. The procedure for departmental voting on whether to grant me tenure was
   highly irregular and unfair; the Ad Hoc and Budget Committees of the University . . . and the Architecture Departmental Committees were not given
   access to my complete tenure submission; I was not given a fair opportunity
   to respond to concerns allegedly raised about my candidacy; and at every
   level of review the procedures employed to evaluate my candidacy were inadequate to permit the reviewing body to comprehend the nature of my area
   of expertise and accomplishments within that area.
2. Subsequently and secretly, the Chairman of the Department had illegally
   solicited and encouraged less than glowing referee letters from persons on
   campus who were not in [my] field of study [they were from the School of
   Engineering] and [these letters were solicited] *after* the faculty voted. Thus,
   a file that was devoid of negative material was infected with ambivalent

letters in a way that was both a serious procedural violation and an intentional sabotage.

The department chair then referred to these "added" referee letters in his summary of her tenure case to the dean. Marie also argued that the department chairman had "ripped out a number of her articles from a bound package, thereby sabotaging my submission of publications, then later defended his 'editing' on the basis of saving on Xerox costs."

Following the review of her grievance by the Privilege and Tenure Committee (P&T), its chair wrote to the Architecture Department chairman stating that they believed Marie's grievance raised sufficiently serious questions or procedural errors that they were requesting a response from the department. After receiving the chair's response, the committee made clear its view that procedural errors had been committed but left open the question whether any of the errors might have been prejudicial to the outcome of her case. The committee found that the chair had inserted a letter from a faculty member outside of the department which contained comments critical of Marie's work, that Marie had been given no opportunity to comment on this letter, and was not informed at the time she requested a summary of the confidential material that this letter had been added to her file following her receipt of a summary of the departmental deliberations.

The P&T Committee recommended that the procedural violations of the first review be remedied by sending the case back to the department for a *new* review, this time including the three external letters from the School of Engineering at the university and Marie's response to the summaries of the three letters now being provided to her. The new department chair's summary letter of this new vote would replace that of the former chair's summary to the dean.

An Academic Senate Committee ordered the Architecture Department to review Marie's case a second time. In 1987, she was reviewed again and again denied tenure. Marie wrote that "the second review was a mockery of due process with the Department strongly voting against [me] this time. There was absolutely no discussion of the merits of [my] scholarly work. Instead, there was protest from faculty members that [I] did not deserve to have a new review."

The committee's memo to the vice-chancellor stated that the agreement for a "normal" rereview was not carried out; however, they also stated that they did not believe that Marie would have been granted tenure in the absence of these flaws because her case "was an extremely weak one." Accordingly, they recommended a negotiated settlement. Marie's description of these events follows:

This committee found procedural violations at multiple levels. The Committee Chair condemned [my] academic record without providing any evidence to refute the overwhelmingly positive extramural reviewers who were experts in this professor's field. . . . The Committee used this outrageous justification for a tenure denial. This second Committee concluded that the procedural violations had no impact on the outcome of the tenure review and that there was no discrimination.

Meanwhile, Marie had filed an Equal Employment Opportunity Commission (EEOC) complaint against the university. University counsel offered her a monetary settlement if she agreed to stop the ongoing EEOC investigation. Marie's attorney wrote back that this was unacceptable to her client.

The chancellor's office and the university attorneys wanted her case to go through an "internal evidentiary hearing" "to determine whether multiple procedural violations affected the outcome." Marie believed that the purpose of such a hearing was to "further bankrupt the victim" by extending the length of time and requirements of an internal grievance procedure, which might discourage her from suing the university. She noted that the last grievant to go through an internal hearing process spent $120,000 in legal fees. By this time, Marie herself had incurred about $150,000 in legal expenses.

> While going through this [tenure battle], I continued to teach, was pregnant, . . . came down with pneumonia, got three cracked ribs, couldn't stop writing despite my doctor telling me to slow down. It took me one year to recover physically. . . . I felt hurt career-wise; it [my career] was destroyed. It was a real downer on my career.
>
> I had thought that my record could stand for itself, but I was resented for my accomplishments. Someone advised me: "You should have campaigned [for your tenure]."
>
> Procedural violations that literally break the rules and regulations of the *Academic Personnel Manual* are the telltale signs of discrimination.
>
> Procedural violations [were] merely the symptoms of a basic problem of bias wherein at the department level, the question of merit is pushed aside for the issue of whether the female or non-white candidate will fit into the "good old boy's club." They didn't want me in the club because of what I am—an Asian American woman who's principled. . . . It was political, but on the part of the Chairman of the department and other members of the faculty it was clearly malicious.
>
> Consider that additional letters, from persons increasingly remote from the candidate's field are solicited in batches. These letters continue to add to the file until one or more letters with even a hint of ambivalence is found. No matter how minute the negative or merely ambivalent reference is, the Department can then blow it up to make a case against the candidate.
>
> The multiple review system is one where a conclusion, even one based on specious information and concocted speculation, could be replicated by passing it on to other committees which rubber stamped it and augmented it with additional specious information and concocted speculation, and fantastic rationalization. . . . The student letters were largely glowing with praise. They were dismissed as biased in my favor.
>
> It is very distressing but this is an omnipresent reality at the University. First, there is the personal ambition of faculty with administrative power who hunger for more administrative power or at least want to remain on the good side of the Administration. Second, there is the fear of retribution and loss of acceptance among most faculty for speaking out about wrongdoing by their own department colleagues. With distressing regularity, individuals at the

University have at best been silent in public about the wrong, which occurs there and at worst . . . have lied about what really happened. The net effect is that there is stonewalling of a complaintant and closing ranks at all levels of the University in treating a tenure grievant as an enemy to be vanquished at all costs.

I went in with a cynical view to begin with. I didn't believe there was fairness. My perceptions of people as basically good was not shattered because basically, I think people are weak, and there are people who are incredibly evil and without integrity. The experience taught me that there are many fewer principled people than I thought.

My attorney thought that as soon as they [the administration] see the facts, they would reverse the original decision. What my attorney did not realize was the extent to which a university would go to block my tenure. I had to hire an army of attorneys.

Marie describes the crucial role played by her spouse.

During my last semester of teaching, the university attorneys told the faculty not to talk to me. Students stopped talking to me. Other faculty talked about my case in their classes. No one would come to my office hours. Other professors were saying how horrible I was. I felt ostracized. If I hadn't had someone to go home to who was so supportive, I would have cracked. I don't know if it would have been possible for me to do this without the financial support that my husband gave me. I could not do it if I was a single mother. . . . My husband convinced me it was important enough to fight and not to worry.

She reflected on her experiences and offers some advice.

After hearing the horror stories of individuals fighting the academic Goliaths, many people rightfully would declare it is not worth the trouble. True, I've incurred about $150,000 in legal expenses thus far and spent seven years in frustrating conflict with persons who have no integrity and in institution that has no scruples. But for me, it was the right decision. I have the satisfaction of vanquishing any doubts that racism, not my own failings, was the engine of my tenure denials. . . . Most important of all, I know that I am doing the right thing.

Detach your emotions from what's happening. Think of it as a principle and know that you are doing the right thing. You should not take it [the denial] personally. It is the process. It should not be seen as a personal issue. If it begins to affect you emotionally, look at it as a hobby. I told myself—I have a fun and wonderful family. I have a wonderful practice. I am a good example for my children. Follow your principles if you can afford to do so.

Although she admits that the money and time she expended on her case were "irretrievable" and was not awarded tenure, she did receive a tax-free settlement of one million dollars.

The Case of Charles: The Paralysis of Professional Invalidation

For Charles, an Asian American professor in a School of Law at a state university, the denial of promotion was devastating. He described the experiences as

> markedly distressing, paralyzing, a loss of total functioning, and extreme depression akin to the death of someone close, an inability to recall the incident, an unwillingness to talk about it, paranoia, the highest order of stress. A loss of self-esteem, self-deprecation, a paralysis in [one's capacity] to [handle] professional responsibilities, anger and permanent bitterness toward individuals regarding the incident, desires for revenge, [feelings of] racial persecution, and the development of a stoic and impenetrable [persona] I became a person who would not engage with others. I developed a kind of scar tissue, the development of cynicism, a total invalidation of my life, of what I pursued, my activities. They made me feel like an inferior person. They weren't judging my competence, only what they thought was relevant. . . . These were totally ignorant people judging me.

Charles believed the denial of his promotion was "probably malicious," possibly a covert way of deterring him from his work with Hawaiians. The same person [on the review committee] had been involved in the tenure denial of a minority activist in another department. Despite this attribution, Charles blamed himself "for not having protected himself better, for not having been better than the average white person, for not having figured out their standards, for not having doubled the number of his publications, for not being two times better than the average golden, fair-haired boys."

To Charles, the Tenure, Promotion, and Retention Committee (TPRC) review appeared "terse. You couldn't tell whether they had read the application. They showed a low regard for the importance of community service. The way they viewed the world was narrow, so different from my own. This reconfirmed that a meritocracy was a façade." He was angry to have to "dignify the act [of his denial] with a rebuttal and counter-argument." Writing a rebuttal "required that the intense anger had to be converted into civil language"; which was very hard, so hard that he had to ask someone to write his rebuttal because he was unable to respond in a coherent way. "I did not successfully cope. I had to rely on the kindness of others." His department colleagues wrote letters of support on his behalf.

Nine months later the denial was overturned. "It was hypocritical, wrong, insulting. I was unprepared for this. I retreated into a shell, a paralysis" that he believed lasted three years. "You have to really tune out how others appraise you and rely on your own evaluations of yourself."

The Case of Nick: Institutional Guerrilla Warfare

Nick, a Japanese American male, was denied tenure at a prominent state university on the West Coast. His battle represented an intense and arduous political and legal campaign. His case was notable for the wellspring of student and community support, which some considered a cause celebre in the struggle for Asian Americans in higher education. As his attorney wrote, "Professor Nick's three-year fight for tenure is probably best described as institutional guerrilla warfare—a classic David and Goliath struggle, pitting an emerging minority community and its allies against a massive institution."

Nick, a graduate of Harvard and Yale, was the acting director of an Asian American Studies Center and held a faculty position in the School of Education. He helped to found the oldest and most widely circulated scholarly journal on Asian Americans, the *Amerasia Journal*. He also served as one of the first presidents of the National Association of Asian American Studies, served on numerous government commissions and boards of many community organizations, and was well respected by many students.

The School of Education had previously denied tenure to two Asian American faculty, and at the time of Nick's review, there were no tenured Asian American faculty in his school. Nevertheless, the denial of tenure was "somewhat unexpected" given feedback he had received from several colleagues privy to the internal review who relayed to him, "Don't worry about it. You have nothing to worry about."

After several postponements of meetings to discuss his tenure file, a meeting was held at which time a secret letter opposing tenure was read to the faculty by the department chair. In a split vote, faculty voted for the denial of tenure. After Nick protested this procedural violation, a second vote was taken that resulted in a two-thirds majority vote in favor of tenure. The campus wide ad hoc review committee later overturned the favorable departmental recommendation, a recommendation that is rarely overruled. The attorney noted that Nick's teaching and service record were considered by the department to be exceptional, and he had received outstanding letters from outside reviewers. However, the ad hoc committee criticized his work as "primarily descriptive." The ad hoc committee was split and a minority opinion was filed. The minority report described the reviewing agencies as evaluating his work with "relentless prejudgment."

The file was then sent back to the department and a third departmental vote was taken. The dean of the school who was a vocal opponent of Nick's sat in on the departmental discussion in an unprecedented act, after which the faculty reversed its previous decision and voted to deny tenure.

> I knew the Dean was opposed to me and was doing everything in his power to make the decision as negative as possible . . . and orchestrating it. To this day, I'm not sure why he did it. I knew him from the first day I got there. We served on committees together. I didn't believe he had a personal animosity toward me. It would be easy to say he was racist, but to this day I can't quite accept that.

As part of the legal claim, his lawyers alleged that he was denied tenure for his outspoken role in exposing admissions quotas against Asian Pacific students at that campus. In addition, supporters suspected that his leadership at the Asian

American Studies Center also stirred political opposition. This warrior had long been an advocate of Asian Americans on campus. The center had strong student and community support and took stands on issues.

> As much as one realizes that things can go wrong or that people act in malicious ways, when it does happen to you, you're not quite prepared for it. For as long as I had been involved in fighting institutions, I had never been trained to fight for myself in this way. . . . Tenure goes to the heart of power in reference to changing who is admitted to the university.

Supporters included alumni, community groups, labor organizations, students, center staff, and faculty outside of the department. Over time, Nick received support from state legislative representatives, local politicians, national and statewide organizations, ethnic media, and Asian American Studies faculty at other institutions.

Nick was cognizant of the symbolic meaning that supporters attached to his case. His tenure battle was waged at a time when Asian Americans were underrepresented in the public and private institutions. The case represented the "glass ceiling."

> I had to accept a celebrity status that I didn't quite want. I realized what my case had become. It helped to me to realize what my case had become. I was a symbol. I had to endure.

The case demonstrated how a legal and political strategy can be combined to win a case. His attorney stated, "I achieved victory because I was able to develop a sound legal argument as well as a larger political strategy, capable of mobilizing thousands of allies nationwide." Nick filed and won two grievances. The second grievance focused on misconduct on the part of the dean and chair. The Committee on Privilege and Tenure made the favorable ruling, stating that "you have also made a *prima facie* case with regard to your allegations concerning Dean X's conduct during and prior to the formal review of your qualifications for promotion and tenure," referring to what seemed to be "a deliberate attempt to deny you tenure."

After lengthy negotiations, the administration agreed to a number of demands, including the removal of negative recommendations from the file, exclusion of the dean from participation in the departmental meeting, and an additional year of employment if the tenure decision were negative. "Winning the grievances accomplished several things, most important of which was to discredit the dean and buy more time to wage the political campaign." In a final departmental vote, the largest number of votes were cast in Nick's favor. It was now up to the chancellor.

Though organizing political support was ongoing, it was at this critical juncture that the weight of the pressure could direct the outcome. A broad range of groups and individuals demonstrated their support in different ways. Nick summarized some of the support he received:

It was after over one hundred and fifty Asian American Studies scholars from across the nation had written letters of support; after the *Los Angeles Times*, *New York Times*, and other media—especially the Asian American press—had done personal stories on my case; after many members of the University of California Board of Regents had called the UCLA Chancellor; after the entire Asian American congressional delegation from Hawaii and California wrote letters to the Chancellor demanding tenure; after the Republican Governor of California, at the urging of the Southeast Asian community in Orange County, had called the Chancellor demanding tenure; after I had won two internal campus grievances; after the Asian American community had sent over three thousand letters demanding tenure; after tens of thousands of dollars were raised in a legal defense fund; after an extraordinary array of major civil rights organizations, bar associations, chambers of commerce, and labor unions had written and endorsed resolutions demanding tenure; after my department faculty had voted for a fifth time to recommend tenure; and just prior to when the California legislature would hold up a sixty million-dollar appropriation bill to build a new business school at [the university].

Students played a very visible role in keeping the issue alive on campus, holding rallies, and integrating the issue into legislative lobbying activities among student activists statewide. On the heels of the redress movement in the midst of empowerment movements among people of color, Nick's case resonated for many people. Nick attributes the success of his tenure case to the following:

It was everything from filing internal briefs to hiring experienced attorneys, using procedural approaches to obtain necessary documents, having the good fortune of having a number of faculty who were willing to deviate from confidentiality to testify on my behalf, receiving support from the types of constituencies who were not just interested in my case but the broader cause.

Nick had several advantages. Because of his position at a major center for Asian American Studies, he had the backing of many staff and students, many of whom were experienced in social and political activism. Second, because this was a tenure case rather than a case of promotion, his case was able to attract greater attention. Finally, his case arose on the heels of the redress campaign, permitting him to tap into the support of these organized movements. The convergence of these and other factors created favorable conditions for overturning the negative decision.

Conclusion

These cases represent an effort to document the functional means and the emotional costs by which negative tenure and promotion decisions were overturned or settled by eight racial minority professors. A report entitled "Race and Ethnicity in the American Professoriate 1995–1996" by Astin, Antonio, Cress, and

Astin (1997), which was based on a 1995–96 nationwide survey of 33,986 faculty respondents, showed that faculty of color accounted for about 10 percent of the professoriate, inching up from 9 percent in 1989. Nonwhites were found to be concentrated in the two-year colleges or in nontenure-track positions. Thus, faculty of color were still represented in small numbers in the 1990s as they were in the 1980s. I assume this to be particularly so for the cases presented, as all were employed at four-year colleges and all were in tenure-track positions.

In addition, Turner, Myers, and Creswell (1999) found that respondents in their Midwest survey identified racial and ethnic bias as the most troubling challenge they faced in the academic workplace. One barrier to the retention of faculty of color that Turner et al. (1999) delineated was isolation from the departments' informal networks, a theme reflected in several of the cases herein presented, that is, the isolation or alienation either within an established department or marginalization of an Ethnic Studies or interdisciplinary department. Turner et al. (1999) also described another barrier to retention for faculty of color: devaluation of "minority" research or denigration of their research interests because their research area is not traditional. This theme is reflected in several cases presented in this chapter, particularly cases in which the research record was strong. Finally, Turner et al. (1999) identified racial and ethnic bias in tenure and promotion practices and policies as a major barrier. All eight warriors perceived their battles with academia as a reflection of bias, whether on the part of one individual or that of the department or institution as a whole. These cases demonstrate that, contrary to the notion that Asian Americans have no problems with discrimination, Asian Americans, like other minority group members, face a glass ceiling in the ivory tower.

On the issue of retention, it should be noted that winning tenure and promotion battles does not guarantee retention. Not all the professors described herein remained in academia despite their victory. Three of the warriors eventually left academia, two by choice. Another moved to another department. While this may seem to be a loss to academia and to generations of students of color who could have learned from these warriors, it does reveal that for minority faculty, there can be another life outside of academia. Some of these warriors fought the good fight, then moved on to a less adversarial life.

These eight cases speak to the common theme of psychological distress experienced by warriors, regardless of the length of time required to resolve their cases. To this point, several spoke of the importance of social-emotional support. I believe it is important to indicate that it is not our purpose to celebrate these cases, although victory over adversity is worthy of celebration. On the contrary, it is a tragic instance that this chapter had to be written at all, for no one but the victim can fully understand what each of these faculty warriors experienced or the lasting impact their experiences had on their lives.

I present these cases in hopes of providing a larger network of support to those who, now or in the future, experience the door of the ivory tower shut squarely in their face. In the interest of and preparing those who would enter the professorial ranks of academia, these cases provide a context in which to understand the experiences of minority faculty who engaged in the respective battles for equity, without which the goal of racial diversification in higher education would be bleak.

Note

1. I wish to thank a contributing author to this chapter, a junior faculty, who prefers to remain anonymous for fear of adding herself to the list of warriors. I am deeply grateful to Franklin Odo, John Liu, Hsiu-Zu Ho, Ray Lou, Don Nakanishi, Marcy Wang, Williamson Chang, Deborah Woo, and Peter Kiang, and also to the Association for Asian American Studies for providing partial funding to conduct the interviews.

Chapter Seven

A Chinese American Woman's Struggle for Success and Self-Discovery in the Academy

Yali Zou

Immigration is the driving force behind a significant transformation of American society taking place at the end of the millennium. Few other social phenomena are likely to affect the future character of American culture and society as much as the ongoing wave of "new immigration." The nature of this change is indeed momentous. . . . [C]ensus projections assume that ethnic and racial categories are enduring and more or less static formations. Given ethnic socioeconomic mobility and the high rates of interethnic marriage in the U.S. along with changing cultural models and practices around ethnicity, there is reason to suspect that these categories, fluid and in constant formation and transformation, may be quite irrelevant in three generations. (Suárez-Orozco, 1998a, p. 5)

Coming to the United States from mainland China is an experience that is only partially comprehensible to Westerners, and very confusing to immigrants themselves. The United States is not only a radically different country but the immigrant's inability to communicate in English can make this experience even more terrifying. The people in China are bombarded with myths about this country as far away from the truth as Western beliefs about China are. Far from being a racially, socially, politically, economically, or ethnically homogeneous society, China is a complex nation with prevalent philosophies and traditions centered on the family and society.

The purpose of this article is to describe my experiences both in China and the United States in order to explore issues of self-identification, the adaptive strategies associated with higher education chosen by immigrants in the United States, and how my dual identity impacts my role as an ethnographer. My case may shed some light on complex problems of clashes in cultural values, long-term efforts to excel in academia, changes in self-identity, and the nature of doing ethnographic research. This chapter will describe my experiences in China within their historical and political context, and will then relate my experiences in the United States and discuss how those experiences have influenced my research. The assumption that prearrival experiences shape immigrants' life in the host country may find some support in this paper and suggestions are made as to how an ethnographer can function effectively in two cultures.

China in the Year 2000 and Beyond

By the middle of the twenty-first century, China will have one of the most powerful economies in the world. The new generations in the post-Mao reform period will vigorously pursue personal wealth in contrast with the current groups of political leaders who fear change. China is, and will continue to be, one of the most complex countries in the world (Starr, 1997). It is a country with many different ethnic groups, languages, traditions, and lifestyles. Even the physical appearance of many Chinese people breaks Western stereotypes of what a Chinese looks like. The challenge of understanding any of the many ethnic groups, or "nationalities" in China is compounded by the series of rapid demographic, social, economic, and political changes that have taken place in the last half century. Since the establishment of the People's Republic of China, dramatic demographic changes have occurred. China maintained a relatively modest population between fifty and a hundred million during most of the eighteenth century. In 1770, during the Qing dynasty the population was about one hundred million. In 1840 this number had increased to four hundred million. But by October 1, 1949, when China became the People's Republic of China, the population was already five hundred million (Poston & Yaukey, 1992, p. 1). The population jumped to an estimated chilling 1.13 billion people by 1990.

The ethnic, social, linguistic, and economic diversity of the Chinese people is overwhelming and complicated. In 1951, China officially recognized fifty-six ethnic groups in China. Among these, the Han was considered the dominant group, both numerically and politically. The other fifty-five nationalities, or the minority groups (according to the 1990 national census), near 92 million, make up about 8 percent of the total population of China. Since 1982, when the Chinese census showed a population of 1,008,175,288, a figure considered extremely conservative by experts (Crespigny, 1992), the policy of one child per family was adopted. The fifty-five ethnic minority groups, however, were exempted from this policy. (For a detailed listing of these groups and their geographic distribution see Trueba & Zou, 1994.) In 1990 the following five largest ethnic minority groups accounted for over 48 million people:

The Zhuang in the south central part of China (with 15,489,630 people)
The Manchu in the northeast (with 9,821,180 people)
The Hui in the northwest (with 8,692,978 people)
The Miao in the southwest (with 7,398,035 people)
The Uygur in the northwest (with 7,214,431 people)

Sixty-eight percent of the land in China is primarily occupied by minority groups. China's borders with Russia, Mongolia, Korea, Pakistan, India, Vietnam, Laos, and Burma all run through areas occupied by minorities. In comparison with the rest of the country, these areas are isolated. Special privileges were granted to minority-dominated geographical areas (which constitute "autonomous regions") by the central government (the Han controlling group) in an effort to retain the loyalty of minority groups and the overall national unity. Autonomous regions were offered administrative, legal, and resource control under specific parameters; in fact, the central government retained supervision and control of major resource allocations.

The Chinese immigrants of today carry with them experiences, backgrounds and home cultural values which sharply contrast to the culture of the United States. Ethnic and racial diversity in China has had a history of confrontation and conflict. Ethnic intolerance, often associated with religious intolerance—anti-Buddhism and anti-Manchuism, for example—are present along with preferences for skin color and other physical characteristics. Ethnic nationalism and religious differences clearly separate the Muslim Chinese (probably close to eighteen million of them live in the northwest part of the country—for a detailed discussion, see Gladney, 1991). In fact, documentation of racial wars at the turn of the nineteenth century illustrates the practices of racial classifications and extinction (Dikötter, 1992).

This is the country in which I lived forty years of my life. Through the description of my life in these forty years, especially during the Cultural Revolution, I intend to give the reader an idea of how these experiences have shaped my value system and educational philosophy. This is the China where I grew up, studied, worked, and where my self-identity is forever attached. Yet, this is also the China that is furthest away from my daily life after having been in the United States for more than ten years.

I Am Profoundly Chinese, but I Am Also American

No other experience in China has had a greater impact on me than having to work in a rural village for two years during the Cultural Revolution. The time I spent in that village changed my life completely. Although I suffered a great deal physically and mentally, this experience nurtured my deep love for poor peasant children, helped me establish a deep relationship with their parents, and it laid the foundation for my future career. In addition, I learned how to face challenges and develop adaptative strategies. Leaving my comfortable family life in the city for the first time when I was seventeen years old, I was sent like millions of other educated young people to live in one of the poorest villages, where there was not enough food to eat (quite often chaff and wild herbs were the only food); there was no running water, electricity, or gas; and communication with the rest of the world was nonexistent. Everyday I labored in an endless field, often for up to fourteen hours under the burning sun or in the freezing winter. In addition, I had to go to the mountains to find tree branches for the evening fire and wild vegetables to supplement the community's meals. I was no different from the cow I had been working with. I was never prepared for this kind of life. I felt depressed and hopeless, and did not know whether I had any future. One day while I was transplanting rice shoots in a rice field with cold water, I felt a sudden pain in my legs. As I looked down at my legs, I saw several leeches attached to my skin. I was so terrified at the sight that I screamed and fell into the muddy field. The villagers came to help me and were sympathetic. The leader of the village came to me and said, "Yali, I feel so sorry for you; tell me what we can do to help." "What can you do?" I replied in despair, "Nothing, just let me die." I felt there was no escape from this life. He smiled as he sat on the edge of the rice field and asked, "Can you read?" "Of course," I answered. "Do you want to teach our children?" "Why?" I asked. He told me that no one in the village of forty-two households with 286 people could read a single Chinese character. His dream was that the children in his village would be able to read and write some day. I was shocked by this reality and told him I would like to try. I started to use my simple living tent as a classroom to teach the village children to read, to write their name, to talk, and to express their feelings. The children looked so poor and hungry! Their faces were dirty and their hair was very long and messy! I wrote to my father and asked him if he could bring a pair of scissors and hair clippers on his next visit to me. When he came with some little gifts and the scissors, I began to cut the hair of these poor children, hair full of lice and dirt. The lice would jump all over me! The children were happy to have their hair cut and their faces washed. They began to trust me and share everything with me. They told me about their families and invited me to visit them.

As I became closer to the students, I was often invited to dinner at their homes and had the opportunity to get to know the parents of my pupils better. I noticed that many of them—although still young (some not yet thirty years old)—were suffering pains in their joints, back, and waist. Some had constant pains all over their bodies, perhaps a result of arthritis or of physical injuries from the hard labor in the field. I realized that I might be able to help them. Because I had suffered from serious migraine headaches quite often, I had brought an acupuncture book, some needles, and alcohol to the village in order to help get rid of my headaches. There were no doctors and no medicine at all in the village. I offered my help to the parents who suffered from pain, assuring them that although I did not know enough, I would do my best with acupuncture to help ease their pain. The needles became magical tools. Many patients recovered dramatically; they could move their hands and legs, walk without pain, some even started working in the fields again. Word of my skills passed from village to village. Many people began coming to me for help. They called me the "barefoot doctor," which in Chinese means a person who practices medicine without a formal education or a license.

Because of my excellent performance in the village as a teacher and a "doctor," I was transferred to an urban area. At that time in China, this was considered a big promotion, since leaving the countryside and going to work in a city was a great opportunity. I went to the Jilin Iron and Steel Plant where I became the inspector for quality control. The plant had seven thousand workers, nine workshop divisions, and one research institute. The Jilin plant was one of the most important iron producers in China (about 60 percent of all iron produced in China came from there). It was managed directly by the Ministry of Metallurgic Industry. Each division had a number of open furnaces with unprotected laborers around, who experienced extremely high temperatures and other hazardous working conditions. While I was there, I had the opportunity to talk to the workers and observe firsthand their difficulties. I was moved by their devotion to their work despite unbelievably difficult working conditions. I spoke on their behalf and asked leaders to improve their workplace.

Because of the Cultural Revolution, in 1966 China's schools and universities were closed down. All former students and professors went to the countryside "to be re-educated by peasants," as Chairman Mao ordered. Eight years later, in 1972, China reopened its universities and began to recruit students from factories, plants, and villages. I was recommended for the Shanghai Foreign Language Institute, where I learned to speak Albanian and became a governmental interpreter. Later I worked in the Chang Chun Film Studio translating Albanian movies to Chinese. I had the opportunity to meet and become friends with writers, actors and actresses, and was able to share with them ideas and concerns. In 1985, I became a professor at the Chang Chun Science and Technology Institute where I found that for over ten years the schools never changed textbooks. All the professors could recite the textbooks they used nearly verbatim. The schools suffered from both a lack of resources and new ideas. I started trying different textbooks and compiled readings that made my students very competitive in the provincial learning competitions. The quality of my teaching and the success I obtained in reforming the curriculum earned me provincial and national awards for excellence in higher education.

Coming to America and Learning the American Way of Life

With ambitious goals and rich experiences in China, I came to the promised land—America. I was excited about my bright future in the United States because I believed that I had enough skills and guts to face the tough challenges ahead of me. However, when I came to the United States, I felt totally lost, incompetent, and dysfunctional. I lost my voice (because I couldn't speak English), my ideas, and even my thinking skills. I could not communicate with people and I couldn't even order my food at McDonald's. People saw me as different, somebody unable to do anything. I became depressed and isolated myself from the outside world. I was afraid to meet people. The only way I could express my bitter feelings was by writing letters to my family and friends in China. I told them that "here is paradise because there is everything you want; but also here is hell because you suffer too much." I felt utterly hopeless. Near this time, one of my American friends, whom I had hired in China to teach English at the university, came to visit me. She introduced me to a professor at the University of California, Davis, who encouraged me to study. I did, but I traveled an extraordinary difficult psychological adjustment journey in doing so.

In order to support my study financially, I had to find a job. After competing with many applicants, I got a position as an instructor of Chinese at the University of California, Davis. It was my first time standing on the stage of an American institution, teaching American students the Chinese language. I was in a panic. Very soon, however, I discovered that I was considered an authority and the students respected me as a teacher with profound knowledge. In the evaluations of my course, students wrote the following: "Professor Zou is a very knowledgeable and effective instructor." "She is humorous and resourceful." "We learned a great deal from her." Teaching Chinese language instilled in me a sense of confidence and power that I needed badly. To be able to say what I wanted, to control the class, to become the professor, and have Americans struggle to learn Chinese (as I was struggling to learn English) gave me interesting insights into the sort of dual personality I had begun to develop. On the one hand, I felt as if I were truly in control when I taught my Chinese class. On the other hand, when I was a student in the Division of Education, I felt, for the most part, patronized or neglected. The professors and students had trouble understanding me. They would speak to me slowly, masticating their words, as if I were stupid. I felt humiliated and depressed. For that reason I loved to teach my Chinese class. It gave me a sense of myself again.

As a Chinese instructor I was a role model, a high-ranking member of the academic community, a person deserving of respect and admiration, a person with social responsibilities, and the power to give grades to American students. Furthermore, I was opening a new world of sounds and ideas, of cultural traditions and practices, of history and philosophy for my students. I felt I was useful. I could contribute to the students' learning because I am a very good Chinese speaker, writer, and professor. But after I would finish my Chinese classes, I would start to worry about attending classes as a student myself. I felt confused, anxious, even stupid. In my classes the Americans looked so smart and competent. I felt I could never compete with them. Many times professors did not give me a chance to talk in public. When they did ask me questions, they were always very simple or just about China. One time in a class discussion it was my turn to discuss some issues about human learning development. The professor openly passed over to the student next to me. I felt embarrassed and humiliated. I raised my hand and requested that the professor give me a chance to talk. The professor did. This was the first time I felt better about myself because I got the chance to express my ideas. I got fair treatment. After the class many students told me how much they admired my courage. However, I had to accept the fact that, no matter how much I knew, I could not express myself well. I hated feeling that way and feeling confused about the future! Later some professors who had faith in me helped me a great deal by giving me specific roles to perform and asking me to do research with them. Still, in my eyes, American students continued to look so eloquent, so articulate. I would tell myself, "I will never reach that level." My sense of self-confidence was shaken from time to time. I would tell myself, "How can I ever complete this assignment?" I was resolved to give all I had, my very best effort, but I was doing this in a language in which I could not express my most intimate thoughts, but one which I understood well enough to analyze meaning and nuances.

Gradually I began to realize that I benefited from knowing two languages and two cultures. This helped me to reach deeper into the structure of the English language and analyze the content of texts better than some American students. I was anxious to read and compare and contrast the two languages. Through this comparison the two languages, the two cultures, and the two countries fascinated me and opened up a new world of knowledge to me. I realized I had found something I was really excited about, but I didn't know exactly what it was.

One time in a class on ethnographic research, my professor asked me to tell the class about Chinese culture and how it differed from American culture. This question was asked of me quite often when I came to this country. When I was in China no one asked me about this, and I never thought about my culture and how different I was from other people. This made me think about my identity more and about who I am. This reflection was very important for me to help characterize my life, the life of my daughter, and the lives of other Chinese immigrants I know—a predominant trait was resilience or the ability to endure hard labor, stress, sacrifices, and to survive until one succeeds in a task. I spent long nights and many hours of work in the library, in my home, everywhere I could have a minute to read, write, and reflect. I realized I was passionate in my dedication to the completion of my work. I would go for many hours without eating until I finished my job. Why did I do that? What prepared me to stand the stresses and the sacrifices and pursue the completion of my tasks at any cost? Perhaps it was my Chinese background, my philosophy of life, and my experience as a child and young adult where I had to endure many hardships in the fields as a laborer and where I learned survival skills.

Becoming an Ethnographer

After I took several courses on minority education and ethnographic research, I developed a great interest in minority students' academic motivations and their achievements. I am especially fascinated by the power of ethnographic research. My passion for the poor peasant children and my commitment to help those children led me to read about the Hmong people, who are refugees from Southeast Asia. Hmong people experience tremendous difficulties in adjusting to this new society. However, they are doing extremely well both economically and academically. I admired their brave spirit, their hard work, and I wanted to know more about this group. Through researching the literature, I found that the ancestors of the Hmong people are the Miao people in China (Trueba, Jacobs, & Kirton, 1990).

After a long period of preparation in the United States, in 1992, my main professor and I began an ethnographic research project in China that focused on Miao university students. The study took place at the Central University for Nationalities, in the heart of the capital of China, and the Guizhou Institute for Nationalities located in the south central part of China. We selected fourteen Miao students for our study. Seven were from the Central University for Nationalities, and seven were from the Guizhou Institute for Nationalities. The Central University for Nationalities is affiliated directly with the State Educational Commission of China and was established in 1951. It has twenty-three hundred faculty and staff and an enrollment of more than seven thousand students from all fifty-six ethnic groups. The Guizhou Institute for Nationalities was founded in 1951 under the leadership of the Educational Commission of Guizhou Province. It has twenty-five hundred students from eighteen different ethnic groups. The fourteen students we interviewed were all originally from rural areas. The parents of these students were mostly uneducated peasants, although a few were teachers, government officials, and village leaders. All of their families had very low annual incomes. However, some of the poorest Miao children who came to study at the university were able to obtain high prestige as members of mainstream Chinese society and were recognized as leaders in their villages. How did this happen? Where did these poor children get the resources for their studies? And how did they succeed?

In order to conduct the ethnographic research project on the Miao I obtained a postdoctoral fellowship at the University of Wisconsin-Madison. Being a native Chinese qualified me as an "insider" in China in the eyes of my professors because I was familiar with the Chinese culture and had the ability to understand and could interpret it to them. On one hand, this perception was correct—I had spent forty years in China and knew the country fairly well (I thought). I had grown up in a Chinese middle-class family, and I knew mainstream ideology and lifestyle as a member of the Han people (the mainstream population that comprises 92 percent of the population of China, or about 1.2 billion people). On the other hand, I was educated in the United States, I understood Western philosophy, I spoke English, and I dressed like an American. All this gave me the credentials to pass for an American in the eyes of the Chinese. Furthermore, I was armed with cultural ecological theories, ethnographic research methods, and, most importantly, I was funded by an American university.

Before entering the research field, my professor and I reviewed the literature, developed a research design, articulated specific questions to be answered by the research, and carefully planned the implementation of the design through gradual strategic steps. In conducting the research, however, we had to wake up to the reality of our own social identities and cultural roles in China, at least as defined by the Miao people with whom we were working. Consequently, I became aware of my dual identity and was caught in a difficult position. I was both Chinese in the opinion of the Americans, and an American in the eyes of the Chinese. But I knew I was neither, or perhaps I was both. That became a serious problem as I continued to think about my own identity, although during the research I did not have enough time to think seriously about it.

As I mentioned earlier, since I saw myself as a Chinese person who had lived in China most of my life, I was placed in the category of "insider" with regards to the Chinese culture. However, because I had come from the Han group, which is viewed as the mainstream cultural group and the "oppressor" or controlling group, I could not really claim to have the same way of thinking as those who are ethnically, socially, and economically different, as in the case of the Miao. They have constructed another set of values and perceptions or what is considered to be a "subculture" of Chinese society, and it was different from my own culture. Therefore, all I could do was describe my understanding of what I heard, what I saw, and what I felt in a way of thinking that I socially constructed in settings dominated by the Han people. Furthermore, I constructed these perceptual frames also from the perspective of Western academia. Indeed, the two cultures, the Han culture and Western academia, filtered my views. After five years of intensive study and training in the United States, I went back to China to conduct empowerment research with the Miao students with whom I was unfamiliar. Therefore, my dual ideological identity placed me in an asymmetrical power relationship with the Miao students. They viewed me as an educated Asian American and consequently as an "outsider" and even superior.

When my professor, my American colleagues, and I went to the Central University for Nationalities in Beijing, we lived in a dormitory on the campus in order to be close to the students. Next to our rooms was the Foreign Affairs Office. All of our activities were under the officials' surveillance; they were responsible for approving who could come to see us, where we could go, and in what rooms we could meet. At the same time, however, the officials were eager to provide us with information after we told them we planned to write a book telling Americans about minorities in China. All the information the officials offered to us was official government policy or government propaganda materials. We asked the Foreign Office for permission to meet with the Miao students. After some negotiations, we got the chance to interview and discuss our research project with some of the Miao students. Before we met them, we prepared a set of questions ranging from their personal background to their opinions about the government policies toward minorities.

The first meeting consisted of fifteen Miao students and two Miao professors. We started asking them questions about their experiences and their journeys from their home village to the university. At first they kept silent, and they seemed to be anxious about the kinds of answers they could give to our questions. We felt a little embarrassed and didn't know what we were supposed to do. Then their professor told us, "Don't feel bad. They didn't prepare for these questions, so they do not know how to answer them." After the meeting we learned that the foreign affairs officials had already prepared the students about what they should say to the Americans. At this time, only three years after the democracy rallies in Tiananmen Square, the Chinese government considered the United States an unfriendly power. Additionally, public expression of one's ideas was closely guarded. Students could not freely say what they wanted to say. In addition, when we arrived in Beijing the Chinese Communist Party Congress had just come to a close. The central theme of the conference was opposition to Chinese intellectual bourgeois liberalism, and the government was worried that students would once again stage demonstrations against the Chinese government. Therefore, the government kept a close watch on the students.

We remembered that on the day the conference ended, we went to Tiananmen Square and saw many military soldiers, policemen, and plainclothes public security personnel watching people's activities. When we asked questions to the unprepared students, they hesitated in answering. The students didn't know what they could tell foreigners and what might get them in trouble. The professor started to enlighten the students and told them in front of us, "You should not worry, you can say what you experienced. For example, you can tell them how the government cares about minority people, and gives minorities preferential treatment, so you have a chance to enter college." Then the students started to recall their hardships both in their villages and in school. For example, Mr. Wang, a twenty-three-year-old student from the Guizhou Province, told us that his Han classmates laughed at his poor clothing and quite often he didn't have money to buy food (Trueba & Zou, 1994). As he talked about the hardships that he experienced and his family's difficult life, he began to cry. His story touched both the researchers and the professors.

On another occasion, a young Miao university professor invited us to observe his class. When he came to our dormitory to meet us, the gatekeeper (a government officer) stopped him and asked him whether he had reported his activity to the Foreign Affairs Office in advance, and the guard would not let him see us. When we came down to the door, we explained to the officer that we had asked the professor to come to discuss one of his courses and his pedagogy in the classroom. Similar red tape and bureaucratic inquiries occurred in situations when phone calls came from the outside, when unexpected students or other visitors attempted to talk to us, or when we tried to change our schedule.

In China, a discussion of oppression cannot be public because it would be considered antigovernment, and it would subject the participants to incarceration and other sanctions. For the Chinese students, however, the ideological position is that the government is always fair, and nobody should view surveillance as oppressive. As we began to think about the consequences of asking people to cooperate with our research, we realized that there was an element of risk and uncertainty associated with critical ethnographic research in a specific context or situation, especially in the context of university students who are often penalized the most for their use of freedom of speech. As researchers, we had to keep in mind that our first responsibility was to the people we studied. Consequently, we had to accept the constraints of the cultural setting in which we functioned. In the end, we kept asking ourselves, how can we, as researchers in a foreign land, pursue our research agenda and still be responsible for the safety of the people we study?

Another dilemma was how as researchers can we best deal with our dominant cultural identity while working with ethnic minority persons? In critical ethnographic research sometimes we unconsciously recreate a context for dominance and tend to impose our values. When we began our research at the Central University for Nationalities, we identified a group of Miao students and professors and organized the schedule for individual and group interviews. We then proceeded to ask our questions regarding their rationale for leaving their villages and becoming university students and professors. We wanted to know how strongly they felt their identity as "Miao," and what role this ethnic identity had in their motivation to achieve academically. We unconsciously conducted our research without reflecting on the automatic assumption about the "subjects" of our research as if they were "objects." This happened until we started to build rapport with the students and professors and heard the individual stories of poverty, struggle, and oppression that had characterized many of their lives. At that moment we turned our methodology around and began to investigate ways in which we could assist them. Gradually my professor and I were adopted as "honorary" members of their clan. It was only after we traveled two thousand miles southwest to the Province of Guizhou and interviewed an entirely different group of Miao university students that we realized the fundamental differences between the two Miao student groups (the one from Beijing and the one from Guizhou).

We were interviewed first at length before we could even get to the points we were investigating. The students and professors in Guizhou demonstrated to us that they felt competent and in control of the situation. They described the Miao as a cosmological ethnic or racial group scattered throughout the entire world, and they interrogated us about the treatment of the Miao (Hmong) in the United States. They also gave us their long-term view of economic and industrial plans to move upwardly the entire Miao group around the world and wanted to know if we were ready to invest in such efforts. This experience made us aware that we had mistaken the first group of Miao students as objects of study, not as persons. We became humble in our visit to Guizhou, a province which has a high concentration of minority populations. As we turned the discussion to the Miao students' plans for the future, we realized that, instead of answering our questions, they would ask us what we thought they could do to help their own people in the future not only in China but throughout the world. Actually, they changed roles and became the researchers, using us as consultants. They were looking up to us for guidance and practical advice; and they were doing it with a unique global perspective and ambition, talking about the Miao being a cosmic group with a bright destiny and a significant international force. We felt obligated to tell them some success stories of minorities in the United States and how the Miao could use their knowledge to develop natural resources in their areas, to communicate with the outside world to attract investments from the Western world, and to participate actively in public events in order to make the Miao group more visible. They followed our thoughts and developed a lot of new ideas. Mr. Tao Wencen, an eighteen-year-old student, said that after he graduates he would organize county cooperatives and business firms, and later he would use the capital accumulated from the cooperatives to establish a Miao city with hotels, restaurants, and other tourist facilities. Mr. Xiaoping Tao said, "I want to help the Miao people become literate; collect and edit Miao folklore and publish a book; write a book on the history of my Miao village." Mr. Xiong Jianliang wanted to become a village leader and use his intelligence to develop his village (Trueba & Zou, 1994).

After our research project was completed, we wrote a book about what we learned about the Miao. I went back to visit our informants on several occasions after the completion of the project. I found out that our research not only helped American students get a better understanding of education, but it also encouraged Miao students to pursue their dreams. Some of them have now become university professors and administrators. My American students were moved by the stories the Miao students told and this motivated them to achieve greater academic excellence.

Personal Thoughts:
Change in Self-Identity and Persistent Continuity

The immigration experience is a never ending venture that continuously redefines one's life and self-concept. As a Chinese woman, becoming a permanent resident and getting to know Americans intimately has given me a new view of life and a capability to see the world from different perspectives and in different dimensions. The Eastern and Western worlds are so vastly different and sometimes conflicting that a Chinese immigrant (from what I have experienced and seen in others) must make heroic efforts to become flexible, bicultural, and committed to learn every day many new and subtle nuances about the American culture and the English language. Perhaps much of the miscommunication between the East and the West has to do with people's lack of ability to learn "new ways of life" and new cultural values. Raising my daughter in this country has opened my eyes to the profound differences in socialization patterns and to the dilemmas faced by Chinese parents in the United States. For me, being a Chinese immigrant is a continued intensive course in acculturation and self-redefinition that will last the rest of my life.

I believe that the foundation for genuine academic empowerment of children of immigrants is a solid self-identity and a clear concept of one's own ethnic community. My daughter and her friends are not only proud of being Chinese, but they are also proud of understanding American culture and using English with a high level of proficiency. The Chinese community around us is very influential, and the competition for achievement is intense. One of the reasons why I have become very interested in self-identity and academic achievement is that I have lived through the pain of trying to compete with native English speakers, and I have seen my daughter work very hard to become a high achiever.

I go back to China every year in order to teach and conduct research among minority groups. This has been an opportunity to retain a profound adherence to my culture without losing my biculturalism; it has forced me to reflect on my own self-identity and has invited me to revisit some theoretical debates and issues related to immigration in the United States. To mention just a few of these, the complex issue of empowerment among Asian Americans, and the need for a liberation, voice, and appropriate space in the instructional process (Freire, 1973, 1995; Freire & Macedo, 1996; Giroux & McLaren, 1986, 1994; McLaren, 1995; Gutierrez, 1994; Gutierrez, Larson, & Kreuter, 1995) is often misunderstood by teachers and academicians. The new Asian Americans of my daughter's generation are not fighting to retain their own ethnic identity and to have a separate voice in schools. They are fighting to acquire an American identity and an equal voice along with other American youth. They will not abandon their own ethnic identity. Their vast networks and frequent communication with other children of immigrants will secure comfort in our own Asian community. But they do not want to be branded different, not even for the sake of recognizing their academic accomplishments.

Regarding the debate on the Asian American "model minorities" (Ogbu, 1974, 1978, 1992), achievement for us, as immigrants, and for our children has been far from easy. It has not been a rapid ascending line to success. On the contrary, we have failed many times but continued to fight. We have had to face our lack of knowledge and experience, but we continue to try because we are building the empowerment of the next generation. Our children struggle, and we force them to continue to try and to make more serious efforts. It has not been easy! Specifically, as we try to adapt, along the lines of Gibson's model of accommodation, not assimilation (Gibson 1988, 1997), we certainly retain the most important family values that brought us to this country: loyalty to our ethnic group and parents, commitment to help each other, commitment to always make the greatest possible effort to succeed, and resilience when we fail. The survival and adaptation of Asian Americans in this country is a complex process (see Trueba, Cheng, & Ima, 1993; Kiang, 1995, 1996). The drastic changes in our multiple identities (Trueba, in press) are directly and profoundly affected by the "transformations" and changes in the children of immigrants and their families (Suárez-Orozco & Suarez-Orozco, 1995a, 1995b) and by the global economic and political currents accelerating migration waves (Suárez-Orozco, 1991, 1998a, 1998b).

As a committed academician, my questions are the following: How can I deal with my multiple identities as I try to conduct objective research? How does experience, cultural background, and ethnic identity impact the result of ethnographic research? What kind of role should my identities play in ethnographic research? How can I turn my identity and experiences into assets? How should I deal with my own ethnic, cultural, and experiential biases? As have many other immigrants, I have had difficult moments adapting. Yet, in the end, I always come out convinced that my biculturalism has enriched my life. Becoming an immigrant often translates into painful experiences that require healing and understanding. In fact, one of my most recent and profound realizations is that I finally became convinced that often conflict across cultures can be resolved through the culture of therapy. I was feeling torn by two extremely different lifestyles and began to realize that I did not have to be both Chinese and American at the same time within the same cultural environment. My mind was opened when I read about cultural therapy as a means to increase our understanding of value conflicts and resolve such conflicts (Spindler & Spindler, 1989, 1992a, 1992b, 1994; Trueba, 1994).

In contrast with the philosophy of Paulo Freire, who sees education and the acquisition of knowledge as intrinsically political, the Spindlers feel that the acquisition obtained through anthropological knowledge about our personal ethnic, racial, and cultural identities is not necessarily political, and leads to "cultural" reflection, a deeper understanding of value differences, and ultimately to conflict resolution. Conscientization (or in the Spindlers' lexicon, cultural reflection) is a means to resolve personal and social problems associated with having the wrong cultural assumptions about other people and their perception of who we are. By learning about ourselves, our "enduring selves" and our "situated selves" and by reconciling them, we can prevent the painful experience of reaching an "endangered self" (confusion and uprootedness from our values). The central concepts of how the enduring self is deeply rooted in the first years of our cultural socialization within the family and community evokes many strong memories in my life. I cannot but accept the fact that my infancy and adolescence as directed by my parents and family left a profound mark on me. Therefore, at the heart of cultural therapy (as I understand it) is the ability to reflect on cultural values, traditions, and personal identity. As a Chinese immigrant, similar to many other immigrants, I have become aware of the need to heal, to piece together my inner self, and to retain my cultural values from both Chinese and American origin (Zou, 1998; Zou & Trueba, 1998).

I assume that at the heart of cultural therapy is the realization that there has to be an acceptance of the self based on a profound historical and cultural knowledge of one's own family. I am aware that in theory, cultural therapy does not assume that each member of humankind needs psychotherapy, or that much of the sad state of affairs in the world today is related to social and cultural conflicts. The condition *sine qua non* for healing from hurts caused by prejudice or bigotry is the possession of a deep cultural knowledge and understanding of human groups and their culturally determined behaviors, as well as an understanding of the mediating role played by language and culture in the acquisition of new knowledge (Trueba, 1994). To the extent that I know the nature of my biculturalism and that I use effectively the Mandarin and English languages, I feel at peace, confident, and competent. However, the price of this peace has been a great deal of work and persistence to survive failure, to stand up and try again.

Chapter Eight

Transnational Linkages in Asian American Studies as Sources and Strategies for Teaching and Curricular Change

Peter Nien-chu Kiang

In the late 1980s, articles and lead stories in both scholarly publications such as the *Proceedings of the Academy of Political Science* and popular media such as *Newsweek* began to urge educators, policymakers, and the American public to recognize the twenty-first century as the "Pacific Century"—a time in which the economic, political, social, and cultural influences of Asia and the Pacific Rim would become increasingly dominant for life in the United States and worldwide (Coughlin, 1989; Pak, 1990). The global impact of the collapse of financial markets in many Asian countries, for example, dramatically illustrated this powerful dynamic during 1998.

One year ago, people throughout the world witnessed China's regaining of administrative authority over Hong Kong after a century and a half of British control. On that day, I noticed Mr. Zhang waiting on a Chinatown street corner for his daily ride to work. As he lit a cigarette to kill time before the van arrived, and sipped black coffee with sugar to get ready for another twelve-hour shift in a hot restaurant kitchen, I watched him purposefully page through four different Chinese-language daily newspapers—his connections to that long-awaited confluence of past, present, and future in Hong Kong. I wondered if anyone—particularly students and teachers—would ever have the opportunity to discover what he was thinking and feeling at that moment. I sensed then, and want to argue now, that it is through those connections with the lived experiences of Mr. Zhang and other immigrant workers on the corner like him, that we can find concrete meaning to ground theorizing about postcoloniality, transnationalism, diasporic identity, and the Pacific Century.

Later that day, I met Sanjeev, an Indian immigrant student in my summer Asian American Studies course, who came to apologize for missing a week of classes. He explained that he had been busy coordinating the Indian Student Association's commemoration of the fiftieth anniversary of Indian and Pakistani independence from British colonial rule. To ease his guilt and explain my own priorities, I told him that while the course is offered every semester, the fiftieth anniversary of his homeland's independence comes once in a lifetime. In an earlier class about immigrant definitions of "home," Sanjeev had described his memories of flying kites on independence day as what he misses most from his childhood in India. During that week of fiftieth anniversary activities, we all understood his choice to miss class, and imagined ourselves flying kites together with Sanjeev.

Through the lives and perspectives of individuals like Mr. Zhang and Sanjeev, we find direct, transnational linkages between Asia, Asian immigrant communities, and students in our own schools. These transnational relationships and themes can serve as compelling sources for teaching and learning. This brief essay suggests some sample strategies for practitioners to facilitate such a process of curricular and pedagogical reform that draws on the potential power of the coming Pacific Century.

Power and Problems of Representation

Research and pedagogical practice show that if teachers are disconnected from the home-family-community identities and contexts of our students, especially those who are immigrants, then we can neither reach them in meaningful ways, nor tap their rich, sociocultural knowledge to share with others in the classroom (Kiang, 1997; Trueba, Rodríguez, Zou, & Cintrón, 1993). Yet, most educators in the United States have had little exposure to authentic Asian and Asian American perspectives through our formal education and professional development. Without opportunities for focused study, our awareness and knowledge base in these areas are typically constrained by media images and personal experience. This is a serious limitation, given the power and pervasiveness of stereotypes of Asians and Asian Americans in mass media as well as in school textbooks and children's literature produced in the United States.

In fact, long before Asian Americans settled in the United States in significant numbers, stereotypic images of Asia and Asians had already taken root in American popular culture and consciousness as a result of the India and China trades in the eighteenth century, and later with the forced annexation of the Philippines in 1898. Colonialism and ideological beliefs in white supremacy have strongly shaped the portrayals and social positions of Asian Americans. From this legacy, contemporary representations of the refugee on welfare, the violent gang member, and the violin-playing computer-nerd coupled with historic images such as the treacherous Fu Manchu, the exotic/erotic Suzy Wong, and the inscrutable Charlie Chan continue to influence how educators, students, and the public perceive Asian Americans and how Asian Americans often view themselves (Leong, 1991; Mazumdar, 1991; Asian American Journalists Association, 1991).

Underlying the stereotypic distortions of Asian Americans and other groups are more fundamental myths of American life that need critical reevaluation, particularly in light of the dramatic demographic changes within our society and the transformation of global relations throughout the world (Mann & Zatz, 1997). For example, the melting pot metaphor, based on theories of immigrant assimilation from the early 1900s when most immigrants came to the United States from Europe, continues to serve as a dominant reference point for policymakers, teachers, and the general public. However, the melting pot paradigm has never adequately represented the realities of African Americans or native peoples who, after many generations, have not achieved structural assimilation in the United States because of unequal power relations, the persistence of racial inequality, and indigenous commitments to self-determination. Similarly, even though today's immigrants share some of the same challenges of adapting to a new language and culture that confronted earlier generations of European immigrants, the melting pot paradigm does not accurately describe the ways that dynamics of racism shape the adjustment process of the post-1965 immigrant waves—most of whom are nonwhite, having come from Asia, Latin America, the Caribbean, and Africa (Seller & Weis, 1997).

Assumptions about U.S. race relations in black and white terms are similarly pervasive and inaccurate. For example, perceptions of and responses to the April 1992 riot/rebellion in Los Angeles following the acquittal of police who had brutalized Rodney King focused on black and white interests, even though the South Central Los Angeles population was half Latino (Chicano/Mexicano and Salvadoran) and two-thirds of the burned stores were Asian (Korean) owned (Gooding-Williams, 1993). Likewise, as a Vietnamese American student reflected on public discussions and media coverage following a race riot at his high school: "I'm not black. I'm not white. I'm Asian. They don't talk about us" (Kiang & Kaplan, 1994, p. 96).

Assumptions about racial categories are also problematic. "Black," for example, includes Haitian and Somali refugees, Jamaican immigrants, and many-generation African Americans; "white" includes Russian and Bosnian refugees, Irish immigrants and Mayflower-descended Yankees, among others. Asian Americans and Pacific Islanders number more than eight million in the United States with Filipinos, Chinese, Vietnamese, Koreans, Asian Indians, and Japanese representing the six largest Asian nationalities. The diversity of Asian Americans, in terms of their various languages, cultures, and histories is undeniable, though often unrecognized, as noted in frustration by a Cambodian store owner:

> He asked the price of beef. Then he said: "You Koreans charge too much." My brother said: "I'm not Korean, I'm Cambodian." But he's mad. He says: "You Koreans rip us off." (Moffat, 1992, p. 1)

Within the same nationality, there are also important differences in regional dialect, religion, class background, educational level, and political perspective as well as distinctions based on generation, gender, and sexual orientation. Two

Filipinos, for example, may have to communicate with each other in English because one's native language is Tagalog while the other's is Ilocano. In a group of Chinese, one may have come from rural China, another from cosmopolitan Hong Kong, a third from war-torn Vietnam, a fourth from Jamaica, and a fifth from Ohio—each with obviously distinct stories to share. Among three South Asian Indians, one may be a granddaughter of early Sikh immigrant farmworkers in California, another may be a university educated Hindu who came to the United States originally as a foreign student, and the third may be a Guyanese-born store owner in Mississippi who attends a Baptist church.

Other factors also contribute to the diversity and complexity of the Asian American population, including the high rates of interracial marriage among some Asian American groups and growing numbers of biracial/multiracial Asian American and Amerasian children (Root, 1996; 1991). Furthermore, many thousands of Asian children, particularly from Korea and China have been adopted by families in the United States who may not be Asian American themselves. One may see, for example, a recently arrived Vietnamese Amerasian teenager who looks just like his African American father but speaks only Vietnamese or an adoptee who may look obviously Asian but might be named Nora Wilson.

As a starting point in exploring transnational links between Asian and Asian American Studies, the process of clarifying stereotypic assumptions, even in the names and labels we use, is a lesson in critical thinking with social, historical, and political dimensions. The very term "Asian American" sharply contrasts with "Oriental" which connotes rugs, spices, and other objects of Western colonialism in Asia, rather than people (Said, 1978).

By explicitly addressing these issues of representation in our teaching, we help students gain self-awareness and metacognition skills in recognizing biases and appreciating multiple perspectives. Beyond deconstructing stereotypes, however, we also must develop new images, concepts, and experiences through making productive curricular and pedagogical connections.

Transnational Thematic Strategies for Curricular Change

Transnational themes such as "defining home" or "changing identities" or "family ties," represent one viable curricular strategy to explore connections of culture, history, economics, and politics across time and distance for specific nationalities such as Koreans, Filipinos, or Thai in both their homelands and the United States. This can be especially meaningful if developed in relation to populations who have significant local presence and community resources to share (Te, Cordova, Walker-Moffat, & First, 1997; Olsen, 1997). In addition, given the standard focus on China and India in world history curricula, a viable strategy based on local/global connections is the theme of "diasporas" which examines the worldwide migrations, settlement patterns, and networks of Chinese or Indian people (or others such as Jews) who have maintained transnational cultural identities, whether they are in London, Capetown, Lima, Queens, or elsewhere (Chaliard & Rageau, 1995).

Thematic strategies can also focus on concepts or processes that cut across the shared experiences of various Asian nationalities in America, in spite of their cultural and linguistic differences and homeland historical conflicts. Using themes such as "exclusion" or "community-building," students can easily draw connections and parallels to the experiences of other groups in a multicultural curriculum. Migration and community themes, like the searching and sacrifice for the American Dream, are central, but not unique to Asian Americans, and can serve as the building blocks of a coherent, integrated curriculum that breaks down barriers between groups in the classroom. Students quickly recognize the power of social forces such as race or class, and also appreciate various human qualities such as having dignity and determination to survive. Experiences of war, for example, offer a powerful, thematic connection between Asia and Asian Americans that deserves deep exploration.

Legacies of War As a Thematic Example

War has defined much of the relationship of the United States to Asia during the twentieth century: from colonization of the Philippines to Japan and World War II to Korea and the Cold War with China in the 1950s to war in Southeast Asia in the 1960s and 1970s. Even economic competition with Japan during the 1980s and 1990s is defined as a trade war (West, Levine, & Hiltz, 1998). Regrettably, this is also how students typically learn about modern Asia through the curriculum (Loewen, 1995).

Images of Asians as the enemy are deeply embedded in American popular culture and consciousness (Dower, 1986), sustained by Hollywood distortions like *Rambo* and *Black Rain* and manipulated by political leaders from FDR to those who more recently proposed to solve the trade imbalance with Japan by re-chartering the Enola Gay—the airplane that dropped the atomic bomb on Hiroshima.

Whenever the United States has been at war in Asia, Asian Americans have paid a heavy price. The forced removal and incarceration of 120,000 Japanese Americans, two-thirds of whom were American-born U.S. citizens, from their homes to concentration camps during World War II is an obvious example. Still, students might be surprised to discover that George Takei—better known as Mr. Sulu in *Star Trek*—is one of many thousands of U.S. citizens whose families were directly and tragically affected by both the camps and the bomb. In his autobiography, *To The Stars*, Takei (1994) reveals that he endured three years of his childhood behind barbed wire at the Tule Lake concentration camp. After the bombings of Hiroshima and Nagasaki in August 1945, Takei recalls:

> The people of Tule Lake were stunned. The quick succession of events was overwhelming. The two bombings, as ghastly as they were, were also deeply

personal tragedies to many. A considerable number of internees had families and close relations living in the two cities. Our family was one of them. Our grandparents, Mom's father and mother, had returned to Japan before the outbreak of war. They had gone back to Hiroshima. . . . It was not till much later, long after we were out of camp, that we learned by some miracle, our grandparents had survived the atomic bombing of Hiroshima. But one of Mama's younger sisters, our Aunt Ayako, died with her baby in the fiery holocaust. (Takei, 1993, p. 59–60)

It is also no coincidence that contemporary Japan-bashing in Congress and Rambo's Hollywood revenge for the Vietnam War have accompanied a sharp rise in racial violence against Asian Americans locally and nationally during the past fifteen years. In 1982, amidst the recession in Detroit, for example, a Chinese American engineer named Vincent Chin was brutally beaten to death by an unemployed autoworker who cursed him, saying: "It's because of you Japs that we're out of work." In 1996, nearly a generation later in a suburb of Los Angeles, Thien Minh Ly, a twenty-four-year-old Vietnamese American was discovered with multiple stab wounds and his throat slashed in the parking lot of his former high school where he went roller-blading. His twenty-one-year-old murderer bragged in a letter to a friend: "Oh, I killed a jap awhile ago. . . ."[1]

With this backdrop of continuing anti-Asian violence, the Japanese American internment experience can serve as a powerful case study for in-depth learning and reflection about how issues of race and power have defined the conduct of United States involvement in Asia, shaping both popular attitudes and government policies. The internment experience and its aftermath raise essential questions about the Constitution and civil liberties, patriotism and loyalty, ethnicity and transnational identity, family and community, the role of the press, and the fundamental meaning of being American—all of which are issues that continue to resonate in American life. A curricular focus on the internment readily lends itself to integrated lessons across subject areas in history, writing, drama, civics, geography, health science, agricultural science, art, poetry, and math. This process also enables students to develop important critical thinking and citizenship skills, enabling them to address contemporary issues of anti-Asian violence as well as to draw parallels with war in the Persian Gulf and anti-Arab sentiment in the 1990s.[2]

Similarly, the Vietnam War experience offers rich material for teaching and learning. With normalization of diplomatic relations and the resulting exchange of many delegations of writers, artists, teachers, doctors, and veterans seeking healing and reconciliation between Vietnam and the United States, teaching strategies and curricular resources are now available to show both sides and present Vietnam (or Laos or Cambodia) as a country, not a war. However, we also need connections to the voices and experiences of Southeast Asian refugees and immigrants who have resettled in the United States as part of the war's legacy.

Powerful, transnational themes of loss, survival, freedom, peace, and healing can be easily explored in the classroom through literary anthologies, oral history collections, and student-conducted interview projects with local Lao, Hmong, Mien, Cambodian, and Vietnamese refugees. It is important for students to know that their Southeast Asian American classmates and neighbors are not "the enemy." Teachers also need to remember that our students were all born long after the war ended, even though images and reference points from that era may still have vivid personal meaning for us.[3]

Ironically, the individual who has arguably done the most to facilitate healing for United States Vietnam veterans is Maya Ying Lin, the Ohio-born, Chinese American who designed the Vietnam Veterans Memorial in Washington, D.C. Since its dedication in 1982, the Wall's healing power for veterans, their families, and for the nation has been movingly described in words, photographs, Academy Award-winning documentaries, and educational CD-ROMs.[4] Yet, the denial of identity and humanity that has characterized the Vietnam War experience for Asian Americans (Kiang, 1991)—from basic training to the highest echelons of military decision-making about the conduct of the war to federal policies of refugee resettlement—is found at the Wall, too, in the stance of Thomas Moorer, former commander of the Pacific Fleet and former chairman of the United States Joint Chiefs of Staff during the Vietnam War. Moorer asserted:

> I've visited the Vietnam memorial and I have mixed emotions about it. I would never have built a memorial like that. I don't like the idea that it was not designed by an American. (Engelmann, 1990, p. 158)

Weaving Connections across the Curriculum

Powerful case studies like the Japanese American internment experience also facilitate the process of teaching and learning across the curriculum from social studies to language arts to mathematics. Research and practice in curricular reform suggest that learning is enhanced when students explore themes in depth and make connections from the combined vantage points of several subject areas. With a thoughtful thematic focus, subject areas can reinforce each other across disciplines and create rich learning opportunities for students, rather than remain in isolation.

Because of commitments to interdisciplinary team-teaching, many middle schools use integrated curricular strategies that address not only larger conceptual themes such as migration or identity, but also very concrete subjects such as "kites" or "walls" that allow for connections across the curriculum. The following example, focusing on "cloth" and Indian culture, is suggested via an electronic mail listserv that links middle school teachers with Asian Studies resource people as part of the Asia Society's national, collaborative curriculum and professional development initiative known as TeachAsia. The message from Don Johnson, a professor of Asian Studies at New York University extends that of Rashmi Singh, director of the California-based resource organization, Education about South Asia-Vidya, Inc., who had responded to one teacher's question about using Indian saris as a curricular focal point.[5]

Date: Fri, 24 Oct 1997 11:05:23
Reply-To: TeachAsia Collaboratives' Conversation
From: Donald Johnson
Subject: Re: TeachAsia related news

In response to Rashmi Singh's post, I think she offered just the right perspective and advice on one of those potentially trivializing introductions to Indian culture. Since cloth is such a crucial part of Indian history (first use of cotton at various Harappan sites), why not use cloth in a deeper way. For example tracing Gandhi's use of the symbol of cloth in the nationalist movement (spinning) boycotts of English cloth, etc. is one useful way to link the two. Also photos of Gandhi's own dress code decisions makes a fascinating visual study of the importance of how what we wear symbolized our values. Just look at his early dress during his days in England as a student and trace his development to wearing the dhoti. Is this progress? Why did he do that? Why did he tell the English king, "you are dressed in plus fours, I am dressed in minus fours? Why do all your kids wear L.L. Bean knockoffs of backpacks? Why do some kids wear baggy jeans and Khakis (Indian word) without belts and falling down? Cloth and clothing can be a great theme for India. All we are asking is to deepen the analysis however you begin.—Don

Just weighing in with my opinion re "dressing up": I have always gone to some length to distinguish between "costume" and what some of the "others" consider regular clothing. As someone who has been asked, "What do you call your 'costume'?" (salwar kameez, kurta pajama or sari) the image that comes to my mind in response is the Halloween concept of "costume" . . . ! And with some of us this does not sit well. It is a fine line—and the Asian Art Museum was able to keep it in the sari portion of their India exhibit, so it can be done, it is just a function of how it is done. And as long as it is only the "hook" and there is real substantive information after that, and the distinction between looking at the subject/area from the outside or inside is clear . . . just like the "meat of the matter" regarding Hinduism does not sit well . . . ! Checking with someone of that ethnicity prior to doing something like this always helps. Good luck, Rashmi

Sharing these brief e-mail communications is useful because they offer rich ideas about thematic content and because this type of dialogue models connections between K–12 teachers and community- or university-based colleagues with expertise in the areas of Asian and Asian American Studies. We need more of these collaborative exchanges which can be facilitated readily through internet technology.

Transnational Connections of Culture and Language

Making connections across the curriculum through themes such as "cloth" highlight the importance of viewing cultures as dynamic and diverse, rather than static and homogeneous. In the process, we are reminded, once again, to examine critically our own stereotypes and assumptions. For example, what do we truly think or imagine is "traditional" or "modern" or "authentic" or "foreign" or "Asian" or "Asian American"? These are challenging but important questions for both our students and ourselves to consider explicitly.

For example, traditional Asian folktales are typically included in U.S. elementary school instruction. If taught appropriately, those legends and proverbs are replete with rich imagery, imaginative characters, and important moral and social lessons reflecting highly developed value systems. Qualities of loyalty, honesty, perseverance, filial piety, and respect for elders, together with emphases on harmony and group welfare over individual interests are highlighted through explicit cues and implicit expectations.

Rarely, however, do teachers and students critically consider how these values and worldviews of various Asian and Pacific cultures, shaped in part by Confucianism, Buddhism, Hinduism, Shintoism, and animism, take root in the United States. What transnational influences do they continue to exert for Asian Americans? More importantly, what positive impact can they exert for the larger society? How might electoral campaigns be different, for example, if political candidates were grounded in Confucian views of leadership or Buddhist principles of harmony and karma?

The need for thoughtful, multicultural teaching and learning of traditional Asian values and worldviews is important for all students but also has particular meaning for many Asian American students. If provided without isolating and exoticizing students, such a curriculum can significantly decrease the distance Asian American children must travel between the linguistic and cultural worlds of home and school, and thereby increase the support and transnational resources available for them to learn effectively.

Demographic projections show that a major shift will occur in the school-age Asian American population during the next twenty years with a spectacular increase in the numbers of American-born children with immigrant parents (Kiang & Lee, 1993). This is cause for urgent concern, given detailed findings by Lily Wong-Fillmore and colleagues (1991, 1991a) in a landmark study providing evidence that as language minority children learn English in the United States, they lose their native language and, by extension, their culture—the younger the age, the greater the effect—due to the dominant status of English in early childhood education programs and the larger society.

Wong-Fillmore clearly shows that as the home language and culture are lost in the process of acquiring English, family relations also erode. The following example represents a likely scenario for future intergenerational relations in many Asian American families with immigrant parents and American-born children:

> An interviewer told the story of a Korean immigrant family in which the children had all but lost the ability to speak their native language after just a few years in American schools. The parents could speak English only with difficulty, and the grandmother who lived with the family could neither speak or understand it. She felt isolated and unappreciated by her grandchildren. The adults spoke to the children exclusively in Korean. They refused to believe that the children could not understand them. They interpreted the children's unresponsiveness as disrespect and rejection. It was only when the interviewer, a bilingual Korean-English speaker, tried to question the children in both languages that the parents finally realized that the children were no longer able to speak or understand Korean. The father wept as he spoke of not being able to talk to his children. One of the children commented that she did not understand why her parents always seemed to be angry. (Wong-Fillmore, 1991, p. 2)

Ironically, the strengths and values of family support which are so often praised as explanations for the academic achievement of Asian American students are severely undercut by the lack of programmatic and policy support for broad-based bilingual instruction and native language development, particularly in early childhood education. The unfortunate cost of such policies is the sacrifice of substantive communication and meaningful relationships across generations within many Asian American families and the squandering of valuable, transnational linguistic and cultural resources for the entire society.

Pedagogical Reform and the Power of Names

While transforming curricular content is the focus of this essay, the realities of our classrooms also challenge us to examine our pedagogical commitments in creating comfortable spaces for ourselves and our students to take risks in sharing and learning together. One particular pedagogical strategy with transformative power and transnational meaning involves recognizing the significance of students' names. Families of all cultures give children specific names for many reasons. Sometimes the meaning of a name embodies qualities that parents hope their children will develop or demonstrate. Sometimes a name is given in honor of another individual who has been important to the family or its society. Sometimes a name is chosen simply because it looks or sounds good. Everyone has stories that accompany their names, although those stories are not always known.[6]

Names have special pedagogical importance for Asian and Asian American students and provide significant insights for all students about issues of language, culture, identity, and power. Many Asian immigrant and refugee students, for example, do not challenge the authority of their teachers or supervisors or even their classmates when their names and identities are mispronounced or misunderstood. According to Toan, a Vietnamese student who has been teased repeatedly because of his family name:

> Under these circumstances, I always responded with a smile. However, my smile did not mean that their joke was funny. I guess they did not realize that a smile can be a mask that hides your fears every time you do not want to disclose your emotion.

Frequently, students adopt new names in order to make pronunciation and recognition easier for others. King Foon (pronounced *Ging Foon*), a Chinese immigrant student, recalled:

> One time my professor called my name "King." I felt so uncomfortable when other students stared at me. Probably they thought my "name" was too boastful. One of my classmates made joke of me. She asked why I did not have the name "Queen" instead of "King" and she said "Queen" was more appropriate for female. In order to be more convenient for me and the professors, I use "Maria" as my name.

On the other hand, when teachers do make the effort to learn and pronounce students' names correctly, the positive emotional and educational impact on students is clear. Uyen, for example, recalls:

> I was so surprised when my professor called my name in Vietnamese. It made me feel at home, just like in my country. After that, I really looked forward to that class.

This is not only the case for Asian and Asian American students, of course. By appreciating the power of names in our pedagogy, we can build on the excitement and motivation expressed by Uyen and redirect the frustration and alienation experienced by Toan, King Foon, and others from all cultural groups in our classrooms. In the process, we can learn much about similarities and differences in language, culture, family, and society in profound and personal ways, while modeling a fundamental commitment that respects students' identities, regardless of background. In classrooms with these pedagogical connections, students like Anthony, a third-generation Italian American, can also reflect:

> Never before have I felt so close and so concerned about a group of people in my life, not even my own cultural background has been able to stir up such emotions.

Learning and Caring in the Pacific Century

Many have written about the necessity for students and teachers to be exposed to a more comprehensive Asian Studies curriculum in order for the United States to maintain or regain a competitive advantage in global politics and business. That rationale does not move or motivate me, however. Rather, I opened this essay by introducing Mr. Zhang and Sanjeev as two individuals among many whose personal lives illustrate the interconnected, transnational nature of Asia and Asian Americans within the context of the coming Pacific Century. The examples of curricular and pedagogical strategies and themes offered here reflect my own efforts to teach in integrative, empowering ways, especially for immigrant students who comprise the majority of my own classroom population.

My students' transnational voices, perspectives, and experiences remind me that even if we design conceptually clear, curricular linkages between Asian and Asian American Studies, that ultimately the most meaningful sources for teaching and learning are found in the lives, struggles, and dreams of real people. By envisioning and establishing genuine curricular and pedagogical connections between Asian and Asian American Studies, we can reground our own teaching and learning within core commitments of societies and cultures where one's context is defined by group relationships, shared responsibilities, and collective identities. In schools and school systems characterized by the pervasive "absence of caring relationships" (Poplin & Weeres, 1994), this is, or should be, the heart of education reform.

Notes

This essay is adapted from "Curricular Connections and Reflections for the Pacific Century," originally written for the Intersections Project, a collaboration led by The Children's Museum, Boston, and funded by The Hitachi Foundation. I also gratefully acknowledge support provided by the Spencer Foundation's Post-Doctoral Fellows Program, administered by the National Academy of Education.

1. A fifty-five-minute video documentary, *Letters to Thien* (1997) is distributed by the National Asian American Telecommunications Association (NAATA). Contact: <http://www.naatanet.org>.

2. Many new books, exhibits, performances, videos, CD-ROM and World Wide Web resources, curriculum guides, and bibliographies about the Japanese American internment experience are available through the support of the Civil Liberties Public Education Fund—a body established by Congress in 1997 to fulfill the final component of the U.S. government's redress commitment (in addition to a formal apology and individual monetary payments to survivors). See: <http://www.acon.org/clpef/>.

3. See: Minfong Ho, *The Clay Marble*, NY: Farrar Straus Giroux, 1991; Katsuyo K. Howard (Ed.), *Passages: An Anthology of the Southeast Asian Refugee Experience*, Fresno: California State University, 1990; Nancy Price Graff, *Where the River Runs: A Portrait of a Refugee Family*, Boston: Little Brown, 1993; Suchen Chan (Ed.), *Hmong Means Free*, Philadelphia: Temple University Press, 1994; Nazli Kibria, *Family Tightrope: The Changing Lives of Vietnamese Americans*, Princeton: Princeton University Press, 1993; and De Tran, Andrew Lam, and Hai Dai Nguyen, *Once upon a Dream: The Vietnamese American Experience*, San Jose: San Jose Mercury News, 1995; Barbara Tran, Monique T.D. Truong, and Luu Truong Khoi, *Watermark: Vietnamese American*

Poetry and Prose, Asian American Writers Workshop, Philadephia: Temple University Press, 1998.

4. See, for example: Sal Lopes, *The Wall: Images and Offerings from the Vietnam Veterans Memorial*, NY: Collins Publishers, 1987; Smithsonian Institution, *Reflections on the Wall: The Vietnam Veterans Memorial*, Harrisburg, PA: Stackpole Books, 1987; Jan C. Scruggs and Joel L. Swerdlow, *To Heal a Nation: The Vietnam Veterans Memorial*, NY: Harper & Row, 1985; the Academy Award-winning film, *Maya Lin: A Strong Clear Vision* (100 min.) by Freida Lee Mock; and the CD-ROM, *Beyond the Wall*, produced by Magnet Interactive Studios, 1995.

5. The e-mail excerpt is included here with permission from the Asia Society's TeachAsia program. See: <http://www.askasia.org> for more information.

6. This section is adapted from the introduction to *Recognizing Names: Student Perspectives and Suggestions for Pronouncing Asian Names—A Guide for the UMass Boston Community*, Boston: University of Massachusetts 1995.

Chapter One

Barone, T. (1992). Beyond theory and method: A case of critical storytelling. *Theory into Practice, 31*(2), 142–146.

Bateson, G. (1979). The mind and nature. New York: E. P. Dutton.

Coe, D. (1991). Levels of knowing in ethnographic inquiry. *International Journal of Qualitative Studies in Education, 44*, 313–331.

Corradi, C. (1991). Text, context and individual meaning: Rethinking life stories in a hermeneutic framework. *Discourse and Society, 2*(1), 105–118.

Galindo, R., & Escamilla, K. (1995). A biographical perspective on Chicano educational success. *The Urban Review*, Vol. 27, No. 1, Human Sciences Press.

Gibran, K. (1923) *The prophet*. New York: Alfred A. Knopf.

Goodson, I. (1992a). Studying teachers' lives: An emergent field of inquiry. In I. Goodson (Ed.), *Studying teachers' lives* (pp. 1–17). London: Routledge.

Goodson, I. (1992b). Studying teachers' lives: Problems and possibilities. In I. Goodson (Ed.), *Studying teachers' lives* (pp. 234–249). London: Routledge.

Goodson, I., & Walker, R. (1991). *Biography, identity and schooling: Episodes in educational research*. Lewes, London: Falmer Press.

Gorelick, S. (1991). Contradictions of feminist methodology. *Gender & Society, 5*(4), 459–477.

Lawrence-Lightfoot, S. (1994). *I've known rivers*. New York: Addison-Wesley.

Richardson, L. (1992). Trash on the corner: Ethics and ethnography. *Journal of Contemporary Ethnography, 21*(1), 103–119.

Richardson, M. (1989). Point of view in anthropological discourse. In P. Dennis & W. Aycock (Eds.), Literature and anthropology. Lubock, Texas: Texas Tech University Press.

Sears, J. (1992). Researching the other/searching for self: Qualitative research on (homo)sexuality in education. *Theory into Practice, 31*(2), 147–156.

Sparkes, A. (1994). Life histories and the issue of voice: Reflections on an emerging relationship. *Qualitative Studies in Education*, Vol. 7, No. 2, 165–183. Taylor and Francis Ltd.

Chapter Two

Baker, D. B. (1992). *Power quotes*. Detroit, MI: Visible Ink Press.

Bertrand, R. (1928). As quoted in *Power Quotes* by Daniel B. Baker, Detroit, MI: Visible Ink Press, 1992 (p. 9).

Bond, H. (1934). As quoted in *The Education of the Negro in theAmerican Social Order*, originally published in 1934 and reprinted by Octagon Books, New York, 1966.

Douglass, F. (1993). *Life and times of Frederick Douglass*. New Jersey: Gramercy Books.

Du Bois, W. E. B. (1903). As quoted in *The Souls of Black Folk* originally published in 1903, but identified in works cited as republished in 1994 (p. 5).

DuBois, W. E. B. (1994). *The souls of black folks*. New Jersey: Gramercy Books.

Ellison, R. (1952). *Invisible man*. New York: Vintage International.

Kennedy, J. F. (1958). As quoted in *Power Quotes* by Daniel B. Baker, Detroit: Visible Ink Press, 1992 (p. 252)

Lerner, M. (1949). As quoted in *Power Quotes* by Daniel B. Baker, Detroit, MI: Visible Ink Press, 1992 (p. 252).

Malcom X (1965). As quoted in *Power Quotes* by Daniel B. Baker, Detroit MI: Visible Ink Press, 1992 (p. 253).

Rothenberg, P. S. (1998). *Race, class, and gender in the United States: An integrated study*. New York: St. Martin's Press.

Terkel, S. (1992). *Race: How blacks and whites think and feel about the American obsession*. New York: The New Press.

Wright, R. As quoted in *Power Quotes* by Daniel B. Baker, Detroit, MI: Visible Ink Press, 1992 (p. 252).

Woodson, C. (1933). As quoted in *The Mis-eduction of the Negro,*originally published in 1933 by Associated Publishers, Washington and republished by AMS Press, New York, 1977.

Chapter Three

Bennett-Alexander, D. D. (1997). Reflections on being an out black lesbian on a southern campus. In B. Mintz & E. D. Rothblum (Eds.), *Lesbians in academia: Degrees of freedom*. New York: Routledge.

Cleary, L. M., & Peacock, T. D. (1998). *Collected wisdom: American Indian education*. Boston: Allyn & Bacon.

Gonzalez, M. C. (1997). Women of color, sexuality, and the academy: A few thoughts. In B. Mintz & E. D. Rothblum (Eds.), *Lesbians in academia: Degrees of freedom*. New York: Routledge.

hooks, b. (1993). *Sisters of the yam: Black women and self-recovery*. Boston, MA: South End Press.

hooks, b. (1994). *Teaching to transgress*. New York: Routledge.

Katz, W. L. (1986). *Black Indians: A hidden heritage.* New York: Atheneum.
Paniagua, F. A. (1994). *Assessing and treating culturally diverse clients: A practical guide.* Thousand Oaks, CA: Sage Publications.

Chapter Four

Delgado-Gaitan, C. (1990). *Literacy for empowerment: The role of parents in their children's education.* London: Falmer Press.
Delgado-Gaitan, C. (1996). *Protean literacy: Extending the discourse on empowerment.* London: Falmer Press.
Delgado-Gaitan, C. (1997). Dismantling borderland. In Anna Neumann & Penelope L. Peterson (Eds.), *Learning from our lives: Women, research and autobiography in education.* pp. 37–52. New York: Teachers College, Columbia University.
Delgado-Gaitan, C., and Trueba, H. (1991). *Crossing cultural borders: Educating immigrant families in America.* London: Falmer Press
Festinger, L. (1962). *A theory of cognitive dissonance.* Stanford, CA: Stanford University Press.
Gliedman, J., & Roth, W. (1979). *The unexpected minority: Handicapped children in America.* Thomas A. Stewart (Ed.). New York: Harcourt Brace Jovanovich.
Goffman, E. (1959). *The presentation of self in everyday life.* New York: Doubleday.
Goffman, E. (1963). *Stigma: Notes on the management of spoiled identity.* Englewood Cliffs, NJ: Prentice-Hall,
Mizel, S. B., and Mizel, Janet P. (1986). *The human immune system: The new frontier in medicine.* New York: Simon & Schuster.
Murphy, R. F. (1990). *The body silent.* New York: W. W. Norton.
Ovando, C. J., & Collier, V. P. (1998). *Bilingual and ESL classrooms: Teaching in multicultural contexts.* Boston: McGraw-Hill.
Pitzele, S. K. (1985). *We are not alone: Learning to live with chronic illness.* New York: Workman.
Sacks, O. (1995). *Anthropologist on Mars.* New York: Alfred A. Knopf, Inc.
Scheer, J. (1984). They act like it was contagious. In S. C. Hey, G. Kiger and J. Seidel (Eds.), *Social aspects of chronic illness, impairment and disability* (pp. 185–207). Salem, OR: Willamette University.
Siegel, B. S. (1986). *Love, medicine and miracles: Lessons learned about self-healing from a surgeon's experience with exceptional patients.* New York: Harper & Row.
Wells, H. G. (1910). *"The Country of the Blind."* London: Nelson.

Chapter Five

Anchor, S., & Morales, A. (1990). Chicanas holding doctoral degrees: Social reproduction and cultural ecological approaches. *Anthropology and Educational Quarterly,* 21 (3), 269–287.
Bruner, J. (1983). *In search of mind: Essays on autobiography.* New York: Harper & Row.
Bruner, J. (1986). *Actual minds, possible worlds.* Cambridge, MA: Harvard University Press.

Bruner, J. (1994). Life as narrative. In A. H. Dyson & C. Genishi. *The need for story: Cultural diversity in classroom and community.* National Council of Teachers of English.

Carter, K. (1993). *The place of story in the study of teaching and teacher education.* Educational Researcher, 31 (1), 5–12, 18.

Cooper, J. E. (1991). Telling our own stories: The reading and writing of journals or diaries. In Carol Witherell & Nel Noddings, *Stories lives tell: Narrative and dialogue in education.* New York: Teachers College Press.

Freire, P. (1992/1970). *Pedagogy of the oppressed.* New York: Continuum.

Freire, P. (1994). *Pedagogy of hope: Reliving Pedagogy of the oppressed.* New York: Continuum.

Freire, P. (1998). *Teachers as cultural workers: Letters to those who dare teach.* (Trans. by D. Macedo, D. Koike, & A. Oliveira.) Boulder, CO: Westview Press.

Greene, M. (1986). Perspectives and imperatives: Reflection and passion in teaching. *Journal of Curriculum and Supervision,* 2(1), 68–81.

Greene, M. (1997). Exclusions and awakenings. In Anna Neumann & Penelope L. Peterson, *Learning from our lives: Women, research and autobiography in education.* New York: Teachers College Press.

Habermas, J. (1984). *The theory of communicative action: Vol. 2. Lifeworld and system: A critique of functionalist reason* (T. McCarthy, Trans.). Boston, MA: Beacon Press.

Montero-Sieburth, M. (1996). Beyond affirmative action: An inquiry into the experiences of Latinas in academia. New England Journal of Public Policy, 2(2), 65–98.

Montero-Sieburth, M. (1997). The weaving of personal origins and research: *Reencuentro Y Reflexión En La Investigación.* In Anna Neumann & Penelope L. Peterson, *Learning from our lives: Women, research and autobiography in education.* New York: Teachers College Press.

O'Loughlin, M. (1996). Facing myself: The struggle for authentic pedagogy. *Holistic Education Review, 5.*

Paley, V. (1979). *White teacher.* Cambridge, MA: Harvard University Press.

Reyes, Maria de la Luz, & Halcón, J. J. (1997). Racism in the academia: The old wolf revisited. In A. Darder, R. Torres, & H. Gutierrez (Eds.), *Latinos and Education.* New York: Routledge.

Rodriguez, R. (1993). Latina feminist carving an institutional niche in academe. *Black issues in Higher Education, 28.*

Sampson, E. E. (1993). *Celebrating the other: A dialogical account of human nature.* Boulder, CO: Westview Press.

Shabatay, V. (1991). The stranger's story: Who calls and who answers? In C. Witherell & N. Noddings (Eds.), *Stories lives tell: Narrative and dialogue in education.* New York: Teachers College Press.

Shotter, J. (1993). *Conversational realities: Constructing life through language.* Thousand Oaks, CA: Sage Publications.

Sleeter, C. (in progress). *Culture, difference and power.* CD-ROM.

Terry, Robert (1993). *A Parable: The Ups And Downs.* In J. Andrzejewski (Ed), *Oppression and social justice: Critical frameworks.* Needham Heights, NJ: Ginn Press.

Torres, M. N. (1995). *Teachers' co-construction of personal and educational perspectives: A sociohistorical approach.* Unpublished doctoral dissertation, University of New Mexico, Albuquerque.

Torres, M. N. (1996). *Cognitive individualism: An impediment to teachers' intellectual collaborative work*. Paper presented at the Annual Meeting of the American Educational Research Association, New York, NY, April 8–12.

Torres, M. N. & John-Steiner, V. (1995). *Impediments to teachers' co-construction of educational knowledge: A sociocultural approach. Proceedings of the International Congress of Psychology*, San Juan, Puerto Rico, July 7–12.

Chapter Six

Turner, Myers, & Cresswell (1999) sited in "External Labor Markets and the Distribution of Black Scientists and Engineers in Academia" *Journal of Higher Education*, Vol. 71, No. 2 (March/April 2000), pp. 187-222 by Stephen Kulis, Heather Shaw, and Yinong Chong.

Yagi, K. and Minami, K. 1990. Estimates of Methane Emission from Paddy Fields. Research Reports of Div. of Environmental Planning of NIAES 6: 131-142. (In Japanese).

Astin, H.S., Antonio, A.L., Cress, C.M., and Astin, A.W. (1997). Race and Ethnicity in the American Professoriate, 1995-96. Los Angeles: Higher Education Research Institute.

Chapter Seven

Dikötter, F. (1992). *The discourse of race in modern China*. Stanford, CA: Stanford University Press.

Crespigny, R. de (1992). *China this Century*. New York, NY: Oxford University Press.

Freire, P. (1973). *Pedagogy of the oppressed*. New York: Seabury.

Freire, P. (1995). *Pedagogy of hope. Reliving pedagogy of the oppressed*. New York: Continuum.

Freire, P., & Macedo, D. (1996). A dialogue: Culture, language, and race. In P. Leistyna, A. Woodrum, & S. Sherblom (Eds.), Breaking free: The transformative power of critical pedagogy. *Harvard Education Review, 27*, 199–228.

Gibson, M. (1988). *Accommodation without assimilation: Sikh immigrants in an American high school*. Ithaca, NY: Cornell University Press.

Gibson, M. (Ed.). (1997). Ethnicity and school performance: Complicating the immigrant/involuntary minority typology. *Anthropology and Education Quarterly, 28*, 315–462.

Giroux, H., & McLaren, P. (1986). Teacher education and the politics of engagement: The case for democratic schooling. *Harvard Educational Review, 26*, 213–238.

Giroux, H., & McLaren, P. (1994). *Between borders: Pedagogy and the politics of cultural studies*. New York: Routledge.

Gladney, D. C. (1991). *Muslim Chinese: Ethnic nationalism in the People's Republic*. Cambridge, MA: Harvard University Press.

Gutierrez, K. (1994). How talk, context, and script shape contexts for learning: A cross-case comparison of journal sharing. *Linguistics and Education, 5*, 335–365.

Gutierrez, K., Larson, J., & Kreuter, B. (1995). Cultural tensions in the scripted classroom: The value of the subjugated perspective. *Urban Education, 29*, 410–442.

Kiang, P. (1995). Bicultural strengths and struggles of Southeast Asian Americans in school. In A. Darder (Ed.), Culture and difference: Critical perspectives on the bicultural experience in the United States. *Critical Studies in Education and Culture Series* (pp. 201–225). Westport, CT: Bergin & Garvey.

Kiang, P. (1996). Persistence stories and survival strategies of Cambodian Americans in college. *Journal of Narrative and Life History, 6,* 39–64.

McLaren, P. (1995). *Critical pedagogy and predatory culture.* New York: Routledge.

Ogbu, J. (1974). *The next generation: An ethnography of education in an urban neighborhood.* New York: Academic Press.

Ogbu, J. (1978). *Minority education and caste: The American system in cross-cultural perspective.* New York: Academic Press.

Ogbu, J. (1987). Variability in minority responses to schooling: Nonimmigrants vs. Immigrants, in Spindler, G. and Spindler, L. (Eds.). *Interpretive Ethnography of Education: At Home and Abroad* Hillsdale, NJ: Lawrence Erlbaum Associates, Publishers, pp. 255–78.

Ogbu, J. (1992). Understanding cultural diversity. *Educational Researcher, 21,* 5–24.

Poston, D. L., Jr., & Yaukey, D. (Eds.). (1992). *The population of modern China.* Series title: The Plenum Series on Demographic Methods and Population Analysis. New York, NY: Plenum Press.

Spindler, G., & Spindler, L. (1989). Instrumental competence, self-efficacy, linguistic minorities, and cultural therapy: A preliminary attempt at integration. *Anthropology and Education Quarterly, 10,* 36–50.

Spindler, G., & Spindler, L. (1992a). The lives of George and Louise Spindler. In L. B. Boyer and R. Boyer (Eds.), *The psychoanalytic study of society. Volume 17: Essays in honor of George D. and Louise A. Spindler* (pp. 1–22). Hillsdale, NJ: Analytic Press.

Spindler, G., and Spindler, L. (1992b). The enduring, situated, and endangered self in fieldwork: A personal account. In L. B. Boyer and R. Boyer (Eds.), *The psychoanalytic study of society. Volume 17: Essays in honor of George D. and Louise A. Spindler* (pp. 23–28). Hillsdale, NJ: Analytic Press.

Spindler, G., & Spindler, L. (Eds.). (1994). *Pathways to cultural awareness: Cultural therapy with teachers and students.* Newbury Park, CA: Corwin Press.

Starr, J. B. (1997). *Understanding China: A guide to China's economy, history, and political structure.* New York: Hill & Wang, a division of Farrar, Straus and Giroux.

Suárez-Orozco, M. M. (1991). Migration, minority status, and education: European dilemmas and responses in the 1990s. *Anthropology and Education Quarterly, 22,* 99–120.

Suárez-Orozco, M. M.. (1998a). State terrors: Immigrants and refugees in the post-national space. In Y. Zou & H. T. Trueba (Eds.), *Ethnic identity and power: Cultural contexts of political action in school and society* (pp. 283–319). New York: State University of New York Press.

Suárez-Orozco, M. M. (1998b). Introduction. In M. M. Suárez-Orozco (Ed.), *Crossings: Mexican immigration in interdisciplinary perspectives* (pp. 5–50). Cambridge, MA: David Rockefeller Center for Latin American Studies and Harvard University Press.

Suárez-Orozco, C., & Suárez-Orozco, M. M. (1995a). *Transformations: Immigration, family life and achievement motivation among Latino adolescents.* Stanford, CA: Stanford University Press.

Suárez-Orozco, C., & Suárez-Orozco, M. M. (1995b). Migration: Generational discontinuities and the making of Latino identities. In L. Romanucci-Ross & G. DeVos

(Eds.), *Ethnic identity: Creation, conflict, and accommodation* (pp. 321–347). Third Edition. Walnut Creek, CA: AltaMira Press.

Trueba, H. T. (1994). Foreword. In George and Louise Spindler (Eds.), *Pathways to cultural awareness: Cultural therapy for teachers and students* (pp. vii–xi). Newbury Park, CA: Corwin Press.

Trueba, H. T. (in press). *Latinos Unidos: From cultural diversity to political solidarity.* Rowman & Littlefield Publishers.

Trueba, H. T., Cheng, L., & Ima, K. (1993). *Myth or reality: Adaptative strategies of Asian Americans in California.* London: Falmer Press.

Trueba, H. T., Jacobs, L., & Kirton, E. (1990). *Cultural conflict and adaptation: The case of the Hmong children in American society.* London: Falmer Press.

Trueba, H. T., & Zou, Y. (1994). *Power in education: The case of Miao university students and its significance for American culture.* London: Falmer Press.

Zou, Y. (1998). Dilemmas faced by critical ethnographers in China. In Y. Zou & H. Trueba (Eds.), *Ethnic identity and power: Cultural contexts of political action in school and society* (pp. 389–409). New York: State University of New York Press.

Zou, Y., & Trueba, H. T. (Eds.). (1998). *Ethnic identity and power: Cultural contexts of political action in school and society.* New York: State University of New York Press.

Chapter Eight

Asian American Journalists Association. (1991). *Project Zinger: The good, the bad, and the ugly.* SF: Center for Integration and Improvement of Journalism.

Chaliard G., & Rageau, J. P. (1995). *The Penguin atlas of Diasporas.* NY: Viking.

Coughlin, E. K. (1989). Scholars turn westward to the Pacific Rim. *Chronicle for Higher Education, 35*(36), 17 May, A1, A10.

Dower, J. W. (1986). *War without mercy.* NY: Pantheon.

Engelmann, L. (1990). *Tears before the rain: An oral history of the fall of South Vietnam.* NY: Oxford University Press.

Gooding-Williams, R. (Ed). (1993). *Reading Rodney King/reading urban uprising.* NY: Routledge.

Kiang, P. N. (1997). Pedagogies of life and death: Transforming immigrant/refugee students and Asian American studies. *Positions, 5*(2), 529–555. Duke University Press

Kiang, P. N. (1991). About face: Recognizing Asian & Pacific American Vietnam veterans in Asian American studies. *Amerasia Journal. 17*(3), 22–40.

Kiang, P. N., & Kaplan, J. (1994). Where do we stand: Views of racial conflict by Vietnamese American high school students in a black-and-white context. *Urban Review, 26*(2), 95–119.

Kiang, P. N., & Lee, V. W. (1993). Exclusion or contribution: Education K–12 policy. In *The state of Asian Pacific America,* (pp. 25–48). Los Angeles: LEAP Asian Pacific American Public Policy Institute and UCLA Asian American Studies Center.

Leong, R. (1991). *Moving the image.* Los Angeles: Visual Communications and UCLA Asian American Studies Center.

Loewen, J. W. (1995). *Lies my teacher told me.* NY: New Press.

Mann, C. R. & Zatz, M. S. (1997). *Images of color, images of crime.* Los Angeles, CA: Roxbury Publishing.

Mazumdar, S. (1991). Asian American studies and Asian studies: Rethinking roots. In S. Hune, H. C. Kim, S. S. Fujita, and A. Ling (Eds), *Asian Americans: Comparative and global perspectives*, (pp. 29–44). Pullman WA: Washington State University Press.

Moffat, S. (1992). Splintered society: U.S. Asians. *Los Angeles Times*, 13 July, 1, 20–21.

Olsen L. (1997). *An invisible crisis: The educational needs of Asian Pacific American youth*. NY: Asian Americans/Pacific Islanders in Philanthropy.

Pak, H. W. (1990). *The Pacific Rim*. NY: Scholastic.

Poplin, M., & Weeres, J. (1993). *Voices from the inside: A Report on schooling from inside the classroom*. Claremont, CA: Institute for Education in Transformation, Claremont Graduate School.

Root, M. P. P. (1991). *Racially mixed people in America: Within, between and beyond race*. Thousand Oaks, CA: Sage.

Root, M. P. P. (1996). *The Multiracial experience: Racial borders as the new frontier*. Thousand Oaks, CA: Sage.

Said, E. W. (1978). *Orientalism*. NY: Vintage-Random House.

Seller, M., & Weis, L. (1997). *Beyond black and white: New faces and voices in U.S. schools*. Albany, NY: SUNY Press.

Takei, G. (1994). *To the stars*. NY: Pocket Books.

Te, B., Cordova, J. M. T., Walker-Moffat, W., & First, J. (1997). *Unfamiliar partners: Asian parents and U.S. public schools*. Boston: National Coalition of Advocates for Students.

Trueba, H. T., Rodriguez, C., Zou, Y., & Cintrón, J. (1993). *Healing multicultural America*. London: Falmer Press.

West, P., Levine, S. I., & Hiltz, J. (Eds). (1998). *America's wars in Asia: A cultural approach to history and memory*. Armonk, NY: M. E. Sharpe.

Wong-Fillmore, L. (1991). When learning a second language means losing the first. *Early Childhood Research Quarterly*, 6(3), 323–47.

Wong-Fillmore, L. (1991a). Preschoolers and native language loss. *MABE Newsletter*, Massachusetts Association for Bilingual Education, Spring, 2.

Index

academic discourse, 79–80, 85–86
academic life: cultural nuances of, 88–89;
    social relations and, 84–88; time
    constraints of, 82–83; working
    groups in, 87–88. *See also* tenure and
    promotion
accommodation, 137
administrative support, 97–98, 109
admissions policies, 27, 119
affirmative action, 28, 30, 31
African Americans. *See* black Americans
Aid to Families with Dependent Children,
    2–3
Amerasia Journal, 119
American Historical Association, 110
American Indians, 34
American Psychological Association,
    100, 105–6
Americanization, 94
Americans with Disabilities Act, xii–xviii,
    6, 57, 73
Anchor, S., 78
anthropology, 10
Antonio, 121–22
armed struggles, 3–4
Asian American studies, xx–xxi, 113,
    119–20
Asian Americans, xvii–xix; admissions
    quotas, 119; culture-language link,
    149–50; discrimination cases, 96–97;
    diversity of, 144; empowerment of,

137; legacies of war and, 145–47;
    significance of names to, 150–51;
    stereotyping of, 142–43; violence
    against, 146
assimilation, 143
Association for Asian American Studies,
    113
Astin, 121–22
Attica Prisoner Revolt, 27–28
autobiographies, 10

Barone, T., 12
Bateson, Gregory, 10
Bennett-Alexander, D. D., 53
bias: Asian Americans, 99–104, 105–8,
    114–17, 118; black females, 36–39,
    46–47; disabled persons, 62–65;
    Japanese Americans, 118–21;
    Latinas, 79–80, 82–89, 90; lesbians,
    52–53; reflected in tenure decisions,
    99–104, 105–8, 114–17, 118, 122.
    See also discrimination; ethnicity
biculturalism, 137, 138, 139
bilingual education, 39, 91–92
biographical positioning, 11
black Americans, xvi–xvii, 16; being
    black in America, 18–19; bias in
    academia, 36–39, 46–47; educational
    opportunities of, 22–23; higher
    education, 21–29; political power of,
    24

163

About the Contributors

Cecil E. Canton (cecanton@csus.edu) was born in Harlem, New York, and was educated in New York at SUNY Stony Brook (B.A.) and Columbia University (M.A., M.Ed.). His doctorate is in educational administration from Columbia University as well. He has worked in adult criminal and juvenile justice and has served as an elementary school teacher, principal, and chief school officer. He currently teaches criminal justice at CSU, Sacramento. His research interests and publications include work in adult corrections, juvenile justice, cultural pluralism and Alternative Dispute Resolution (ADR) programs and principles. Dr. Canton is a conflict mediator with a national and international portfolio.

José Cintrón (cintron@csus.edu) is professor of education at California State University, Sacramento, College of Education and chair of the Bilingual/ Multicultural Education Department. He teaches multicultural education, bilingual education, and social/psycho-educational foundations courses in the multiple subjects teacher credential program. In addition, he teaches advanced multicultural education and field studies courses in the Bilingual/Multicultural Education Masters Program. Dr. Cintrón has consulted and trained bilingual teachers and staff throughout the state of California. He is currently codirector of the Migrant/Optimal Learning Environment (M/OLE) Project at CSU, Sacramento, a balanced literacy staff development training project for migrant education teachers working in K–6 classrooms.

Eugenia D. Cowan (gcowan@csus.edu) completed her undergraduate work at Biola University in La Mirada California, receiving a B.A. in sociology in 1978. Her master of arts degree is in counseling psychology, received from the Professional School for Psychological Studies, San Diego, in 1983. Doctoral studies were completed at the University of California, Santa Barbara, in education in 1992, with an emphasis in confluent education.

169

Concha Delgado-Gaitan (conchadg@inreach.com) is an award-winning ethnographic researcher and scholar on oral and written traditions in immigrant communities. She is the author of three books, *Literacy for Empowerment, Crossing Cultural Borders* (with H. T. Trueba), and *Protean Literacy*. She is the coeditor of *School and Society* (with H. T. Trueba). Many of her articles appear in scholarly journals, among them, *The Harvard Educational Review, Anthropology & Education Quarterly* and the *American Educational Research Journal*. She is an independent writer and resides in the Bay Area.

Lila Jacobs (jacobsl@csus.edu) completed her undergraduate work at the University of Wisconsin, Madison, and her graduate work at the University of California, Santa Barbara. She's a professor at California State University, Sacramento, and the coordinator of a unique urban leadership program, which she initiated four years ago. Her research areas and published work span a variety of topics, such as female-headed households, welfare to work programs, and Hmong students in U.S. schools, including a book entitled *Cultural Conflict and Adaptation,* with H. T. Trueba and Dr. E. Kirton. In addition, she is involved with international issues as well as local politics.

Peter Nien-chu Kiang (peter.kiang@umb.edu) is an associate professor at the University of Massachusetts, Boston, where he teaches graduate courses in social studies curriculum design and directs the Asian American Studies Program. Peter's research and advocacy related to Asian Americans in both K–12 and higher education have been recognized by the National Academy of Education, the Massachusetts Teachers Association, the Massachusetts Association for Bilingual Education, the NAACP, the Anti-Defamation League, and the New England Resource Center for Higher Education. He holds a B.A., Ed.M., and Ed.D. from Harvard University and is a former Community Fellow in the Department of Urban Studies and Planning at MIT.

Chalsa M. Loo, Ph.D. (loo@lava.net)is a licensed clinical psychologist in private practice and a clinical research psychologist at the National Center for Posttraumatic Stress Disorder at the Department of Veterans Affairs. She received her Ph.D. from Ohio State University. She is the author of numerous articles and two books—*Chinatown: Most Time, Hard Time* and *Chinese America: Mental Health and Quality of Life in the Inner City.* She received the 1991 Distinguished Contribution Award from the Asian American Psychological Association, has been the principal investigator for three large research grants, and currently conducts research on trauma and racism.

George D. Spindler is appropriately recognized as the "Father of Educational Anthropology." He is one of the most knowledgeable and distinguished ethnographers in the world today. In addition to having edited over 200 case studies in anthropology, George Spindler was the editor of the *American Anthropologist* and played a key role in developing a number of subfields in anthropological linguistics, ethnoscience, the ethnography of law, and educational anthropology. His major theoretical contributions (through his teaching of over 14,000 students over the last 50 years and his numerous publications) were focused on the nature of cultural transmission and cultural adaptation. As a psychological anthropologist, George Spindler described complex processes of self-identity formation and adaptation. His long-term impact in the fields of psychology, educational anthropology, and research methodologies will have relevance for a very long time. His classic pieces, many that he authored with his late wife, Dr. Louise Spindler, are read and discussed in graduate and undergraduate seminars around the world. These include *Education and Cultural Process: Towards an Anthropology of Education* (1974, 1987, 1997), *The Making of Psychological Anthropology* (1978), and *Pathways to Cultural Anthropology: Cultural Therapy with Teachers and Students* (with L. Spindler, 1994), and *Fifty Years of Anthropology and Education 1950-2000: A Spindler Anthology* (2000).

Myriam N. Torres (myriamtor@aol.com) has a Ph.D. in educational foundations from the University of New Mexico, 1995, an M.S. in experimental psychology from the Universidad Nacional Autónoma de México, 1983, and an M.A. in school counseling from the Universidad Pedagógica Nacional, Bogota, Colombia, 1980. Myriam has taught from elementary grades to graduate school. After receiving her Ph.D., she worked in the University of New Mexico teaching educational research and educational psychology courses and then on to California State University, Monterey Bay, working in the teacher preparation program. She is currently a program coordinator for the Santa Clara County Office of Education.

Yali Zou (yzou@uh.edu) is an associate professor in the Department of Educational Leadership and Cultural Studies and director of the Asian American Studies Center of the University of Houston. She obtained her masters and Ph.D. in education from the University of California at Davis. She has conducted ethnographic research in both the United States and China, has coauthored and co-edited four books on ethnic identity and multicultural issues. The two most recent are: *Power in Education: The Case of the Miao University Students and Its Significance for American Cuture* (1994, Falmer Press), and *Ethnic Identity and Power: Cultural Contexts of Political Action in School and Society* (1998, SUNY Press).

Made in the USA
San Bernardino, CA
28 March 2017